The Impact of Print-On-Demand on Academic Books

Chandos

Information Professional Series

Series Editor: Ruth Rikowski
(Email: Rikowskigr@aol.com)

Chandos' new series of books is aimed at the busy information professional. They have been specially commissioned to provide the reader with an authoritative view of current thinking. They are designed to provide easy-to-read and (most importantly) practical coverage of topics that are of interest to librarians and other information professionals. If you would like a full listing of current and forthcoming titles, please visit www.chandospublishing.com.

New authors: we are always pleased to receive ideas for new titles; if you would like to write a book for Chandos, please contact Dr. Glyn Jones on g.jones.2@elsevier.com or telephone +44 (0) 1865 843000.

The Impact of Print-On-Demand on Academic Books

Suzanne Wilson-Higgins

Chandos Publishing is an imprint of Elsevier
50 Hampshire Street, 5th Floor, Cambridge, MA 02139, United States
The Boulevard, Langford Lane, Kidlington, OX5 1GB, United Kingdom

Library of Congress Cataloging-in-Publication Data
A catalog record for this book is available from the Library of Congress

British Library Cataloguing-in-Publication Data
A catalogue record for this book is available from the British Library

ISBN: 978-0-08-102011-1 (print)
ISBN: 978-0-08-102019-7 (online)

For information on all Chandos publications
visit our website at https://www.elsevier.com/books-and-journals

Publisher: Glyn Jones
Acquisition Editor: Glyn Jones
Editorial Project Manager: Lindsay Lawrence
Production Project Manager: Joy Christel Neumarin Honest Thangiah
Cover Designer: Mark Rogers

Typeset by SPi Global, India

Contents

Preface

The past 30 years have witnessed an unprecedented pace of change in communication including scholarly communication, and print-on-demand has played an important role in that change. This book is written from the perspective of a practitioner publisher, a digital books on-demand print service provider, and a library supplier which have made up the past 27 years of my working life, assisted by an undergraduate interest in history and postgraduate interest in business. My specialist topic is not the nature of the scholarly monograph, academic textbook, or specialist tome itself, but as a publisher who engages with the commissioning, presentation, selling, and distribution of books. I observed the changing nature of academic content and participated alongside some of the leading scholarly publishers who not only grasped new publishing opportunities presented by the convergence of services founded on new print-on-demand digital technologies but innovated services and products around them. Many of those innovators have kindly consented to provide case studies or short summaries of their company's experience with print-on-demand for academic books. This book couples a history of a specific business innovation: digital print-on-demand, and the impact that innovation had on three types of academic book: the monograph, the textbook, and aggregate book collections. For some, business and scholarship are not always happy bedfellows, but with respect to print-on-demand for academic books they have in fact been most complimentary.

To place this business innovation in context, I reviewed much of the literature covering the past two decades of discourse regarding the academic book and especially the impact of digital technology on it. The past two decades have witnessed ever accelerating digital technological change—not least developments in digital composition, automated workflow for book creation, digital asset management, digital printing innovation, web-based ecommerce, improved book supply chain logistics, and bookbinding technologies which have given birth to self-publishing on an unprecedented scale and fuelled digital book creation services. Some academic books, such as the constant output of scholarly monographs, might even be viewed as a particular subset of author-driven 'self-publishing', tempered by peer review and editorial comment. Publishing a quality academic book carries real and significant origination costs as recent studies have surveyed, calculated, and reported, regardless of the means of distributing or reading a completed book. Some studies assert that printing is only 11% of the cost of producing some books because origination of the book is so costly. However, digital print-on-demand for books necessitates a completely fresh approach to composing, making, distributing, and even selling an academic book. 'On-demand' is not just about the printing and binding, it supports a 'digital first' publishing model and it delivers books with an immediacy that changes the supply paradigm. Virtual inventory print-on-demand for books requires engineering discipline to execute. From templated digital composition through to digitally enabled distribution and tracking, it reduces the total costs and liberates new revenue streams to academic publishers that were not accessible before its innovation.

Academic libraries have increasingly embraced an all-digital world: supporting digital open access models which facilitate search, accessing published datasets and multimedia research results, utilising digital discovery tools, purchasing digital book collections for access by academic user communities at ever more granular level (chapters, images, tables, etc.). It may be that the future takes the academic book to an entirely screen-dominated world, but today the ascendance of the digital screen has not entirely eclipsed the role of print on paper for books. There remains a residual and significant demand for printed on paper and bound editions of academic books by scholars, researchers, students, interested enthusiasts, and even some libraries. The majority of print editions of academic books would simply no longer be readily available without print-on-demand and these books carry economic and social benefit for authors, publishers, printers, distributors, retailers, readers, and yes, even libraries. So I encourage the reader to celebrate the story of the print-on-demand book revolution and consider its positive impact on the world of academic book publishing both now and in the future.

Acknowledgements

I must thank many individuals for their tremendous support throughout this book project. George Knott, Commissioning Editor at Chandos (an imprint of Elsevier), who first approached me about writing this book and Lindsay Lawrence, Editorial Project Manager at Morgan Kaufman (an imprint of Elsevier), who endured my submission delays and writing trials and Joy Christel Neumarin, Production Project Manager at Elsevier. Then those who shaped my development and understanding of business, academic publishing and digital print-on-demand, and of course those who granted permission to reproduce their words or work in case studies, as well as those who generously gave their time and opinions to me during the preparation of this book. Alphabetically listed here, thank you to: Larry Bennett, Daniel Berze, Kirby Best, Philip Blackwell, Toby Blackwell, Larry Brewster, Ken Brooks, Robert Campbell, Richard Charkin, Phil Clark, Y.S. Chi, Mitchell Davis, Frank Devine, Peter Drucker, John Edwards, Joseph Esposito, Richard Fidczuk, Rick Anderson, Doug Fox, Pam Granger, Kathryn Grant, Terry Gridley, Lewis Gunn, Verge Hagopian, Heiko Hess, Chris Higgins, Michael Holdsworth, John Holloran, John Ingram, Gareth Jarrett, Michael Kelper, Martin Klopstock, Emile Kranendonk, Rory Litwin, Paul Major, Ed Marino, Colin Moir, Rufus Neal, Edwin Ng, Charly Nobbs, Yvette Nora, Neil Hood, Angus Phillips, Ad Plaizier, Rebecca Pool, Frank Romano, Michael Schultz, David Taylor, Lynn Terhune, Xuemei Tian, Brian Wilson, Stephen Young and all my friends, colleagues and family not listed who have always given me encouragement. Lastly (and of course first), the living God Jesus Christ who has upheld me throughout my personal and working life, even when I turned away or stumbled.

Why read this book?

Everyone who at times prefers reading academic books on printed pages in a bound format might find this book of interest. With the rise in online book collections, e-book downloads, and online learning environments, one might think that all academic book reading has migrated to screens but that is not yet the case and may never completely happen. Academic books printed on-demand seem to be perceived differently by publishers and librarians, and this book tries to tell the story of how the academic book has been saved and reinvented by print-on-demand over several decades, and that print-on-demand for books in future has the potential to reduce costs and revolutionise the academic book by enabling peer reviewed academic self-publishing as well as supporting traditional academic book publishing models.

Librarians, publishers, and the new breed of publishers/librarians should find this book useful in terms of informing their professional work. Students of librarianship and publishing ought to be aware of the widespread use of print-on-demand for books in academic publishing today as well as considering the potential future impact. After all, this book is in a series aimed at the professional librarian.

While I was writing this book, I came across the results of a survey of librarians in the United States which evaluated their perceptions of print-on-demand books. Rory Litwin undertook the survey and published the results. He runs Litwin Books, an independent academic publisher of books about media, communication, and the cultural record including an imprint called Library Juice Press and group blog called *Library Juice* [1]. The summary of the survey appears in Appendix 1 with his consent. Released in March 2017, the survey included 218 academic/college librarians amongst the 408 respondents. Litwin concludes that 87% of the respondents were misinformed about print-on-demand books. The answers from staff in academic libraries to the two key questions suggest that many are unaware of the big picture regarding print-on-demand academic books and the positive impact that print-on-demand has had and continues to have on academic book publishing. They seemed to have a poor opinion of books printed-on-demand, while, at the same time, most indicated that they could not even tell if a book was printed-on-demand (which should be excellent news to publishers).

In the 2017 survey, academic librarians were asked the question: *What are some of the words you associate with print-on-demand?* Words like 'expensive', 'cheap', 'vanity', 'self-published' and 'poor-quality' compete with 'convenient', 'economical', 'quick' and 'cost-effective'. Here is a word cloud generated from the 218 responses specifically from academic, consortia, and community college librarians and staff:

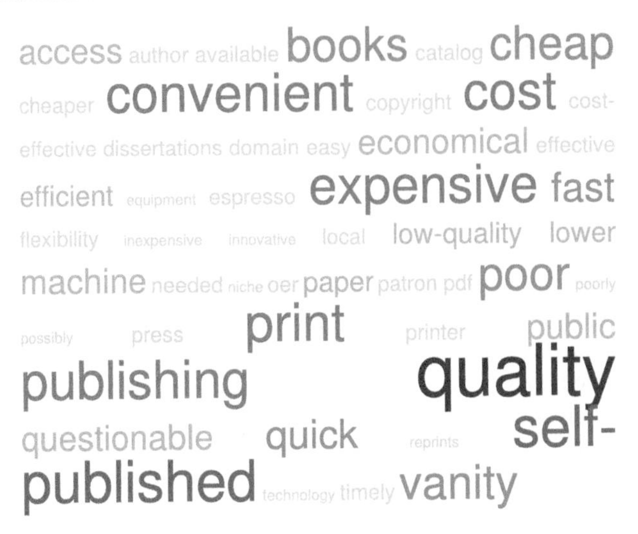

This lack of consensus of vocabulary and with a few pejorative words thrown into the mix, the results suggest a very different understanding across participant librarians and potentially across different academic libraries. In addition to stating words associated with print-on-demand books, academic librarians and staff were asked: *In the context of your job, do you know if a book is print-on-demand, and if so, how do you find out?*

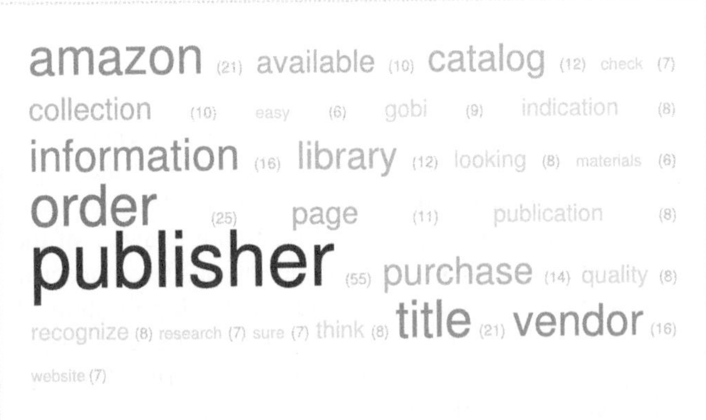

Some 25% of respondents had no way of telling if a book was printed on-demand at all, and for those who did, the publisher was the primary source of knowledge. So this survey suggests that while publishers are either proudly declaring that their books are available print-on-demand, or inadvertently labelling books in metadata or passing on information through intermediaries like Amazon and Gobi, the librarians are at best ambivalent towards the 'print-on-demand' label. At worst, they are prejudiced against books printed on-demand, but possibly from a perspective of being misinformed.

Through the case studies and interviews in this book, you will see that leading academic publishers and industry commentators believe that print-on-demand for books has in fact saved the printed academic book (most especially the monograph), sustained book sales revenues, and assisted the migration of library customers to e-book collections by enabling researchers and students (and sometimes even librarians) to continue to choose printed books in addition to institutional screen access. In addition, the availability of printed on-demand academic books has upheld the economic value of the academic book as a printed artefact for the reader to read, own, share, archive, and even resell.

This book seeks to celebrate the story of academic book printed on-demand so far and hopes to reveal to the sceptical librarian, publisher, academic, or student through case studies and interviews that the impact of print-on-demand has been largely positive on academic books. The future of the peer-reviewed academic monograph and perhaps even the customised textbook is fundamentally changing. New business models like Open Access for books and, possibly more importantly, new academic self-publishing integrated with peer review services are challenging the established academic publishing world. Print-on-demand has been both a catalyst and an enabler of these new publishing models. Be it welcomed or unwelcomed, the impact of print-on-demand on academic books has certainly been significant and far-reaching.

Part One

Convergence and two decades of print-on-demand innovation 1995–2015

Introduction to part 1

What is print-on-demand? According to the Oxford English Dictionary the first citation of this noun was in the *Financial Times* in 31 January 1983, the spelling should be 'print-on-demand' and the definition is

> *"A system or process by which small numbers or individual copies of a text may be printed to order, esp. (in later use) using computer technology; abbreviated POD."*

Of course this definition includes books but might also refer to other types of literature produced through digital printing-on-demand. Here we are concentrating on books printed-on-demand. By August of 2000 the *Wall Street Journal* was reporting that:

> *"Most of the large publishers have arranged to digitalise their [book] catalogues and offer such computer-based services as e-books and print-on-demand."*

It may or may not have been true at the time that 'most large publishers' were actively digitising their books, but by 2000 print-on-demand for books had arrived. Large academic book publishers formed the vanguard of book publishers to embrace this new approach to delivering books to readers.

While we are clarifying definitions, we need to ask: What is an academic book? The authors of *The Future of the Academic Book* (2017) most recently asked themselves this question and concluded:

> *This is as difficult as defining the academic disciplines. The conventional definition is that it is a long-form publication, a monograph, the result of in-depth academic research, often over a period of many years, making an original contribution to a field of study, and typically of 80–100,000 words in length. Articles, in contrast, are shorter (7–10,000 words) and usually less wide ranging. However, the distinctions are becoming increasingly blurred, as digital publishing means that many of the restrictions imposed by print no longer apply. [2]*

John B. Thompson in his book *Books in the Digital Age* (Polity, 2005) makes a distinction between what he calls 'academic books'—by which he means monographs or specialist texts; and books for 'higher education'—by which he means textbooks or books for professional development [3]. There is a chapter dedicated to each of these forms in turn in Part 2. For ease of use throughout this book which focuses on a publishing ecosystem of delivery, i.e. print-on-demand for books, I have chosen to refer to both specialist research monographs and education, training and development textbooks used in higher education collectively as 'academic books'.

The core thesis of this book is that yes, print-on-demand has had a significant impact on academic book publishing and on the academic book over the past 20 years and asserts that print-on-demand will continue to exert some influence over academic book publishing for the next 20 years. How did this come about? How are different forms of academic books impacted? And what does the future hold for print-on-demand academic books? This book brings together some responses to these questions through the voices of key participants in the print-on-demand story: interviews, unpublished case studies (new and old), recent surveys and some published articles. This book offers a macro-level view of a particular consequence of technological innovations coming together in the academic publishing ecosystem. Innovations which have affected a paradigm shift in the book publishing industry in general, but particularly impacted the availability of academic books as well as the way in which they are composed, compiled, assembled, disseminated, and read. This book is an outcome of many micro-level observations from the author and key participants in the revolution: book printers, book publishers, print equipment manufacturers, prepress service providers, online book retailers, book wholesalers, and book distributors. Print-on-demand has enabled change across the academic book supply chain and the markets it serves by supplying robust and profitable revenue streams to publishers embracing it.

Most readers will have some experience of digital transformation either as a digital native or as a digital immigrant in their personal and professional lives. I have spent all of my publishing career knee deep in the digital transformation of the publishing industry, especially the academic and specialist book publishing industry, but also alongside scholarly journals, professional databases and multimedia learning environments. With nearly a decade working with Ingram to establish its UK print-on-demand facility, I felt there ought to be a documented summary of what has happened and the amazing impact that print-on-demand has had on the academic book. Certainly print-on-demand impacted how the academic book is actually made and how it is delivered, and potentially has impacted the very survival of the printed monograph. Not only monographs but also other forms of academic books like custom textbooks, professional training books, grey literature, and book collections have been impacted by print-on-demand. Across all these forms, ensuring availability through print-on-demand increased demand while removing infrastructure costs from the delivery of a specialist book to its reader. At its best, by sustaining revenue streams for academic book publishers, print-on-demand offers the printed academic book the potential to flourish alongside the e-book, e-book collection or online learning environment and giving scholars the choice of a printed interface in a digital world.

Business innovation and creative engagement with technological innovation underpins the print-on-demand revolution. The testimonies that follow illustrate continuous change taking place in book publishing. As a novice business books commissioning editor in 1990, I had the pleasure of preparing to reissue for Butterworth–Heinemann Peter Drucker's classic management books and in doing so re-read *Innovation and Entrepreneurship Principles and Practices* [4]. The book was originally published in 1985 when I was studying for a Masters in Business Administration in Scotland and was required reading. It contained significant ideas about innovation in business. Peter Drucker viewed innovation as the instrument by which entrepreneurs exploit change as an opportunity, and Drucker asserts that innovation is capable of being learned not only practiced and that the systematic analysis of the opportunities offered up by change leads to economic or social innovation. Drucker' populates his book with many corporate examples. As MBA students were taken to IBM's East Kilbride, Scotland to see the just-in-time manufacturing plant in action as living proof of institutional innovation. Drucker's ideas concerning institutional innovation were manifest throughout the 2000s in digital publishing and digital printing technology companies like IBM, Xerox, Adobe, Hewlett Packard, and Kodak. These companies had technological innovation as a core competence and acted as the fundamental enablers of digital print book manufacturing and much of the innovation of print-on-demand services for books today was built on their technologies. They embodied institutional innovation as reflected in Drucker's 1985 writing and became leaders in the creation of the digital composition and digital print which has ultimately revolutionised book publishing by unleashing self-publishing of books, community publishing of books, and sustaining academic books by reaching new markets where a modest rate of demand for a title could be enjoyed over time.

A decade after Peter Drucker's book, the January–February 1995 issue of *Harvard Business Review* contained a significant article [5] encapsulating new thinking about business innovation from Clayton M. Christensen (then the Kim B. Clark Professor of Business Administration at Harvard Business School) and Joseph L. Bower (then the Donald Kirk David Professor Emeritus at Harvard Business School). The idea was essentially a thesis born of observation in many businesses that disruptive technologies often surprise leading companies who are so absorbed in listening to their mainstream customers that they miss the next generation of innovation for what seem small but are emerging markets. To address this problem the writers recommend businesses create and invest in organisations that are independent of their mainstream business.

Kodak notably became a victim of this type of surprise by ignoring the disruptive technology of digital photography. Ironically, Stephen Sasson at Kodak invented the first digital camera in 1975 but even as late as 1993 Kodak's management could not see beyond their market leadership position delivering what their current customers wanted in film-based colour printed photography. As early as 1990 Danka International Services Inc., part of Kodak Digital Printing, clearly a cradle of institutional innovation, collaborated with IBM to solve the problem of just-in-time computer manual manufacturing. Less than a decade later that software solution and its development team became the bedrock of Lightning Source Inc.'s print-on-demand for books success. Once it was married up to a powerful online bookselling catalogue this in turn became a disruptive technology in the book industry by enabling the self-publishing revolution. Many academic book publishers engaged with this service and Ingram's Lightning Source features in several cases and interviews that follow.

From 1995 to 2005 these ideas about institutional versus disruptive innovation provide a context for the emergence of digital printing, digital media, online retailing and digitally enabled logistics. The Xerox Corporation pioneered the way for managing documents and printing them on-demand, eventually in bound book form, when they released the DocuTech Production Publisher Model 135 in 1990, subsequently attaching these machines to computer networks and by 1993, like Danka, had a complete document service model for companies. Xerox became 'The Document Company' with a digital X in its logo symbolising the transition of documents between the paper and digital worlds. Meanwhile in August 1991 the first website went online from Tim Berners-Lee starting the worldwide web on the Internet which subsequently saw exponential growth thereby captivating Jeff Bezos' attention and he started Amazon in the summer of 1994 in his garage. The book selling website went live in the summer of 1995. Innovations born in Drucker's institutional innovation era and innovations born of disruption, as reflected in Christensen/Bower's ideas, were now set on trajectories to converge in the publishing world by 2000. The academic book was caught up in the centre of these changes.

In 2006 Professor Ron Adner, The David T. McLaughlin Chaired Professor and Professor of Strategy and Entrepreneurship at the Tuck School of Business at Dartmouth College conducted business innovation research and wrote in *Harvard Business Review* that innovation takes place in 'ecosystems' and that these:

> *... are characterized by three fundamental types of risk:* initiative risks—*the familiar uncertainties of managing a project;* interdependence risks—*the uncertainties of coordinating with complementary innovators; and* integration risks—*the uncertainties presented by the adoption process across the value chain. [6]*

Print-on-demand for books illustrates an innovation ecosystem and all three of these risk types can be observed in the interviews and case studies that follow concerning print-on-demand for academic books. The academic book publishers were early adopters of the publishing and supply chain solution that the newly integrated technology offered. Hearing from both innovators of services to publishers and the publishers who used those services to innovate is a core purpose of this book. Those innovations have in turn benefitted scholarly communication and the academy.

Part 1 of this book dedicates a chapter to each of the four critical innovations that had to be present in the publishing ecosystem to enable print-on-demand to impact academic book publishing and consequently the academic book. These are: digital prepress for on-demand which comprises digital composition, digital workflow and digital asset management; digital print and book manufacturing on-demand; bookselling on-demand; and book fulfilment on-demand which is the 21st century book supply chain complete with order management, Electronic Data Interchange (EDI), barcodes and pick, pack, fulfil automation. The interviews and/or case studies in each chapter help to ground the reader in the practical working out of this convergence and implementation of print-on-demand for academic books in university presses, profit-making book publishers and the data services suppliers.

Book pre-press for on-demand printing

1

The first of the four contextual factors that enabled print-on-demand to make a significant impact on academic book publishing was the establishment of digital book publishing pre-press including digital composition, digital workflow management, and digital asset management. Pre-press is an adjective according to the Oxford English Dictionary "Of, relating to, or designating procedures carried out on a publication prior to printing, such as typesetting, composition, and colour separation." [7] In the 1980s and 1990s, digital pre-press processes fundamentally changed the way books were composed and printed. In the early days, laborious steps were taken to create new digital files that could be passed to printers. Many old books were scanned from print editions and books that were held on film as the printers had to be converted to digital files for digital printing. New books began to be created on desktop publishing systems using computers using new tools. However, even those digitally composed books were being conventionally printed.

Perhaps nothing is new! In 2001, Michael Kelper, then a professor in the School of Printing Management and Sciences at the Rochester Institute of Technology, published a magnum opus *The Handbook of Digital Publishing Volumes I and II* (Prentice Hall, 2001). He cites in a footnote that the first print-on-demand books ever made which were actually produced in 1938:

> *when Eugene Power started a microfilm archive for the purpose of preserving intellectual property owned by the British Museum. In the mid-1950s, he is credited with the original print-on-demand production [of books] at University Microfilming International—UMI [now part of Proquest]. [8]*

So conceptually and in practice, print-on-demand for books had its origins in scholarly preservation in post WW2 Britain. However, the hand-crafted production of a single copy or two copies of dissertations and a thesis using positive images from microfilm is a small-scale, hand-crafted approach to on-demand printing and publishing. What opened up academic book publishing to new possibilities and significant revenue streams is the speed and volume of digital print-on-demand delivery in a 21st-century publishing ecosystem. By 2000, digital composition for the creation of books was established; digital workflow for tracking digital components of books as they were newly composed was in place; and the basic tools for digital asset management were available to academic book publishers.

The Impact of Print-On-Demand on Academic Books. https://doi.org/10.1016/B978-0-08-102011-1.00001-8

1.1 Digital composition

An integral part of the digital publishing process for books is the evolution of digital composition. In digital composition, publishers use computer software to lay out text, photographs, and illustrations and then traditionally create either plates or film negatives for every book page to be printed. Prior to the introduction of digital workflow, software tools that might reside on personal computers, office networks, and most recently the cloud, publishers originally undertook and later outsourced much of the pre-press process to specialist typesetters. Typesetting is essentially composing text by means of arranging physical type, processes which were laborious, slow, and error-prone. Here is a summary of Romano's six-step history of typesetting technologies [9]:

- handset typesetting (1440–1970)
- machine typesetting including hot metal typesetting (1886–1976)
- photosetting/photocomposition (1950–1990)
- laser image setting (1978–2008)
- direct to plate (1981)
- laser computer to plate (CTP) (1991–present).

Even in the late 1980s, UK printers and design agencies employed full-time typesetters with specialist typesetting equipment; in less than a decade that equipment would be obsolete and the role reinvented. The advent of digital composition was a precondition for academic print-on-demand books to succeed.

Understanding the rapid change around digital composition at the end of the 20th century is worth briefly reviewing as these developments were essential enablers of print-on-demand for academic books. Digital composition uses stored letters/symbols called glyphs in digital systems, retrieving and ordering those symbols according to a language's orthography for visual display. Pioneers in digital composition of text include IBM with their SCRIPT procedural markup language, which led to IBM's generalised markup language (GML), which is a descriptive markup language that is the basis for Standard General Markup Language (SGML), Hypertext Markup Language (HTML), and Extensible Markup Language (XML). Even as recently as the 1970s, mathematicians and computer scientists fell foul of the traditional typesetting process where equations had errors introduced by typesetters. In order to exchange mathematical equations with accuracy, Donald Knuth developed TeX, which in effect is a typesetting system [10]. Digital markup languages such as SGML and TeX profoundly influenced the preparation and accuracy of scientific research publications, particularly in the fields of mathematics and physics. Leslie Lamport developed the document preparation system LaTeX which used plain text and is useful not only in accurately marking up mathematics and a range of scientific disciplines but also manages multilingual works with complex characters with accuracy [11]. Companies that own and operate online collaborative LaTeX editors include Overleaf (founded by John Hammersley) who acquired the company ShareLaTeX (founded by Henry Oswald and James Allen) in 2017. Today there is a LaTex editor user community of two million authors primarily in academia or professional research [12]. They have seen sustained growth in usage in recent years, not only by institutions and enterprises, but even by students writing up projects.

Following the personal computing revolution, innovators like Adobe Systems (founded in 1982) created Postscript and led the desktop publishing revolution in the late 1980s. Publishing tools like Adobe Photoshop (1988), Adobe Acrobat, and Reader 1.0 (1993), digital fonts, and the PDF (Portable Document Format) led to software tools Adobe InDesign (1.0 released in 2000) [13]. These tools were rapidly adopted by professional book designers for composing books and preparing files which are then handed over to the book printer. Scanning technology also improved at this time and was taken over with the arrival of high-quality digital photography. It became possible to rapidly and accurately shoot pages and save them as digital files. Cost-effective and accurate scanning/digital photography suitable for printing purposes meant archived books could be captured and turned into print-ready files to replicate those books. With parallel development in WYSIWYG (What You See Is What You Get) desktop publishing software, by 2000 mechanical composition was essentially superseded by digital composition in the commercial printing and publishing world. Academic publishers routinely had the in-house ability to produce digital files for black and white text integrated with images and colour cover files, a prerequisite to taking advantage of print-on-demand for books services. New academic books continue to be created using digital composition tools. Adobe's CreativeSuite is now run as a software service in the cloud and web-based self-service platforms for authors provide pre-designed templates into which authors can place their text and images. Automated processes can create files which are compliant with standards for digital printing. Manipulating content within these software tools enables files to be created for print and electronic delivery (either downloads or for web platforms). In addition, books from a pre-digital age might be optical character recognition scanned, rekeyed, or shot with digital cameras to create print-ready files. Two decades of publishing software tool development means that original, newly created books, scanned printed books from archives, or even e-book collections are rich sources for the digitally printed academic book.

1.2 Digital workflow management systems

In the academic publishing context, digital workflow for journal publishing was the precursor to completely digital workflow for book publishing. The availability of print-on-demand for books gave publishers a commercial imperative to get their book content and digital workflow in order. In the early 1990s, the academic journal was radically changed not only by the creation of e-journals for the library to purchase and the researcher to read, but behind the scenes digital workflow software solutions for journal publishers began to engage authors in a new way of submitting and peer reviewing articles. For example, Aries Systems in Massachusetts, USA developed a product called Editorial Assistant which was a typical desktop manuscript-tracking application. This tool was used by journal publishers from the early 1990s until 2008 when it was superseded by Editorial Manager, a flexible web portal solution in the cloud capable of ingesting journals, books, and all manner of content [14]. Publishers embraced these digital workflow tracking tools. Some scholarly institutions and some large academic publishers developed their own in-house systems during that period too, moving to web-based ingestion of data elements such as text, figures, photos, and abstracts.

Meanwhile, book publishing was slower to follow suit, not least because of the absence of a profitable revenue stream for digital books until the advent of the downloadable retail outlets, learning environments, and subscription collections online. Downloadable e-books and print books require different digital files and simply managing those files on Digital Asset Management (DAM) platforms poses a challenge and expense for publishers. Several publishers and publishing system vendors have adapted their journal content ingestion systems to be suitable for book ingestion through web portals. For cost-effective and scalable publishing, this move towards a self-service web-based and automated ingestion workflow was critical for academic publishers to profitably embrace print-on-demand for books.

In parallel, the consumer-centric author services companies enabled the self-publishing books revolution for authors of all types. According to the Authors Earnings Report 2016, author income from self-published consumer book sales via Amazon.com has potentially grown in value (depending on how value is measured) to be greater than author income from commercial book publishing [15] and even Nielsen reported in 2016 that 22% of UK e-books sales were of self-published e-books [16]. Now everyone can be a published author. To do this an author must be prepared to pay for the service, conform their files to templated specifications and enter their content into a web portal for easy ingestion by the publisher. Barriers to entry for authors are lifted and the cost of book publishing has been driven down. It is worth mentioning this consumer self-publishing phenomenon in a book about academic publishing, not least because in 2016 new self-publishing vendors began to offer the peer-review process as a service on their menus. Like Open Access, self-published peer-review books on-demand have the potential to radically challenge the economics of conventional academic book publishing in the future. More on this topic will follow in Chapter 10.

1.3 The on-demand book digital workflow

In order to achieve single copy one-off print-on-demand at any economic scale, the process requires workflow software and a file submission web portal to assist with user-friendly uploading of new books to the process. At first, those web ‘front-ends’ were being used in a business-to-business context and were backed up by sound digital workflow. The entire print-on-demand process for books end to end requires digital workflow software to track the book from ingestion, through preparation of files, to printing and delivery of books to users. That process has a number of digital content management steps as well as manufacturing and delivery steps.

One of the earliest documented process summaries of one-off print-on-demand for books is found in a US patent submission [17] made in 1995 by the On-Demand

Manufacturing Company or ODMC. Five of the twelve steps noted are specifically related to retrieving, storing, and reproducing digital text and images. The court record is paraphrased here below and the digital pre-press related steps are highlighted in bold:

The method of high-speed manufacture of a single copy of a book comprises the following steps:

1. **storing the text of a plurality of books in a computer;**
2. **storing a plurality of covers for books to be printed in said computer, said covers being stored in a bit-mapped format;**
3. storing sales information relating to said plurality of books in a computer;
4. providing means for a customer to scan said sales information;
5. enabling the customer to select which book or a portion of a plurality of books;
6. commanding a computer to print the text of said selected books and a cover in response to said selection;
7. **retrieving the text of said selected books from a computer;**
8. printing the text of said selected books on paper pages;
9. binding said paper pages together to form said selected one of said books;
10. **storing graphical information corresponding to the cover of each of said books;**
11. **commanding a computer to reproduce said graphical information on a book cover;** and
12. binding said paper pages together with said cover there around.

Connecting each step in the digital printing process and monitoring a book's progress through the print-on-demand process requires identifiers to be present in the digital file and that identifier needs to be printed on the constituent elements in a high volume but single copy printing environment. Naming conventions need to be applied to files for swift automated retrieval. Ingesting new books as files with the correct names, preparing and pushing those files to print direct to plate (both black and white book block files and colour cover files), and then binding with glue the correct book block to the correct cover file followed by trimming the book to the correct size and finally shipping the correct book to the right customer sounds simple until the process is scaled up to thousands of books per day. Scalable print-on-demand at economic prices could not be achieved without effective digital workflow processes and software (Fig. 1.1).

Technological developments in pre-press composition and digital workflow management were made possible by the convergence of new digital communication tools (not least the worldwide web) with new underlying technology enabling efficient and scalable production. Accurate file preparation suitable for digital printing, for example ensuring crop marks were removed and images bled off the page, was necessary. To ensure consistently uniform files, the 'pre-flight check' discipline (as per the aerospace industry and embedded in Adobe's Acrobat software) is applied. Digital printing demands that all aspects of the files are reviewed and checked before ingestion as any instructional notes like crop marks will be reproduced on the page. The image of the page will be faithfully reproduced in print. Not only is ensuring absolute conformity of submitted book pages (PDFs) and images (JPEGs) important but utilising clear naming conventions on each file in order to automate ingestion is also important. Applying prescriptive rules around the book specification types, the paper stock, trim size, and

Pre-digital prepress workflow steps	Pre-digital prepress workflow meanings	Digital prepress workflow steps
1. Typesetting	To set the text using manual typesetting with moveable type, hot metal typesetting or phototypesetting	Word processed text submitted. Transfer to pre-designed layout templates
2. Copy-editing		Correct the word processed text before transferring
3. Markup	Annotations conveying print layout and correction instructions	Text styles embedded or tagged within the design program, corrections tracked in word processing
4. Proofing	Printing out sheets of typeset text galleys or proofs	Completed on screen using digital proofs. Occasionally print galleys or proofs
5. Proofreading	Manually checking the proofs for errors and marking them up	Can complete on screen in word processing track changes or print and markup
6. Screening and adjusting the tone of images		Half-tones and grey-scale adjustments made on screen
7. Imposition	The combination of many pages into a single signature form.	Automated single pages rendered by the computer to plate
8. Separation	Specifying images or text to be put on plates applying individual printing media (inks, varnishes, etc.) to a common print	A raster image processor (RIP) produces a raster image also known as a bitmap. Such a bitmap is used to produce the printed output. The input may be a page description in a high-level page description language such as PostScript, Portable Document Format, XPS or another bitmap
9. Manufacturing of plates	Rubber, plastic, aluminum plates OR film which is the photomechanical exposure and processing of light-sensitive emulsion on a printing plate	Manufacturing of a high-quality print (PDF) file
10. Paper selection		Papers suitable for digital print are pre-selected and loaded on print equipment

Fig. 1.1 Pre-digital vs digital pre-press process workflow.

finishing of the cover enabled scalable, one-off book print-on-demand. Different print vendors established different digital file standards for their configured equipment in line with their print equipment manufacturer's requirements. For all these solution providers, there is a trade-off between flexibility and scalability.

By 1995 in the United States, digital pre-press had gained ground in the book printing industry, and in 1996 Frank Romano from the Rochester Institute of Technology in New York published a book called *A Pocket Guide to Digital Pre-press* [9] aimed at professionals in all segments of the US printing industry, not only the book printers. It offers a comprehensive snapshot of digital pre-press at a time when digital processes and tools had just come of age. In his introduction, Romano asserts that there are five evolving technology tracks in graphic communications. Two of these technology tracks specifically evolved to enable on-demand book publishing. First, the typewriter through line printer to dot matrix printer to various laser printers to integrated printer bindery, culminating in **on-demand printing/publishing**. This technology track is particularly pertinent to the preparation for printing the black and white 'book block'; and second, drawing through digital scanning to computer art and design to **on-demand colour printing to colour publishing**, which is the technology track pertinent to digitally creating the designed colour cover of a book. These cover files can be submitted as TIFF or JPEG files as well as PDF.

By 1996, digital pre-press or premedia infrastructure was accessible to academic publishers to serve up print-ready digital files and, at the same time, enabling book printers to manipulate those files and deliver them to new digital printing equipment. Digital workflow software was available to publishers for the creation of the print-ready file (either from digital origination tools like Adobe Suite or via a scanning process, but digital workflow also tracks an individual book throughout the manufacturing process and through to the supply chain for distribution and delivery. The convergence of these capabilities led to businesses offering print-on-demand services for books at cost-effective prices and academic book publishers began experimenting and later ramping up print-on-demand programmes built on these digital foundations.

Professor Michael Kelper published his magnum opus *The Handbook of Digital Publishing Volumes I and II* in 2001 [18]. Kelper's handbook, being a comprehensive and technical tome, is a synthesised time capsule of digital publishing innovation and practice at the turn of the 21st century and written from a print industry perspective. Vol. 1 has 20 chapters and Vol. II has 24 chapters. Each hardback volume is over 600 pages in American letter size packed with half-tones and with colour plate sections. Rereading it from the perspective of the publishing world in 2017, half of the book has been completely superseded by digital technological change, but surprisingly there are five chapters of the 24 chapters in Vol. II which still offer a robust summary of digital workflow and print-on-demand versus offset printing. Specifically, Part Two, entitled 'Digital Workflow and Job Engineering', comprises four comprehensive chapters covering Digital Workflow, Digital Asset Management, Digital Job Engineering (which describes how printers effectively and efficiently manage print jobs), and Connectivity and Digital Data Flow. Vol. II ends with Chapter 24 On-Demand Publishing Technology, which was the new innovation at that point [19]. For anyone keen on technical detail, I commend it to you. Kelper summarises the technical bedrock and the digital management principles on which many of today's digital pre-press practices at the printer are based. The essential difference between digital print workflow and offset printing workflow is that digital workflow builds in the possibility of continuous revision and iterations. Version control and version management becomes an issue if static files are being stored, and the need for digital printing standards arose to assist book publishers and printers in managing their digital assets. Digital Printing Standards have been defined and are curated by organisations like SWOP (Standards for Web Offset Publications, USA) and Fograf (Germany) today.

During the period 2000–03, British sociologist John B. Thompson undertook a deep dive research study into 16 firms, interviewing 230 individuals associated with academic and higher education publishing through numerous interviews with publishers and vendors. Subsequently, the study was published under the title *Books and the Digital Age* (2005). Thompson's research as a social scientist is rigorous and comprehensive. It takes an in-depth look at many aspects of the academic book publishing industry but dedicates an entire chapter to **The Hidden Revolution: reinventing the life cycle of the book.** The first two parts of the revolution are digital workflow and digital asset management:

> *It's a quiet revolution, a hidden revolution... which is steadily and profoundly transforming the working practices and business models of the publishing industry, indeed transforming the life of the book itself. It's not so much* a revolution in the product *as* a revolution in the process*: while the final product may look the same as the old-fashioned book, the process by which it is produced has been, and is being, radically transformed. [3]*

The third part of the revolution that Thompson covers is digital printing and print-on-demand, discussing in detail its rise in the United States and United Kingdom for English language books (2000–04) but also noting the potential for books in other languages and markets. He eloquently writes up a summary of services from two suppliers. First, the 'supply chain provider' Lightning Source Inc. owned by the Ingram Content group, i.e. the largest book wholesaler in the United States [20], followed by the BiblioVault services from the Chicago Distribution Center operated by the University of Chicago Press and supported by the printer Edward's Brothers offering short-run digital printing for the warehouse [21]. Both of these services have at their core digital asset management systems which are scalable and robust. Both offer smaller academic publishers solutions for managing their print book and e-book content, and they both integrate with reselling services either business to business, as in Lightning Source's case, or a specialist business to consumer shop window which Bibliovault provides. The ability to discover and sell books has been fundamental to print-on-demand for success of academic books. We look at this in more detail at the end of this chapter through an interview and in later chapters through two key individuals behind those services, John Ingram, owner of Lightning Source (in Chapter 4), and John Edwards, owner of Edwards Malloy (in Chapter 2). They each reflect on their part in this hidden revolution.

The creation of these services was utterly dependent on digital workflow and digital asset management technologies deployed to manage publishers' digitally composed book files. The University of Chicago Press operated BiblioVault not only provided the digital repository for about a dozen university presses in 2004 (in 2017, that number is ninety scholarly institutions which remain mostly university presses), but also BiblioVault provided an incentive and a route to market for university presses to fully participate in the digital pre-press and printing revolution. Similarly, Ingram's Lightning Source incentivised publishers by supporting the digitisation of print books, even sharing the conversion costs with some, in order to build the database of books and to plug it into the emerging online retailing channels which could generate sales revenue.

Digital asset management is now a core book publishing competence which is either outsourced or supported in-house by all publishers including scholarly and higher education publishers. The number of book publishing digital assets continues to grow. Over three decades, there has been much discussion and debate about how publishers should manage the creation and storage of digital assets. Some advocate using tools like SGML and then XML to tag data elements enabling a multiplicity of file outputs suitable for online website display, downloadable e-books, offset print files, and digital print files. Others advocate creating, naming, and storing a multiplicity of PDFs, each fit for the purpose. Some outsource the storage of these files, whereas others have in-house systems. Each publisher has adopted its own set of solutions, and the technology is rapidly improving and changing. All academic book publishers today are creating and managing digital assets using digital tools in order to make printed books, e-books, and even websites at the point of publication. There is even a shift away from print-ready files for offset towards print-ready files for on-demand digital printing. An industry expert from a composition and data management service provider based in Chennai, India told me that even in 2017:

> *We are seeing a shift in the end deliverables being requested by our academic publishing clients. Increasingly, we are being asked to deliver e-Book files (EPUB and MOBI) and print-on-demand PDFs at the completion of a project, rather than traditional print PDFs. It is our inference, therefore, that the academic publishing community is seeing a positive impact and increased use of print-on-demand technology. From the perspective of resource consumption, print-on-demand seems to be more sustainable than the traditional print-run focused production model. [22]*

Digital print compatible 'on-demand ready' files typically today comprise a book cover file and a book block file. These are being routinely being produced to standards compatible with the print service provider's specification which is driven by the print manufacturers.

The *Fogra Digital Printing Handbook* of 2014 [23] summarises the latest tools like XLM which are moving towards a completely neutral set of stored digital assets that can be outputted to a multiplicity of file types for digital display and print purposes. This is not quite routine practice in book publishing today, but progress is being made in this direction.

This chapter concludes with an interview with Ed Marino, Chairman and CEO of codeMantra today and previously President of Lightning Source Inc., followed by a case study from Cambridge University Press. Thompson's study of academic and higher education publishing contained an excellent snapshot of a point in time (c.2003) when university presses and other scholarly publishers were just beginning to ramp up their own print-on-demand programmes. Contemporaneous with Thompson's study is the case study at the end of this chapter which describes the early days of Cambridge University Press's print-on-demand programme (1997–2006). It illustrates a pioneering example of the process of preparing to bring books back to life by using print-on-demand to tap into new sales revenue streams (Fig. 1.2).

Fig. 1.2 Ed Marino, Chairman and CEO of codeMantra.

Interview: Ed Marino, Chairman and Chief Executive Officer of codeMantra LLC USA (2017)

Ed has served as CEO of codeMantra since October 2015. With more than 30 years of business experience, he spent 16 years in Chief Executive Officer level roles for public and private companies in the technology, business-services, and marketing sector including Presstek and Danka Services International (previously Kodak Imaging Services). He was a Co-Founder, President, and Chief Executive Officer, Lightning Source, owned by the Ingram Content Group. He has or had leadership roles at the Electronic Document Systems Foundation (EDSF); New York University's Graphic Communications Advisory Board; and the Graphic Arts Technical Foundation (GATF). The National Association for Printing Leadership published his book *The Loyalty Payoff* (2005) concerning customer loyalty. Ed has a BS in Electrical Engineering (Temple University) and MS in Electrical Engineering and Computer Science (Drexel University) and sees the book publishing industry through the eyes of an innovative problem-solving software engineer.

I have nothing but respect for Ingram who stepped up with investment and vision to allow print-on-demand technology to impact the book industry and, as it turned out, especially the academic book publishers. The catalyst for the success of print-on-demand was presenting publishers with a way to monetise their backlist by harnessing the power of the Amazon search engine and catalogue which enabled all consumers, including those in the scholarly community, to discover books for the first time and express their wish to buy those books. Ingram Book Company captured the back orders from all bookstores (also known as dues in some markets) which demonstrated the latent demand for an ISBN. Armed with that information, Lightning Source could show publishers the untapped book sales potential expressed in real numbers—sales ready for the taking that academic publishers might never have known about or accessed.

The secret to successful execution of the print-on-demand service was the software. Amazon's systems captured daily orders and our 'Amazon sweep' picked up those daily orders, passed them to Lightning Source for manufacturing, invoiced Amazon, and pushed the finished book to the floor for shipping. To make that happen, the software was acquired from Danka Services International. The acquisition was a complete one-time source code purchase and the transfer of the software development team. The origins of Danka's print-on-demand software was in their business-to-business service to create, manufacture, and deliver printed computer manuals just-in-time, not least for IBM and was in operation as early as 1990. The system included order management and order collation, which pushed the orders to the print floor and enabled fulfilment.

The software included a full-order cache management system which was also a manufacturing workflow tracking system. The technical team led by Phil Clark originally built the software to solve IBM's document management problems with a library of 18–20,000 documents to which individually might need to ship to order. One of the technical challenges was managing variable spine widths and a solution was implemented with the help of a finishing equipment business in Canada. Matching the book blocks to the book covers was also an important part of the manufacturing process and innovative voice software was integrated with the Duplo perfect binder which declared a 'book match' or 'mismatch' when the barcoded ISBNs on the edge of the untrimmed covers and the back of the book block were brought together. It was effective if somewhat amusing to those touring the facility.

Once the files were submitted and set up by the pre-media team, for the publisher this was a 'lights out' operation; they were simply paid for the book sales. Amazon was a discoverability tool for books which enabled the compelling opportunity for the publisher to monetise backlist when coupled with the Lightning Source full service "order to cache" capability and led to exponential growth in print-on-demand for books, including academic books.

Today at codeMantra, where we deliver digital composition services to many publishers, including academic publishers, we are seeing more publishers who are creating digital first content. Digital first means the publisher is capable of going to the market before committing to print. There is also a definite recent trend from publishers who are requesting more digital print-ready files. Generating a digital print-ready file today is much easier than it was 15 years ago. There are still deep backlist books being converted into files suitable for digital printing and ebook release by some publishers, but "digital only" new books with optional print versions of those titles is the direction of travel. Following the demand **if** it is there for a printed book rather than setting it up just in case is a feature of this new digital landscape (Fig. 1.3).

Case study

Cambridge University Press (2006) by Rufus Neal, Digital Publisher from 1997 to 2010 and abridged by the author and Rufus Neal. This 2006 case study highlights some of the Cambridge strategies in the late 1990s for opening their backlist as a profitable asset and allowing books to remain available.

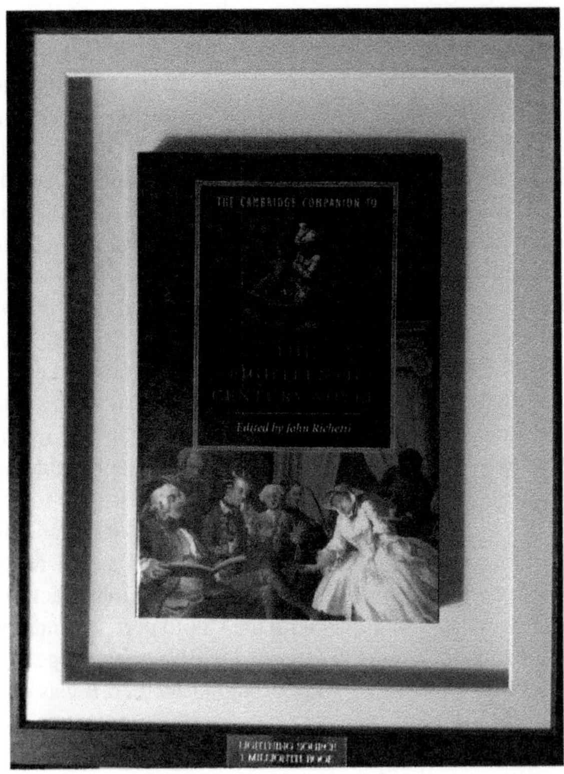

Fig. 1.3 The 1 millionth book printed on-demand by Lightning Source UK Limited for Cambridge University Press: *The Eighteenth Century Novel* from the Cambridge Companion series.

Cambridge University Press was founded by a royal charter granted to the University of Cambridge by King Henry VIII in 1534. It is the oldest printer and publisher in the world, having been operating continuously since 1584, and is one of the largest academic publishers globally. The Press has always set standards in design and typography, and continues its long history of excellence and innovation in the current era of digital publishing.

In the mid-1990s, personal computers, email, and the internet were still rarely seen outside universities. However, it was clear that phenomenal growth in this new digital world was inevitable and that it would impact on all areas of publishing, from the way in which books were typeset, to how they were printed, used, and sold. In 1997, the then Global Director of Business Development, Michael Holdsworth, set up a small working group of digital enthusiasts (Computer Integrated Publishing Initiative—CIPI) to exploit the emerging digital technologies. CIPI aimed *inter alia* to: (a) create new types of product; (b) tackle ongoing revenue loss from books being forced to go out-of-print when declining annual sales no longer enabled a conventional reprint to be economically viable; and (c) secure rights for future electronic and online exploitation of titles.

For some time, typesetters had been producing electronic files for supply to printers, but in a plethora of different proprietary formats that could not be easily reused by another supplier. Files were rarely delivered to the publisher: they were often deleted by printers or, if retained, stored on floppy disks or magnetic tape kept in shoe boxes. As part of the CIPI Initiative, a digital asset store was created and workflows emplaced to ensure that ALL new printing files were correctly delivered, tested, and stored as PDFs. The short-run reprint programme was started in 1997 as part of the CIPI Initiative.

Digital workflows and file preparation was the starting place to implement a solution in partnership with a digital printing manufacturer: In 1998, more than 8000 of Cambridge's academic ISBNs sold fewer than 100 copies per year, of which 5000 sold fewer than 50 copies, and 2000 sold fewer than 10 copies. It was simply not possible viably to reprint this cohort of books using conventional means and, consequently, between 800 and 1200 academic ISBNs, of annual sales value £1,000,000, were being declared out-of-print each year. In 1997, digital printing meant that if a book was selling 10 copies a year in hardback, or 100 copies a year in paperback, we could probably keep it in print. Putting a book out-of-print therefore became a **choice,** not an inevitable necessity, for a proportion of titles. Cambridge also had immense physical stocks of books that are never going to sell, and much of this surplus stock came from over-optimistic reprints driven by the need to get acceptable margins using conventional reprinting.

Early stages of the short-run reprint programme 1997–99: In 1997, a book selling 10 copies or more a year in hardback, or over 100 copies in paperback, with no colour, was usually accepted into the programme. The relevant editor and the author were consulted. The Cambridge answer code for the book would be changed to UCC. The answer code in our other publishing centres (New York, Australia) would be changed to IOC: all short-run stock was centrally and exclusively held in Cambridge and 'imported-to-order' to fill orders from the overseas branches. We set up 16 ISBNs in our short-run programme in late 1997 (15 hardbacks), over 100 in 1998 (80 hardbacks), and over 600 new ISBNs in 1999 (200 hardbacks). Annual income was less than 0.1% of total academic income in 1997, 0.3% in 1998 and 1.5% in 1999.

There were still major problems with the 'new' processes. Although the list of digitally printed ISBNs was growing rapidly, in essence the whole reprint process remained analogous to the conventional reprint process—with the single difference that we were sending orders to be printed on a new type of printing machine. The time and expense needed to make a conventional decision, do associated paperwork, process each new ISBN individually, to order subsequent reprints, and supply orders to branches was far too great and not proportionate to the income being generated. Technical limitations meant reprints had ugly plain covers produced from templates. At the end of 1999, paperback reprint production was moved to what would become Lightning Source. Lightning charged a set unit price (which was the same whether printing 1 or 100 copies), produced reprints of high quality with full colour covers and crucially printed and delivered new stock in response to an electronic request triggered automatically when stock levels were low. Initially, Lightning only offered paperback reprints, but soon also offered hardbacks, and after a short time supplied stock directly to the US as well as UK warehouses.

From that point on, there were no further old-style reprint decisions: In partnership with Lightning, we drastically streamlined our internal systems and processes, as well as developing a completely new restocking paradigm that consigned almost all of the conventional reprint processes to the bin. Our reprint process was now akin to simply moving new stock into our forward distribution bins from a different warehouse location—in this case, the 'virtual warehouse' at Lightning. Taken together, these developments provided the foundation that, over the next 5 years, saw **the number of 'out-of-print' decisions reduce to a trickle, backlist income grow exponentially, and excess stock levels reduced dramatically.**

By the end of 2006, 65% of Cambridge in-print ISBNs were in the short-run programme; **sales revenue from the titles—titles that would previously have gone out-of-print and of no further sales value—generated 15% of total Academic book income** (and was still increasing exponentially) and were achieving overall gross margin percentages that were better than new book publications. As a bonus, authors were extremely pleased to see their books maintained in print, whereas **the new systems and processes required us to produce and store good quality, consistent digital files** of short-run titles as well as to clear digital usage rights with authors, which facilitated the subsequent e-book and online exploitation of this cohort.

Digital print and book manufacturing on-demand

2

The second essential precondition for print-on-demand to impact academic book publishing was the innovation of cost-effective digital printing equipment and tracking software to manage print workflows suitable for books, and rolling out that new technology to book printers who were prepared to take a risk. In 1990, practically all books were printed using the offset printing technique. Offset printing continues for books today but it is rapidly being replaced by two types of digital printing: toner and inkjet. Offset printing involves an inked image being transferred from a plate to a rubber surface and then transferred onto paper. Digital printing lays down a digital image directly onto a variety of media. For books this of course means paper and, initially, paper that could tolerate high temperatures from lasers. In the early days of professional digital printing, large format laser printers capable of high-volume printing were utilised. Now both laser printers and inkjet printers are widely used. Photoelectronic digital 'printers' were originally more like industrial strength photocopiers laying down toner on top of paper via a heat intensive process rather than pressing and absorbing ink into the paper. Just-in-time manufacturing of computers in the 1980s and 1990s developed to a sophisticated level and enabled made-to-measure computers for consumers or businesses. As an MBA student in Glasgow in 1986, I toured the IBM computer assembly plant in East Kilbride, Scotland, UK and witnessed just-in-time computer manufacturing for its business customers. Packed into those boxes, beside the computers, were printed manuals. Those printed computer manuals forged the way for book publishing print-on-demand. This is highlighted in interviews with both Ed Marino in Chapter 1 and Edwin Ng, CEO of Markono in Chapter 4.

Digital printing also allows for the modification of the page image used for each impression, which is referred to as variable data printing and is the basis of custom publishing. Digital printing from files, via electrophotographic lasers and inkjet, has simply transformed book printing. The transformation was incremental and there were several very early adopters in the printing community with several disruptors who came along in the late 1990s.

Independent book printers Antony Rowe were the first printer in the UK to digitally print and bind books using the first Xerox DocuTec. When they presented samples to me and my colleagues at Butterworth-Heinemann (a professional books publishing division of Reed International Books in 1994), frankly we were horrified. The samples looked like poorly reproduced photocopies stuck together in a shoddy manner with generic makeshift covers. The quality was too far removed from the traditionally offset printed and sewn books we were used to publishing. However, the toner, paper stocks, and hot glue perfect bindings improved, and by 1997 digital printings met the basic requirements of enough black and white academic and professional books to start engaging all the big academic publishers.

The Impact of Print-On-Demand on Academic Books. https://doi.org/10.1016/B978-0-08-102011-1.00002-X

The economic appeal was and continues to be significant for academic publishers. Typically, 30% of academic book print runs were wasted and academic publishers routinely priced their books at a level which could cope with the higher unit cost of manufacturing which the early days of digital print demanded. Digital printing would come to dominate academic book publishing over the next decade and that was driven by the digital print service providers who innovated print-on-demand services that delivered new sales by integrating with book sales channels.

It seems appropriate to start any discussion regarding digital printing with a mention of R.R. Donnelley headquartered in Chicago, Illinois, USA and with a long and distinguished printing history. They were the printers of the Sears retail catalogue which started in 1888 (a precursor to online retailing) and the original telephone directories. As early as 1994, a technology consultant and journalist wrote:

> *Donnelley also plans to soon implement digital presses for small-volume jobs and a relational database from Oracle Corp. to store client files so reprints of books or catalogues can be made more easily, as well as in different sizes.* **It is expected that converting to digital technology will eventually make books-on-demand services possible in the future** *[24] Appleby, 1994. (highlighting added).*

As early as 1990, Donnelley were acting as the pioneer printing partners with Kodak software and printers for McGraw-Hill's Primis (now Create) custom textbook programme (see Chapter 6 for the case study). In 1994, Donnelley installed a state-of-the-art digital book production system in Crawfordsville, Illinois, USA and in the same year secured exclusive contracts with HarperCollins and Reader's Digest. They then opened a 60,000 square foot plant in Memphis, Tennessee, United Statesfor 'print-on-demand publishing' (meaning digital short-run printing with batches as low as 100 units of a single title). In 1995 with $5 billion sales, Donnelley were ranked as the No.1 US printer by American Printer [25]. A proportion of those sales were from textbook printing including digitally produced coursepacks. By 2001, books accounted for $708 m of Donnelley's sales [26], by 2002 $705 m [27], and then in October 2016 Donnelley completed a spin-off of LSC Communications including all book, directory, and magazine printing and books. Their six month results January through June 2017 stood at $501 m [28], so book, directory and magazine sales may be around the $1 billion mark by the end of 2017. LSC Communications have print facilities on two continents and offer in-warehouse digital printing for educational publishing groups including HarperCollins and Pearson. The Primis case study in Chapter 6 recounts Donnelley's early engagement in digital printing and proactive partnering with publishers and print technology companies. Compared to some of the other declining print market segments, their book printing services actually held up quite well and it might be reasonable to speculate that this is in part due to growth in digital printing on-demand.

Meanwhile in continental Europe, Xerox opened a research and development centre in Grenoble, France in 1993 and a few years later, Timothy Bovard co-founded CPI in 1996 and acquired the nearly bankrupt French book printer, Bussière. Bovard adopted an acquisition-led growth strategy for 12 years turning CPI into Europe's largest printer of monochrome books, acquiring the UK-based Antony Rowe amongst others in the process. He left CPI in 2008, and when he did, Bovard spoke to journalist Simon Nias. Bovard reflected in the article "CPI co-founder Bovard in surprise departure from company", **Print Week,** Thursday 09 October 2008:

> *The growth of CPI has been a project that has been as fascinating as it was unexpected. I would have never imagined from our beginnings at Bussière that we would build such a formidable group. We were able to seize the opportunities that arose and to consolidate the market. Through the acquisitions we made and through our focus on quality, we were able to save and turn around many printing companies that would no longer be in business today if they were not part of CPI. Today, CPI has a unique position in the industry and* **a rare opportunity to lead the industry's evolution with the arrival of high-performance digital printing technologies** *[29].*

CPI in France today has some of the most forward-looking technologies for print-on-demand in place including in-line binding and robotics.

The development of the digital printing industry, and specifically book printing, can also be traced through a succession of professional publications aimed at the print industry and post-graduates studying print technology. The distinguished digital printing expert Professor Frank Romano (now Professor Emeritus, Rochester Institute of Technology, New York) in 1997 published a book that signalled the establishment of digital printing as a new graphic communication discipline: **Delmar's Dictionary of Digital Printing & Publishing** (Delmar Publisher, 1997) [30] The book is a treasure trove of terms covering definitions of PDF and Post-script, a detailed entry on half-tones, entries on Standard General Mark-up Language (SGML) and Hyper-Text Mark-up Language (HTML) with much detail (XML is notably missing in 1997). There are a few profiles of companies and their new technologies like Belgian print equipment manufacturer Xeikon where he describes a print engine driven by the PostScript code, fusing toner particles to paper and web-fed paper rolls. 'Drop on-demand' is a very detailed description of inkjet and 'continuous inkjet' printing at the time, technologies which are now economically in use for digital book printing 20 years later.

Much has been written about the distinction between digital printing and on-demand printing of books. Frank Romano in his book with Howard Fenton **On-Demand Printing: The Revolution in Digital and Customised Printing** (Graphic Arts Technical Foundation 1998) defines 'on-demand' as being 'short notice and quick turnaround' [31] and "we do not associate any particular technology with the concept of on-demand" [32] and he defines digital printing as "any printing completed via digital files" [32]. Their point is that digital presses may not necessarily be on-demand presses and that the definition of digital printing is fluid and evolving.

This chapter has a sequence of images highlighting some distinctive aspects of on-demand book manufacturing versus just digitally printing batches of books from digital files. For example there are two ways to feed paper into digital printers: cut-sheet (loading pre-trimmed paper into printers to print book blocks) and web-fed (large rolls of paper that are fed into printers and cut in the process to create printed book blocks). Web fed printing can be a faster, scalable method (and therefore more economic/efficient) means of printing books on-demand. See the sequence of images from rolls to bar coded book blocks ready to be matched with bar coded covers. Speed and efficiency are critical to successful print-on-demand book operations (Figs. 2.1–2.3).

Short-run digital print versus one-off digital print. Ingram initiated a collaboration with IBM in 1997 called Lightning Print which became Lightning Source by 1999. About the same time, Dell computers had a global consumer advertising campaign: **Buy it. Build it.** This 'first sell, then manufacture' just-in-time commercial model, born of the need for computer manuals on-demand, depends on having effective processes, systems, and a workflow in place plus the book supply chain to make it happen. The Dell slogan encapsulated what then happened in book print manufacturing as just-in-time order management capability hit the book supply chain when Ingram set up the first one-off print-on-demand book service and the consumers discovered the books through Amazon. The one-off manufacturing process and workflow enabled completely different titles with common production attributes to be batched as illustrated in the binding process below (Figs. 2.4 and 2.5).

Fig. 2.1 Web-fed digital printers at Lightning Source, La Vergne TN c 2010. Photo reproduced with permission from Ingram Content Group.

Fig. 2.2 Paper feeding through cutters to make two sets of book blocks. Photo reproduced with permission from Ingram Content Group.

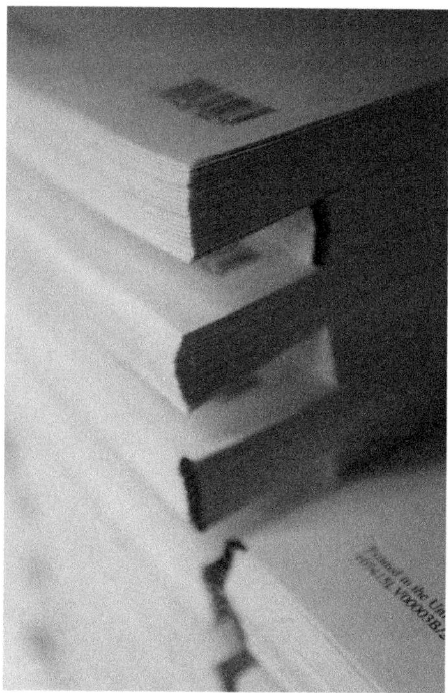

Fig. 2.3 Barcoded book blocks stacked prior to binding. The bar codes enable book blocks and covers to be matched correctly in the binding process.
Photo reproduced with permission from Ingram Content Group.

Fig. 2.4 Computer workflow monitor with operator preparing 'book blocks' *(lower right)* for hot glue binding using the stack of covers on upper left of the photo.

Fig. 2.5 Covers bound to book blocks with hot glue. Untrimmed books being conveyed to guillotine trimmer. Note that four different titles are being manufactured in this batch enabling truly one-off manufacturing of books.
Photo reproduced with permission from Ingram Content Group.

Meanwhile, university presses and commercial academic publishers were engaged with the ascendency of the digital scholarly journal subscription and facing the decline of printed monograph sales as library budgets were squeezed. They were looking for solutions. BiblioVault launched in 2001 catering to university presses and was supported by short-run digital book printer Edward's Brothers in the Chicago Distribution Centre warehouse. Short-run digital book printing coupled with book warehousing is certainly more efficient than the long-run offset printing model, but it falls short economically for the publisher in that it still incurs cash negative upfront printing costs rather than simply turning on a new revenue stream. Academic publishers fell into two camps: those who clearly understood the cash benefit of a stockless digital printing solution, were prepared to hand over control, and were in a position to benefit by rethinking their distribution and warehousing arrangements versus those who were not. Some were not in a position to really benefit from a digital print stockless model due to exclusive relationships with book distributors or wholly owned distribution and warehousing facilities within their corporations. So short-run printing (hundreds) and ultra-short-run (tens) printing to warehouse or in-warehouse printing complemented the stockless print-on-demand model.

It is important to understand the two digital printing models of short-run and one-off stockless print-on-demand. Printers refer to single copy (stockless), ultra-short-run (printing tens of copies), or short-run printing (typically hundreds of copies). There is much discussion in the literature and the industry about how many books make a 'short-run' and charts covering 1 to 1 million units in a printing [33]. Print-on-demand books are invariably printed from files to either laser printers using toner or Inkjet printers. Since 2014, Inkjet printing for books has gained a significant market share.

Digitally printed books typically have a higher cost per printed page than traditional printing methods. However, the higher page rate is covered by both avoiding the need to make printing plates, reducing labour costs incurred at the printer, and, more importantly, the ability to minimise the publisher's investment into the number of printed books that have not yet been sold. Other cost savings include the reduction of warehousing costs and reducing the shipping distances by distributing files to multiple print locations rather than shipping physical books. Distributed print allows books to cross borders without customs intervention and delays and reduces the delivery time and shipping cost, and these are explained further in Chapter 8 when we look at the trends in book manufacturing on-demand. At this point in the story, understanding the economic difference between offset printing and digital printing is enough. Academic publishers grappled with the pros and cons of managing the costs of digitally printed books when services were first made available. In 2004, Thompson, an academic sociologist and industry outsider, summarises the economics of the offset book versus the digitally printed book well in layman's terms:

> *Once the file has been made available, there are no significant set-up costs for digital printing, but above a hundred copies there are no significant economies of scale either – the cost per copy is roughly the same for printing a hundred copies or a thousands copies. (The unit costs tend to be higher...).*
>
> *In the case of offset printing, there are significant setup costs that have to do with plate preparation, etc., but there are also significant economies of scale: the more that are printed, the lower the unit cost. If you chart the costs of printing between one and say a thousand copies using digital and offset printing, the lines will cross at a certain point: below that point it will be cheaper to print digitally and above that point it will be cheap to print on a traditional offset press. ....*
>
> *Developments in digital printing technology have brought down the cost per copy and enabled digital printers to push up the level at which they can compete with offset*

> *printers. At the same time, traditional offset printers have responded to the challenge from digital printers by choosing to compete for short print-runs when previously they would not have been interested in this work ....*
>
> *At any point in time, the switch-over point is the outcome of these two processes which are driven by technology and by the competitive logic of the printing field [34].*

The optimal unit cost switchover point will differ from product to product, publisher to publisher, and vendor to vendor as they use different print solutions with different associated costs. Focusing solely on the unit cost of a book can be very misleading because it is the whole cost of supply and even the cost of cash tied up in stock that needs to be evaluated by the publisher. In any case, the reduction in the unit cost of digital printing has marched on and the quality has improved to the point that most offset printers have now incorporated digital printers into their shop floors as part of their service mix to remain competitive.

The technical differences between offset and digital printing are well documented by Kaj Johansson, Peter Lundberg, and Robert Ryberg in their book **A Guide to Graphic Print Production.** It came out in the third edition in 2011 and their chapter on printing differentiates between *printing presses* which use static image carriers (like plates) which means every printed product will look alike as opposed to *printers* that do not use any printing plates, which means that every printout can be unique. Digital printing for these authors means that "the machine being used is based on the techniques of printers but has such high capacity that it can compete with the traditional printing press" [35].

On-demand printing of academic books and short-run digital printing of academic books has grown exponentially between 1997 and 2017, unleashed new commercial value of academic book sales for publishers, and created new printing volume for digital print service providers by making books available that simply would have gone out of print and preventing warehouses being filled by overprinted books that would end up written off in publishers' accounts and pulped (Fig. 2.6).

Fig. 2.6 Print floor at BoD.de 'Books on Demand' in Hamburg, Germany. BoD.de have introduced an academic book publishing service in 2017.
Photo reproduced with permission from BoD.de.

Surely, having a 'scholar of digital printing' is a testimony to the maturity of digital printing and the digital printing of academic books. Emeritus Professor Frank Romano had written 50 books by 2017 in the field of graphics communication, much on the subject of digital printing. For those readers who are very keen on book manufacturing and digital printing I commend the Romano bibliography to you. He was a visiting Scholar of Digital Printing in 2013, 2015, and 2017 at Cal Poly San Luis Obispo's Graphic Communication Department (located in California, USA) which specialises in all aspects of graphic communication management, Web and digital media, and design reproduction technology. Digital printing of academic books has already come of age and Chapter 9 examines some of the key trends in book manufacturing and printing that might feature in the future of academic book publishing. This chapter concludes with and interview with printer John Edwards, CEO of Edwards Brothers Malloy and a vintage case study from 2008 featuring the establishment of an on-demand academic book program with books produced by Lightning Source Inc. for John Wiley & Sons.

Interview with John Edwards, CEO of Edwards Brothers Malloy (2017) USA

Established in 1893 in Ann Arbor, Michigan, USA and now based in the states of Michigan and North Carolina, the printing company Edwards Brothers Malloy has always been a short-run book manufacturer serving the academic monograph space (Fig. 2.7).

Fig. 2.7 John Edwards, CEO, Edwards Brothers Malloy based in Ann Arbor, Michigan, United States.

We could see in the late 1990s that the run lengths were coming down due to shrinking library budgets and other factors. We knew that traditional sheet-fed offset would not be competitive in the long term. Direct to film and direct to plate helped to lower costs, but not enough. We started with a few Xerox Docutec imaging devices to find a cheaper way to produce short-run books. From the beginning, for straight text only monochrome books the image quality was okay. For titles with a lot of images, the quality was not good, so, for many years, we continued to run illustrated titles offset. With the advent of the Nuevera and Oce (now owned by Canon) technology, the image quality really improved and from that point many titles with images were produced digitally for our customers and this was cut sheet printing only.

As the internet grew and ultimately the Kindle and other e-readers, the pressure to produce short-run books economically became a primary focus for us. We continued to expand our digital printing footprint, to print local and in publishers' warehouses to reduce costs. Also, binding technology continued to improve and Inkjet became more cost-effective, particularly for single-colour books. Four-colour quality is still not as good as offset, but it is getting better. We now have two Inkjet devices and twenty cut sheet monochrome toner machines and seven four-colour toner devices connected in the network. As of 2017, digital printing is about 25–30% of our business producing 10–20 times the number of different book titles each year and printing much smaller runs of each. In 5 years or less, I would expect our digital volume to exceed 50% of our business.

We have successfully partnered with printers in the UK (CPI), Australia (Griffin), and Singapore (Markono) to move files closer to the end user of the books we make. We have been doing this for about 10 years. We have a number of customers who have eliminated inventory and transmit EDI orders to us daily to manufacture and ship to end users daily.

Single copy book printing on-demand or the 'book of one' is not cheaper to produce; however, on a total cost basis, it can be. The publisher needs to really understand transportation, storage, and cost of money to understand. They real key is not the cost of the book made and sold; it is the total cost of the books made divided by the units sold. Traditional offset or longer run digital still makes sense for a large percentage of titles produced today, but not for all. We set up EDI feeds from our customers so they can eliminate inventory or go to 'micro' inventory to minimise obsolescence. Our connection is through the traditional academic publishers.

I believe print-on-demand technology has kept the printed monograph alive because producing quantities via offset 'just in case' that might not be sold and end up being wasted makes them too expensive. Looking ahead, I believe by 2020 more than half of the physical books printed will be via Inkjet, toner, or some print technology that does not even exist now (Fig. 2.8).

Case study: John Wiley & Sons Collaborating with Lightning Source (2008)

The First Decade of Print-On-Demand for Books [36] Case study reproduced with permission.

For over 200 years, Wiley has evolved to meet the needs of its customers – from letterpress pamphlets to digital apps and interactive online learning tools. The Wiley family's involvement in the business continues, now into the seventh generation. The company may be a far cry from Charles Wiley's small Manhattan printing shop, but its emphasis on quality and commitment to customers haven't changed since 1807 [8].

In 1998, Lightning Source paid a call on Wiley's office in midtown Manhattan [9]. According to Lynn Terhune, (then) POD and USR (ultra-short-run) Administrator, "We listened to what they had to say and were intrigued. As a result of that meeting, we agreed to pilot a short- run program for a handful of test titles, which ultimately grew to 200 titles. In this short-run program, we used Lightning Source to print small quantities for inventory and distribution by Wiley through normal channels." Terhune

Fig. 2.8 Lynn Terhune in 2008 at Lightning Source Inc., La Vergne Tennessee, United States. In 2017 Lynn is Global Digital Print Manager, Strategic Sourcing & Procurement at John Wiley & Sons, Hoboken, New Jersey, United States.

reports that the company launched an internal project with a clear directive to find a way to optimise distribution utilisation and eliminate lost sales due to the unavailability of inventory when customer orders arrive. Wiley turned to Lightning Source to explore an expanded relationship. Terhune says, "We decided to add a print-on-demand (POD) component to our short-run pilot. With short-run, publications are both inventoried and returnable. But with the POD program, while Wiley would still be receiving the customer orders, Lightning Source would take care of the distribution for us. In that instance, materials are neither inventoried nor returnable. It was a radical departure from traditional practices."

"Having made a decision to move forward with Lightning Source, Wiley re-engineered its workflow to seamlessly integrate direct electronic ordering through its systems to make it transparent to the customer," states Cliff Kline, Senior Vice President for Customer and Product Support Operations at Wiley. This included establishing a robust EDI (electronic data interchange) interface for two-way communication between Lightning Source and Wiley. Terhune points out, "This allows us to send orders directly to Lightning Source multiple times daily with little intervention on our part. When Lightning Source receives the order, they provide us with a purchase order acknowledgment, as well as an advance shipment notification upon shipment. This is all standard EDI methodology, but we knew up front that if this program was going to grow, we had to remove as much manual intervention as possible and make the process as automated as possible."

The programme was launched in June 2003 with 20 titles and today (2008) encompasses over 10,000 titles. Wiley is now adding between 150 and 350 titles per month to the programme, or approximately 2000 titles per year. Terhune indicates that some titles in the programme start with electronic files, but a large number of the backlist titles continue to be scanned. In that case, says Terhune, Wiley uses Lightning Source's scanning services to convert titles for inclusion in Lightning Source's digital library. Terhune has seen the paper/digital mix begin to shift to more digital source files in the past few years. Furthermore, to reduce the cost base and improve both the overall efficiency of the programme and the quality of the product, Wiley has assigned dedicated resources to acquire digital files for both covers and text for as many publications as possible.

In the US, Wiley operates a POD programme that allows it to offer titles to customers without stocking them at any of its US distribution centres. In this application of POD, orders are taken by Wiley, processed and passed electronically to the print vendor, and drop shipped by the print vendor, sometimes one book at a time, directly to the customer. As a consequence, orders never go on backorder, and Wiley does not miss any sales due to out-of-stock situations. In the US, Wiley's service standards to fulfil POD titles are the same as if the title was supplied from one of the company's US distribution centres. "The POD model gets product in our customers' hands quickly without Wiley having to make a risky reprint decision," says Terhune.

Wiley's EMEA customers prefer a different model. The company uses the ultra-short-run (USR) model, for which it keeps a 'trickle stock' (about one month's worth of sales) of all POD titles in its European Distribution Centre (EDC). This ensures that orders that include both POD and non-POD titles can be shipped immediately in one consignment to customers. A Wiley software module constantly monitors demand and inventory at the EDC and indicates when additional stock is required. For the EDC Customer Service Books team, "it's a good script to have: It's on the shelf, we'll ship it today.," says Charly Nobbs, VP and Distribution Director for EMEA (Europe, the Middle East, and Africa), who has responsibility for Wiley's UK facility in Bognor Regis. Since 2001, Wiley has had the ability to utilise Lightning Source's UK plant to streamline European distribution, and the company has ramped up its UK title accession over the past four years. According to Terhune, "Using Lightning Source's US and UK plants has been a huge boon for us – one enormous plus we didn't take into consideration at the inception of the program. In the past, by the time we got a European order for out-of-stock items, produced them, and shipped them back by sea freight, it could take up to three months." Now Wiley in the UK places daily orders with Lightning Source UK for any items required – an improvement that eliminates freight cost and provides better [service]. According to Charly Nobbs, "For more than 200 years, Wiley has recognized the importance of satisfying the changing requirements of its customers. This is particularly true in today's digital print environment. Wiley is working with Lightning Source internationally to achieve persistent product availability for all our customers across our wide range of publishing." In addition to its UK USR operation, Wiley is fulfilling POD orders to its subsidiary locations in Singapore, Australia, and Canada as quickly as if they had come from a US distribution centre, with Lightning Source handling the distribution logistics.

Terhune says, "Lightning Source told me that once we launched the POD program, we would be shocked at how easily the orders would flow. They were right."

In its Fiscal Year 2008 (ended 30 April 2008), Wiley produced more than 561,000 units with Lightning Source through its Demand Print Programme. In January

2009 alone, Lightning Source produced a record of approximately 65,000 units for Wiley globally. Terhune reports that all Wiley divisional Inventory Managers have wholeheartedly embraced the USR and POD programmes. Also, the process for activating titles at Lightning Source has been streamlined as well. Terhune says, "When we first started the program, we had to enter all the metadata relating to each title into Lightning Source's web site or upload an Excel spreadsheet. Now there is a two-way transfer of information every night, and we know immediately when a title goes live. Additionally, we have found that exception reports, which document titles with pending action items, have been an invaluable addition to the process. If a title is in wait/hold status requiring action, we are alerted and can immediately take the appropriate action. It removes the potential for human error from the process."

David Taylor, (then) President, Lightning Source, commented: "Through POD, Wiley has cut costs, reduced risk, and leveraged resources to seize greater competitive advantage for the company and ultimately deliver on its promise to the book industry: to deliver any Wiley content whenever, wherever, and however a customer wants it. I am delighted Lightning Source could contribute to Wiley's tremendous accomplishments, and I very much look forward to the next 12 years of our ongoing collaboration."

"Lightning Source definitely has the process down for one-off and ultra-short and short-run book production," says Terhune. "Because Lightning Source started by building a process specifically for this model rather than that of a traditional printer and binder of books, they made one-offs work financially as a business for them and for the publisher."

As to the future, Terhune is looking forward to working with Lightning Source in the production of longer runs, books with more colour content, and first printings. She says, "They are already doing runs of 100 and above for us on a regular basis. We are talking with them about higher quantities. With the infrastructure we have in place, there is nothing preventing them from producing other types of orders. We are delighted with the business model shift Lightning Source has enabled for us, and we expect to see a wide range of new applications emerge over the next three to five years."

One new capability Terhune would like to see is the availability of digital demand printing facilities in all of Wiley's subsidiary locations so that files can be distributed to the production facility closest to the customer, saving shipping time and freight costs and reducing carbon impact. She says, "The UK Lightning Source facility has demonstrated the value of this approach, and in today's global economy, the volumes to justify these additional plants should develop quickly."

Author's note: Since 2008 when the above case celebrated 10 years of printing books on-demand, John Wiley & Sons have become a digital knowledge and learning company as their 2016 and 2017 financial results commentaries detail below. The volume and value of printed education textbooks, professional development books, research books and reference books are in decline but print-on-demand books have enabled efficient and consistent supply of print books in line with demand. Meanwhile the decline in book sales value at Wiley is off-set by author-funded access (Open Access) and a variety of added value online services.

2016 vs 2017 Wiley's Financial Results commentary June 2017 [37]
Full year 2016–17 revenue of $1719 million, up 2% at constant currency and down 1% excluding the impacts of foreign exchange, shifting to time-based journal subscriptions, and contributions from acquisitions. GAAP revenue flat including a $43 million unfavourable foreign exchange impact. Full year adjusted EPS of $3.00, up 13% at constant currency or up 1% (favourable to guidance of mid-single-digit decline) excluding the impacts of foreign exchange, the journal subscription shift, dilution from acquisitions, and unusual charges and credits. GAAP EPS down 21% primarily due to an unfavourable tax decision in Germany. **Revenue from digital products and services now 68% of total revenue, up from 63% in the prior year.** Calendar year 2017 Journal Subscriptions up 1% on a constant currency basis with approximately 97% of targeted business under contract.

2015 vs 2016 Wiley's Financial Results commentary June 2016 [38]
June 2016: In the fourth quarter, Wiley's revenues declined 1% to $434.3 m (£305.8 m). Within that, **education textbook sales dropped 23% and research book sales fell 8%**, but those declines were offset by growth in journal subscriptions, up 1% and double-digit growth in the corporate learning business, up 35%.The strongest businesses for Wiley during the year were **Author-Funded Access, with sales up 21%**, Online Test Preparation, up 27%, Online Programme Management, up 18%, Corporate Learning, up 31%, and WileyPLUS Course Workflow, up 10%. **Sales in Education books, Professional Development Books, Research Books and Reference Books declined.**

The company also shifted more of its business to digital over the financial year.The percentage of revenues from **digital products and services increased to 63% from 60% the year before, whilst revenues from print books declined to 23% from 25%.** Mark Allin, president and c.e.o., said the company's fourth quarter results were in line with expectations: We continued to make good progress in our transition to a digital knowledge and learning company, with **nearly two-thirds of our revenue now generated from digital products and services.** Our solutions businesses again delivered double-digit top-line growth, notably online test preparation, corporate learning, and online program management, **offsetting much of the market-driven revenue decline in traditional book publishing**.

Bookselling on-demand

3

The third technological and market development that was necessary for print-on-demand to impact the academic book was the revolution in academic bookselling. Discoverability of books through new online bookselling catalogues on the web joined up to print-on-demand titles databases. Then in-store print-on-demand machines sought to bring those books physically closer to book buyers. Online catalogues were extensive enough to include even obscure monographs provided the metadata were supplied to them and academic publishers were quick to take advantage of these changes.The Internet Bookshop, Amazon.com, The Book Depository, and more became places where readers could readily search, select, and buy academic books through their computers, and eventually through their smartphones. It is hard to believe from a 2017 perspective that in 1993 online bookselling did not even exist!

The past 25 years have seen retailing in general, online bookselling of any type of book, and therefore retailing of the academic books fundamentally changes. There has been a shift from physical 'bricks and mortar' bookshops powered by intelligent selection by human book buyers to data driven online retail web portals that remember your selections and suggest more of the same. For consumer books in some locations, data generated by consumer buying behaviour have entirely replaced the intelligent human buyer. Consumer transactional data and customer reviews are today entirely powering physical bookshops like Amazon.com. For the collection building academic library, consumer retail channels may not have been as influential as the library acquisition systems development where collection management and associated acquisition management is assisted by online services. In the past 25 years, these services migrated from locally held desktop software tools supplied by library suppliers to online buying portals.

Academic book publishers in the late 1990s experienced the tangible success of Amazon's online book sales of academic books and the associated sales revenue which was delivered to them less Amazon's substantial percentage. Spurred on by this online success, academic book publishers built and enhanced e-commerce enabled websites and started selling academic books directly to authors, researchers, students, and even librarians. This took place in parallel to building online web portals for institutional access to journal content and eventually ebook collections viewed online within institutions. Gathering journal subscribers and forming customer direct relationships through new library consortia deals, as well as supplying authors offprints and article reprints, meant that much of the online direct selling and accessing infrastructure was in place or in development. Throughout the noughties, publishers collaborated with vendors to integrate on-demand book printing services through Electronic Data Interchange (EDI) so that individual books could be drop-shipped to readers.

New digital workflow, improving production quality, and increasingly affordable unit cost for single copy printing of books were literally connected to Amazon's sales

The Impact of Print-On-Demand on Academic Books. https://doi.org/10.1016/B978-0-08-102011-1.00003-1

channel through book wholesaler Ingram Book Company and made a zero-stock strategy achievable for academic publishers. For several years, Ingram supplied Amazon.com books from their book wholesale operations, but as Amazon rapidly moved to extending their product range beyond books to jewellery, sporting goods, clothing, and white goods, they established fulfilment centres in the United States and abroad.

Amazon.co.uk set up its own fulfilment centre, but they also collaborated with large book wholesalers like Gardner's based in Eastbourne, UK to assist speedy supply. In the same way that Amazon.com integrated with Ingram Book Company and Baker & Taylor in the United States, they integrated with wholesalers Bertrams and Gardner's in the United Kingdom. Offering print-on-demand services that complemented this integration was an important move. Ingram set up Lightning Source UK Limited in 2000 in association with Bertrams and printer Antony Rowe set up on-demand print facilities in Gardner's warehouse at about the same time. Looking back from 2017 over the past 20 years, Simon Morley, Purchasing Manager at Gardner's, shared their experience:

> *Our view of print-on-demand has been nothing other than positive. It has allowed titles to remain available that in the past would have become unavailable and therefore we would have lost sales. As a seller of deep backlist this has kept many titles live and profitable. Print-on-demand has enabled the smaller niche publisher and self-publishers to enter or remain in the market as the economics of publishing are made viable.*
>
> *The supply chain is simple and easy with just a handful of printers offering a one-stop solution to multiple titles. Quality and speed has improved so the end user is not compromised. If one was to roll back the clock, the biggest self-made barrier was telling the book trade that a book was manufactured print-on-demand because that put up artificial reasons why not to promote the book. How and who was printing a book is of no relevance to 99% of the book industry. [39]*

Seamless integration of online bookselling and print-on-demand services was key. The customer experience had to feel the same as sourcing a book from stock and that book needed to be of comparable quality. In parallel, the wholesaler Libri in Germany had Amazon.de open on its doorstep and Libri integrated with Amazon along with wholesaler KNV. Libri then invested in BoD (Books On Demand), which initially served the growing German language consumer author services or self-publishing market, but swiftly grew to offer not only self-publishing services in six languages across Europe. BoD also resold many academic print-on-demand titles too as databases of book titles could be plugged into bookselling channels online. Channels to market were opening up through online bookselling and print-on-demand was integrating with those new channels.

In 2004, a UK-based ex-Amazon employee got together with a shipping logistics expert and an IT systems developer and started The Book Depository building up an impressive service stealing market share from both online and bricks and mortar shops in its target markets. Integrating their systems to print-on-demand vendors like Lightning Source enabled them to leapfrog to virtual inventory, assembling the books to be shipped out on the same day they were received. For the customer, The Book

Depository coupled the ability to accept payment in multiple currencies with these sophisticated logistics. By purchasing container space in real time, same day, they could reach even Australia or New Zealand cheaply and swiftly. Offering freight free books to those underserved markets allowed The Book Depository to seize market share. Even textbooks could be sold and shipped at competitive prices from one market to another and publishers' price barriers between markets were challenged. Their success culminated in The Book Depository winning the UK's Queen's Prize for Export in 2009, and then The Book Depository was bought by Amazon in 2011, the same year bricks and mortar bookseller Borders USA went into receivership and liquidated. Print-on-demand academic books played a part in fuelling that rapid sales revenue growth as academic publishers unleashed unavailable books at higher than average retail prices into international markets.

At about the same time that The Book Depository started up, economists were considering how consumer demand was playing out through online downloading and retailing. The supply of books and the role print-on-demand might play was under discussion. Chris Anderson, Editor of *Wired Magazine*, wrote an important article describing 'long-tail' demand in an editorial published in October 2004 and he subsequently expanded his ideas in a book *The Long Tail: Why the Future of Business Is Selling Less of More* (*with the strapline: How Endless Choice is Creating Unlimited Demand*). He eventually issued a revised edition of the book in July 2008 [40]. Although the book focuses on consumer demand, there are definitely parallels with academic book demand. Anderson writes about the emergent supply chain and 'long-tail' sales patterns for music (Rhapsody), movies (Netflix), and books (Amazon). The patterns of demand for individual music tracks had sales patterns which when plotted on a graph over time inevitably showed a 'long-tail' of demand which the new technology of digital downloads could satisfy. Digital technology could keep tracks, no matter how obscure, permanently available. Similarly, the sales life cycle of books commences, rises, plateaus, and then tails off and this is true of the sales pattern for academic books. Essentially, the long-tail is a graph of the rate of sales in units sold. For academic books, there are prepublication sales (referred to as back-order or dues in the book publishing industry) that build up over time, for example, from up to 9 months prior to publication, sales are then shipped on publication, and sales then continue to build reaching peak levels and then plateau, then gradually or suddenly decline to a steady low level (often erratic demand). That steady rate of sale which typically never reaches nil is the long-tail of demand (Fig. 3.1).

Here is a sales graph for a monograph book that illustrates Anderson's principle:

Anderson eloquently describes the Amazon economic story from Amazon 1.0 (1994) online catalogue business to free consigned stock submitted by suppliers (Advantage 1996) to virtual inventory storefront for other retailers in (Marketplace 1999) [41]. Fulfiling sales via print-on-demand pushes a retailer and a publisher away from holding stock of printed books just in case a sale might be made to a just-in-time (JIT) manufacturing model whereby orders are placed and the product is manufactured in response to the order. This is the purest definition of print-on-demand books: stockless and inventory free where individual books are printed, bound, and shipped in response to a placed and paid for order online. A JIT manufacturing in response to

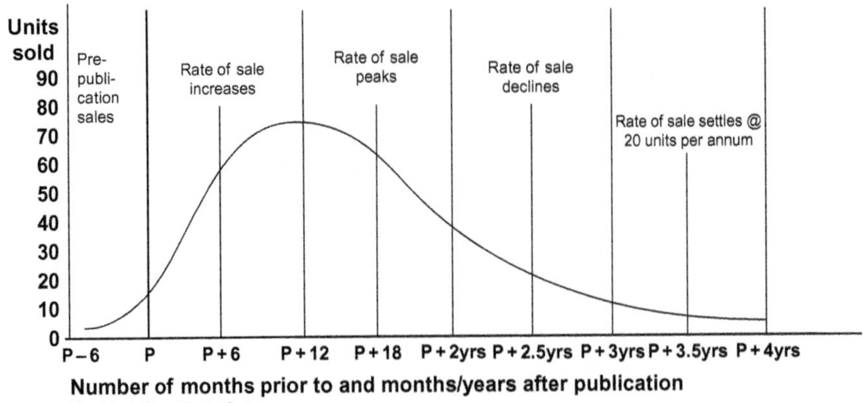

Fig. 3.1 The long tail: monograph sales over 4 years.

orders is achieved in print-on-demand services from Amazon's 'inventory free' service, or Ingram's Lightning Source buy–sell 'DI' (Distribution) wholesale reselling service and UK wholesaler Gardner's 'POD service' powered by printer CPI (originally in warehouse printer Antony Rowe). All three of these providers offer stockless supply of books services as part of their service mix and by necessity are closely integrated to the supply chain channels to market rather than simply shipping batches of books from traditional print book manufacturers to book distributors. Like Dell's computer manufacturing on-demand service and advertising slogan declared: Buy it. Build it.

An alternative to stockless fulfilment is short-run digital printing which can mean anything from 50 to 500 units printed, which might mean printing batches more frequently but keeping stock at a minimum number of units. A hybrid of these approaches was developed in the form of auto-replenishment whereby an algorithm predicts the demand for the next period based on historical purchasing, e.g. 6 weeks, and generates an EDI replenishment order (electronic data interchange order information sent computer to computer) in appropriately sized batches. Vendors like wholesalers Gardner's, Bertrams, Baker & Taylor, and Ingram started integrating with print-on-demand book facilities or running their own print-on-demand for books.

Embracing Anderson's long-tail demand economics, in August 2007 Amazon started print-on-demand services for books and acquired CreateSpace creating a comprehensive creative author services portfolio. Amazon Print-On-Demand was offered as a service to publishers so that their titles would constantly remain available even when physical book deliveries had not been made. Amazon was long-tail thinking incarnate and the next step was to offer author publishing services to their consumers. Informed by sophisticated marketing data regarding customer star ratings and regional sales data, it felt surprising when in November 2015 Amazon came full circle to launch its first physical bookshop. An Amazon bookshop's range is defined and fine-tuned as a local showroom reflecting local consumption patterns practically in real time with minimal stockholding and books presented covers out for impact. Online bookselling

Fig. 3.2 Espresso Book Machine in bookshop c.2005.

had reached maturity by 2015 when online customer bookselling data took control of the Amazon bookshop shelves. At present, these are consumer book stores, but why not inform and create the campus bookstore in the same manner? The case studies below cover three aspects of (online delete) bookselling as it relates to print-on-demand for academic books: first print-on-demand at the physical point of purchase; second, a look at the rise of online retailing for books; and finally, a consumer direct monograph offering linked to an institutional subscription business model (Fig. 3.2).

Case study: Espresso Book Machine

On Demand Books, the proprietor of the Espresso Book Machine (EBM), was founded in 2003 by its Chairman, Jason Epstein, a renowned innovator throughout his nearly 60-year publishing career, and business executive Dane Neller, who left his role as President and CEO of Dean & Deluca in 2005 to focus his full energies as CEO of On Demand Books. The EBM was featured in a Time Magazine cover story as a 'Best Invention of 2007'. Website: www.ondemandbooks.com.

In October 1999, Jason Epstein gave a lecture at the New York Public Library and later wrote a book entitled *Book Business: Publishing Past Present and Future* in which he predicts a paradigm shift towards print-on-demand and digital access to books: "a shift potentially more influential than the one precipitated by the invention half a millennium ago of moveable type" [42]. The book is a half publisher memoir of Epstein's career, and half publishing book business history including references to Wiener's 1950s *Cybernetics* which foreshadowed the internet and worldwide web. He concludes that "On the infinitely expandable shelves of the World Wide Web, there will be room for a virtually limitless variety of books that can be printed on demand or reproduced on hand-held readers or similar devices" [42]. He also reflects on the potential for publishing to return to its cottage industry origins. Epstein put his thinking into practice and in 2003 invested in the On Demand Books (ODB) which prototyped and later manufactured Jeff March'sEspresso Book Machine. In April 2006, a beta version was installed at the World Bank's bookstore in Washington, DC, USA, seemingly an ideal way to print their copious grey literature repository as well as any other books available in the database. I visited the World Bank shortly after the installation but there were technical problems. With only one machine on site the potential for a single point of failure to occur when retrieving the files, then printing, collating, and binding each copy was highly likely. It was a bold move of the World Bank to embrace this new technology.

The New York Public Library's Science, Industry and Business library was the first library to install the Espresso Book Machine in 2007. Since then, others have invested and tested the espresso book machine, including the University of Utah, University of Michigan, Darien Library, Brooklyn Public Library, Sacramento Public Library, and the Riverside County Library. Priced between USD $125,000 and $150,000, the primary benefit to investing in this new innovative technology is "to support a creative and intellectual community by giving anyone the opportunity to independently publish their work for a nominal cost", according to the librarian at the University of Syracuse Dorotea Szkolar in 2012 [43]. In 2008, Lightning Source (Ingram Content) launched a pilot programme linking its content database with the Espresso Book Machine (EBM) from On Demand Books. Participating publishers included John Wiley & Sons Inc., Hachette Book Group, McGraw-Hill, Simon & Schuster, Clements Publishing, Cosimo, *E*-Reads, Bibliolife, Information Age Publishing, Macmillan, University of California Press, and W.W. Norton. The pilot service enabled these publishers to enhance the availability of their titles at point-of-sale EBM locations. Approximately 85,000 titles from these publishers became available for purchase at EBM locations in the United States in May 2009. Following a pilot programme, publishers that print and distribute books with Lightning Source then had the option to add the EBM channel. The EBM, which was named a Time Magazine 'Invention of the Year', is essentially an automated teller machine for books. Placed primarily in bookstores and libraries, the machine automatically prints, binds and trims perfect bound paperback books on-demand, at point of sale. "We see the Espresso Book Machine as an innovative and exciting way for publishers to get their books out into the market", said David Taylor, then the President of Lightning Source, in 2008. "There is clearly a place for the in-store print-on-demand model in the emerging landscape of globally distributed print". Mr. Taylor continued, "Working with On Demand Books allows the many thousands of publishers with whom we already work the chance to get their books into this new distribution channel with minimal effort. In the times in which we are living, publishers need to be looking at every option to ensure that their books can be immediately available to people who want to buy them" [44].

A host of publishers supported and welcomed the Espresso Book Machine available catalogue when piloting a programme with Ingram to add more content to their available library. "The EBM& Lightning Source pilot program is an exciting next step in the evolution of digital printing and direct fulfilment of Wiley's must-have content to our customers, wherever and whenever they need it," said Lynn Terhune, US print-on-demand and ultra-short-run administrator at John Wiley & Sons. "Our rich content is being discovered by our customers in channels that were unimaginable five years ago" [44].

"Providing McGraw-Hill content to our customers around the world is core to our strategy", said Philip Ruppel, President for McGraw-Hill Professional. "Espresso's ability to make thousands of our key titles available on-demand gives us another vehicle to achieve that goal" [44].

"Norton is delighted to have joined the Espresso/Lightning source pilot program and especially to include in it, Jason Epstein's insightful volume Book Business, which makes the case for this initiative that will help achieve the widest possible distribution for our books", said W. Drake McFeely, Chairman and President, W.W. Norton and Company [44].

"The University of California Press has had a long and active partnership with Lightning Source, and we're very pleased to have the opportunity to extend that partnership to the Espresso Book Machine pilot program", said Erich van Rijn, Director of Publishing Operations, University of California Press. "This program will further our efforts to make the greatest amount of our published material available to the widest possible readership. The point-of-sale printing model is truly an exciting development for the book business" [44].

"On Demand Books is delighted that the Espresso Book Machine is playing such a central role in a program that is blazing a trail to the future of book publishing", said Dane Neller, CEO of On Demand Books. Mr. Neller continued, "With the book business facing dramatic changes and challenges, we believe the timing of the EBM could not be better. Publishers, retailers, and libraries alike see the appeal of the machine that collapses the supply chain, boosts backlist sales, matches supply with demand, eliminates returns and powers new, high growth sales channels for publishers" [44] (Fig. 3.3).

Fig. 3.3 Espresso Book Machine c.2009.

Rick Anderson is Associate Dean for Collections and Scholarly Communication in the J. Willard Marriott Library at the University of Utah. (delete: Writing in 2011) Article [45] reprinted here with the permission of the author. Originally published: "The Good, the Bad, and the Sexy: Our Espresso Book Machine Experience" The Scholarly Kitchen August 2, 2011 https://scholarlykitchen.sspnet.org/2011/08/02/the-good-the-bad-and-the-sexy-our-espresso-book-machine-experience/

Having an EBM has been fun, exciting, and frustrating, and I fully expect that it will continue being all of those things for the foreseeable future – with the mix gradually shifting away from 'frustrating' and towards 'fun' as the technology matures and as we keep discovering new ways to put the EBM to good use for our patrons.

Technically speaking, the EBM does print books very quickly. It takes about 5 min to print a 300-page book – as long as the machine is warmed up. If it is not, you have got to let the glue melt, which will take 45 min to an hour. Of course, 3,000,000 titles sounds like a lot of content, but much of it consists of very old titles in the public domain, only some of which represent content that anyone cares about. We knew this going in, but it has still been a bit disappointing that more current content has not been added more quickly to the database. (On the other hand, one of the great strengths of the EspressNet book database is its depth: shortly after installing our EBM, we were able to find and print an obscure 300-year-old German text for a faculty member who had been trying, unsuccessfully, to find a printed copy of the book for years. That EBM-powered serendipity changed the structure of his course.)

Great concepts do not print books; functional machines print books: We were very fortunate in being the second desert-climate library to purchase an EBM. The first was Brigham Young University, and ODB had to scramble to repair some unanticipated (and, to be fair, probably unanticipatable) climate-related problems. One of the more amusing ones involved static electricity: since the ambient air is so dry, pages would not pile up cleanly as they emerged from the text-block printer. ODB had to send a technician to Provo to cut a hole in the top of BYU's machine and install an ionising fan. However, being a young technology, other technical problems remained: we had issues with balky and leaking inkjets, malfunctioning sensors, and recalcitrant cover feeds, all of which have been fixed or mostly fixed at this point. We are still waiting for a colour text-block printer that will communicate effectively with the machine, despite having been offered that option initially. For now, we are still making do with black-and-white (we can print covers in colour without any problem).

No matter how sexy the delivery mechanism, the content matters more: As I mentioned above, we have been disappointed (though not shocked) that publishers are generally slow to allow frontlist titles to be printed and purchased through the EBM. To some degree, this can be explained by the EBM's very small installation base: 45 machines in 41 locations worldwide, 12 of which are libraries (where publishers might not expect many sales to happen).

No matter how sexy the search interface, bad metadata means bad search results: The real problem with search in EspressNet is not the inflexibility of the interface, but the abominable quality of its metadata, much of which comes from Google Books. At this point in time, searchers cannot assume that their results are accurate, which is hugely frustrating. Inflexible search is a problem, but bad metadata in a 3,000,000-title database is an *enormous* problem, one that cannot be solved without significant expense.…we have been startled by the unanticipated ways in which the EBM really has caught people's attention: there's significant demand for blank-page journals that we print up on the EBM, bound in covers featuring images from our library's rich digital collections; we sell these, steadily, for $7. We experimented successfully with printing and shipping the annual proceedings for a scientific society, and have seen great demand for our self-publishing services. We are currently in talks with our campus bookstore about cooperative selling arrangements, whereby the EBM can act as a sort of expanded backlist warehouse.

Being an early adopter is expensive: The EBM has 'eaten' a lot of [library] staff time and energy, and we fully expect that it will continue to do so for a while….

Start-up companies do not always fully know what they are getting into: The EBM and its attendant technologies are not only new to us and our patrons; they are also new to the company behind them. My impression is that ODB is still struggling to figure out the right balance between treating the EBM as a retail tool and a library technology. *The Good, the Bad, and the Sexy: Our Espresso Book Machine Experience by Rick Anderson, Scholarly Kitchen August 2, 2011* [45].

Case study: Online bookselling: Amazon, The Internet Bookshop, and Alibaba (2017) US/UK/China

This case is a reflection by the author on three contrasting online bookselling businesses that developed in the 1990s and summarises Amazon's entry into print-on-demand services from the publisher user perspective. Amazon's control of publisher content to delight their customers contrasts with Alibaba's open business to business services portal approach which enables the publisher to connect with a number of print-on-demand for books vendors by region.

In the first quarter of 1994, an online bookshop started up called www.bookshop.co.uk based in Oxford, England in the United Kingdom. This may appear logical at the time as Oxford is a traditional academic book buying town due to the ancient university and the highly regarded bricks and mortar Blackwell Bookshop which was serving academic libraries around the world with books. However, Oxford was not one of the UK's book distribution hubs which requires cheap labour, cheap property, and proximity to ports and airports to sustain a strategic move into disrupting the book supply chain. The Internet Bookshop served its owners well but had no real aspirations or capability to change the bookselling paradigm. However, in the United States in July 1994, another online bookshop started called www.amazon.com based in Seattle, Washington state. Seattle harbours a software development talent pool due to the aerospace industry (Boeing) and software companies (Microsoft). In addition, Seattle has proximity to west coast book buying towns west of the Rocky mountains (a geographic logistical barrier for distribution) and crucially Roseburg, Oregon which is equidistant between San Francisco and Seattle, and was the largest west coast book distribution warehouse operated by the Ingram Book Company.

Over 1 million book titles were listed on each of these nascent websites which created a new user experience whereby academic books could be readily found as quickly by a researcher or student as a librarian using a library acquisition tool. At the American Library Association's 1996 midwinter conference in San Antonio, I attended an academic acquisitions librarians' session run by a young and enthusiastic Jeff Bezos who gave a presentation about his fairly new online bookshop Amazon.com. He was selling the merits of online bookselling for academic institutional book purchases. He also asked librarians about their book ordering habits and what facilities they might require on the website. He treated these potential customers with substantial book buying budgets with respect and listened to them. He embodied a customer-centric mindset throughout. The library booksellers present and most of the librarians were sceptical of this new approach to ordering books as they had bespoke systems and collection management tools for libraries and lacked the imagination to see how online bookselling was poised to push substantial book sales revenue directly to academic publishers and serve as a powerful, user-friendly search and discover tool for the academic book reader. This was disruptive innovation in action and print-on-demand was poised to become an integral part of it. Academic book buyer accessibility through an online catalogue plus rapid availability achieved through an order management system that could serve up printed books daily to an efficient US book supply chain partner in Ingram meant books previously unavailable became visible and available for the first time. Coupled with Amazon's aggressively discounted pricing, this would inevitably attract ever more academic book buyers and acquisition librarians. Print-on-demand proved so effective that within the decade Amazon would buy their own on-demand capability for their warehouses.

In 1997, The Internet Bookshop (Oxford) Limited was worth USD \$10 m [46] and selling books worth USD \$400 k per quarter, which is not bad for a three-year-old start-up business. However, over the same period, Amazon had raised USD \$11 m, was spending USD \$4 m in marketing per quarter, was discounting all books at 20% off list price, had world class book distribution in the background supplied by Ingram, and was selling books worth USD \$16 m per quarter. In short, Amazon was aggressively revolutionising bookselling. In the space of four years online bookselling, led by Amazon.com, had become a new market force and was immediately impacting on the niche academic book business. By June 1998, the Internet Bookshop, which was a nice little earner for its founder but lacked any ambition to be more, was sold to United Kingdom high street bookseller and stationer WH Smith's. By contrast, Amazon's financially aggressive approach, proximity to world-class software developers, slick marketing, attractive discounting to consumers, and robust book distribution pushed Amazon forward to stealing serious market share from bricks and mortar bookshops including campus bookstores and specialist outlets. Amazon.co.uk opened supported by its Amazon International's first regional book fulfilment centre at Marston Gate in the United Kingdom in 1998 and in the same year Amazon.com announced diversifying away from bookselling. Amazon began its trajectory to becoming a world-class reseller of all goods and a software services business.

By December 1998, halfway around the world, Jack Ma launched online seller Alibaba.com in China as a business to business marketplace, followed by Tmall where sellers set up their shops and consumers buy goods from them. The 'marketplace' model was born along with the idea that a web portal might outsource all the fulfilment of a book order but own the customer transaction, customer data, and track their buying behaviour. Alibaba charged sellers a modest commission of 2%–5% per transaction (as opposed to Amazon's 17%) and provided marketing tools. It may be due to this 'enable others' mindset that they are now the largest online retailer in the world. Tmall sells many products including academic books. Together with Taobao, (a consumer-to-consumer marketplace like *E*-bay), AliPay (the largest payment system in China like PayPal), Alibaba Cloud (a data mining technology company), and Alimama (a marketing services provider to assist sellers), Alibaba grew to exceed a market capitalisation of USD 200 billion by 2015 and exceeded Walmart as the world's largest retailer by 2016. Alibaba operates in 200 countries [47]. Key in 'print-on-demand books' into Alibaba's search engine and refine the search to 'minimum order of 1' and 20 vendors offering digital book printing services on-demand are displayed. Some are consumer oriented services like customer children's books, but many are proper print-on-demand book service vendors.

Around the world from 1998 to the present, online retailing including bookselling has grown exponentially. Academic textbooks and monographs were among the initial commodities that started the revolution, and print-on-demand services were fully integrated by 2000. Lightning Source was supplying Amazon.com print-on-demand books from the 1990s and in 2000 BookSurge was started by Mitchell Davis (see his BiblioLabs interview in Chapter 7) in Charleston, South Carolina, USA. BookSurge established a competing business targeting publishers and independent authors with on-demand printing and online distribution services. In 2005, Amazon.com acquired BookSurge LLC and its founder went to Amazon to assist with the integration. Amazon formed CreateSpace in 2005 when rebranding another acquisition: CustomFlix Labs Inc., which was launched in 2002 for independent filmmakers to distribute their work. BookSurge was subsumed under the CreateSpace brand in 2009. Today they claim to be: "the publishing and manufacturing on-demand leader for independent content creators, publishers, film studios, and music labels" [48]. Amazon print-on-demand services (the publisher facing name) aka CreateSpace (the author services name) started signing up many publishers including many academic publishers with full service

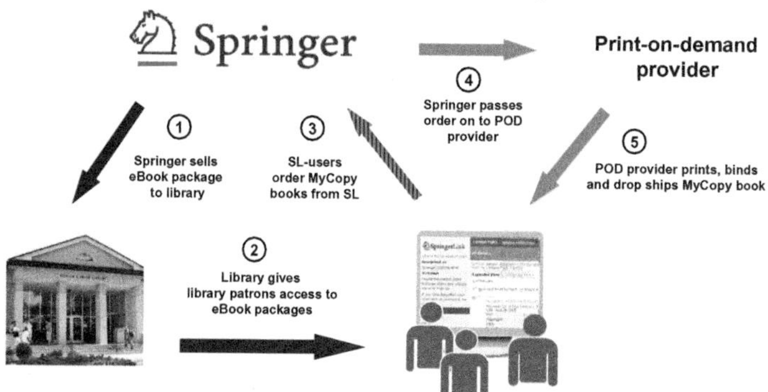

Fig. 3.4 A diagram explaining the Pioneering MyCopy service to academic libraries and patrons from Springer in December 2009.

print-on demand book reselling services. Amazon took away the ability to set reselling discounts and discounts were set as per the publisher's conventional selling discount. In this way, Amazon clawed back a significant share of the net sale price. In particular, Amazon offers two types of on-demand printing for books: inventory free and in stock protection print-on-demand. Inventory free means just that, a stockless without holding any inventory of a book which works well for monographs where the rate of sale may be single figures per month. In-stock protection is a complimentary service for books held on consignment at Amazon which might suddenly sell out with a spike in sales. In-stock protection protects Amazon from ever being out of stock and therefore disappointing a customer wishing to buy a book. More importantly, Amazon are gradually accumulating the files of all books from publishers (files to print covers and insides aka book blocks) and amassing a huge virtual library of books that can be manufactured on-demand for as long as rights permit (Fig. 3.4).

Case study: The MyCopy Service from Springer (2008) NL

Reproduced from the My Copy website August 2017 http://springer.com/mycopy [49].

MyCopy is an innovative online bookselling service which is supplied directly to academic libraries that subscribe to SpringerLink ebook collections. Individual members of an academic institution can order their own personal softcover edition of Springer eBook titles for just 24.99, including shipping and handling, provided their library subscribes to the ebook collection. Available to registered patrons of libraries that have purchased Springer eBooks, MyCopy is available for thousands of book titles. **MyCopy is currently available to library patrons in 30 countries and is extremely popular with students and researchers.** MyCopy is simplistically and economically priced (costs 24.99 USD, EUR, or GBP) per eBook copy and the price includes shipping and handling to the purchaser's address (excludes local VAT/Sales tax where applicable).

MyCopy is currently available on thousands of Springer's English language eBooks and for new eBooks added to SpringerLink. Academics and students have the choice to read or download titles electronically on link.springer.com through their institutional library and/or order a personal printed paperback book with the MyCopy service. In addition to the contemporary ebook collections, the Springer Book Archives date from the 1840s through 2005. Patrons can select the MyCopy option on titles from an even larger range of eBooks. Pay securely with our credit card service or with PayPal. Ships directly to the customer with no additional handling and shipping costs. Available only to institutions that purchased one or more of Springer's eBook collections. The printed copy includes a colour printed softcover and the content is printed in black and white.

How does it work? Visit link.springer.com, find the Springer eBook you are interested in buying, and look for the 'MyCopy' button. Simply click on the Buy Now MyCopy button, add the book to the shopping cart, and follow the payment instructions. Pay securely by credit card service or PayPal and receive a print copy within 8–10 business days.

The pricing is incredibly simple across three currencies: All books will be sold at the same price of 24.99, regardless of the currency, and the currency is set based on the shipping address. VAT or GST is added depending on your location. MyCopy books can only be ordered if your library has purchased the title as part of one or more Springer eBook collections. The entire ordering and shipping process will be handled by Springer in cooperation with a specialised print provider. For the most current list of countries where this unique service is available, visit springer.com/mycopy. Here are three reviews quoted on the My Copy website by users based in the United States, United Kingdom and Switzerland:

Yes, the book did match my expectations. I certainly will buy again – the most attractive thing is the considerable savings in the price this is simply unbelievable and not matched by any other o er from any bookseller! Please keep it up, said Dr. Manika Jayawardena, trainee radiologist, associated through the University of Liverpool.

This project represents a very innovative way in which to look at both publisher and library services for electronic content in the future, and MyCopy is a great value-add to our site license for these eBooks. Wendy Allen Shelburne, Electronic Resources Librarian at the Library of the University of Illinois at Urbana-Champaign.

My belief is that this service will explode. Jens Vigen, Head Librarian of the European Organization for Nuclear Research, CERN.

Book fulfilment on-demand

4

The fourth area of technological and market development that was necessary for print-on-demand to impact the academic book was book fulfilment, which comprises the book supply chain. This includes all aspects of book fulfilment to enable sales through all possible retail channels. Book wholesalers like Ingram in the United States and Gardner's in the United Kingdom were uniquely placed to deliver the behind the scenes book fulfilment capability, automatically gathering orders several times a day and pushing them to the print floor for printing and despatch. Most importantly, in addition to the order management systems, there were four critical elements of the book supply chain that needed to be in place to make scaled up print-on-demand sales happen. First, electronic data interchange (EDI) of orders for books including shipping messages; second, effective book metadata describing each individual book in defined industry standards which one computer can pass to another; third, encoded metadata information into barcodes to speed up handling processes for thousands of unique books; and finally, supply chain innovations in the wider business ecosystems which made small parcel logistics cost-effective for customers. These developments, which I always viewed like the plumbing within a building, may sound rather dull in comparison to breakthroughs in digital composition, digital print innovation, and the dawn of online bookselling, but without an effective book supply chain to deliver physical books quickly, print-on-demand academic books would have flopped.

Professor Ron Adner, mentioned in the introduction to Part 1 of this book, published a widely acclaimed book about successful and unsuccessful innovation, *The Wide Lens: What Successful Innovators See That Others Miss* [50] (Portfolio, Revised edition June 25, 2013). Adner teaches lessons in supply chain and market alignment where product offerings might struggle to match consumer expectations. Successful innovators do not ignore our interdependent world and the innovation ecosystem which their business inhabits. One of his case studies is that of the Sony e-book reader which failed because "even a great e-reader cannot succeed in a market where customers have no easy access to e-books" [51]. Amazon Kindle succeeded where Sony failed by providing that access coupled with a good enough e-book reader. For print-on-demand books, the supply chain had to work seamlessly and efficiently in order to provide customers access to academic publishers' print-on-demand books and to become an innovation success.

The plumbing: The book supply chain had been going through significant change since the 1980s and 1990s as consumer goods supply chain management developed into sophisticated processes driven by siloed systems which could exchange data through EDI. Book publishing industry associations like Book Industry Communications (BIC), Edi-t-Eur, and the US Book Industry Standards and Communications (BISAC) were busy commissioning supply chain studies for books and writing standards for machine-to-machine communication that all parties in the book supply chain might implement in their systems. In particular orders, order acknowledgements and order despatch notifications are critical to swift book supply and underpinned the prompt

The Impact of Print-On-Demand on Academic Books. https://doi.org/10.1016/B978-0-08-102011-1.00004-3

time to market for print-on-demand manufactured books, i.e. same day despatch or next day despatch.

Academic book publishers were active participants in these initiatives which helped take costs out of the day-to-day book distribution business. That preparatory work enabled the implementation of EDI for print-on-demand book supply to take place over a few short years between 2004 and 2009. Integrating drop-ship consumer direct supply of books from publisher distribution systems using EDI communications was vital in the swift success of print-on-demand book sales for academic books. Costs were kept to a minimum provided the exchange was machine to machine: from publishers the orders being passed to a print vendor, with order acknowledgements instantly back if the book was found on the server followed by despatch notification for billing systems to issue customers compliant e-invoices. For virtual inventory print-on-demand books, this was vital because, unlike conventionally ordered books held as inventory which were picked from warehouse shelves, packed into boxes, and despatched to the retail customers who then unpacked, sorted, shelved, and repacked books for either retail bookshelves or for despatch to consumers, stockless print-on-demand books were printed to order and often despatched directly from the printer to the customer, thereby shortening the supply chain.

Traditional 'goods in' booking slots for arrival at retailer's distribution centres did not necessarily apply because a print vendor would only know a day in advance which books they were actually going to despatch.

Metadata and barcodes: Another fundamental development necessary for the success of print-on-demand was book metadata, i.e. data describing the book. Machine-to-machine exchangeable metadata needed to be present to enable the rapid and accurate identification of books within a just-in-time manufacturing and fulfilment operation. For the first time, book metadata became systematically standardised in 2000 with the publication of ONIX for Books 1.0; subsequent releases followed with 2.0 in 2001, 2.1 in 2003, and 3.0 in 2009. ONIX brought together all the key descriptive data elements that booksellers might require from a publisher to inform a buying decision and the core ONIX data elements can also be used to produce book advance information sheets, catalogues describing books and other promotional material, populate publisher websites, and to meet the needs of the wider supply chain.

One key element of the descriptive data used by the wider supply chain is the ISBN (International Standard Book Number). The ISBN was developed much earlier in the 1960s as an aid to inventory management in warehouses and was established as an international standard in 1970 with at least 150 countries using ISBNs by 2017. It is a fundamental tool which facilitates discovery of books, book sales, and even the digital print manufacturing process. The use of barcodes were first widely utilised in the grocery business logistics. Eventually, the ISBN was turned into a machine readable EAN/USP barcode. Barcodes enable scanners to identify a physical book accurately and swiftly move it through a process. For example, the picking, packing, and dispatching process. With the advent of book distribution systems and stock management systems, locations of stock were numbered and those numbers were translated into barcodes to enable devices to read and match books to storage locations. These locations can efficiently be reassigned to stock different books. By the advent of print-on-demand for books, the generating and assigning of ISBNs with associated book level barcodes printed on the covers of books was common practice in the book industry in many countries. Most academic publishers' warehouses and their picking staff were also using scanning technologies to match warehouse locations with book barcodes to manage the picking and packing of conventionally printed books.

EAN/UPC Barcodes were not only critical for despatch of books to customers but also as an integral element of the digital printing workflow process as described by Ed Marino in Chapter 1. System generated EAN/UPC barcodes printed on book covers and print production ISBNs printed on the last page of book blocks enable them to be united in the trimming and binding stage of the print-on-demand process. Combining the wrong book cover with the wrong digitally printed book block is essentially a business disaster waiting to happen even if the mismatched pairing might be humorous at the time. Barcodes enable the software to alert operators who might rework the books correctly (Fig. 4.1).

Small Parcel logistics: If any readers are keen to understand in detail the evolution of small package delivery technologies and practices, William T. Dennis wrote an excellent book in 2011 detailing the US experience called *Parcel and Small Package Delivery Industry (2011,* ISBN1461021545). The 'hub-and-spoke' logistics system was pioneered by Federal Express (FedEx) in 1973, and by 1977 they were able to establish an air-based system capable of delivering small packages—including mail—overnight throughout most of the US. In March 2000, FedEx launched a home delivery service to support new online and catalogue retailers. Dennis distinguishes between traditional delivery and e-commerce delivery systems [53].

In 1999, automatic replenishment programmes were evident in the logistics literature and specifically were being tried by the grocery industry; in 2004, auto-replenishment of books was taking place in academic book publishers' warehouses as described by Paul Major of Oxford University Press in Chapter 5. Using predictive algorithms that forecast demand for each book over a given period, a perfectly valid alternative of ultra-short-run and short-run digital printing in warehouses was being developed taking an auto-replenishment approach. While the stockless or virtual inventory print-on-demand model for academic books was the most radical departure from conventional book supply chain holding preprinted stock for extended periods, auto-replenishment takes a hybrid approach where the warehouse is still being utilised (rather than outsourcing all stock availability to a wholesaler) and small stock holding is optimised in line with forecast demand. Making book fulfilment happen in a timely fashion was key for print-on-demand books, not quite as fast as picking from stock, but delivering a book to a customer within a couple of days from order placement was good enough for most circumstances.

Two interviews conclude this chapter with leading print-on-demand service suppliers who have served in different markets successfully and have successfully integrated order management, book distribution, and digital printing: John Ingram, Ingram Content Group, and Edwin Ng, Markono. These are followed by a triple case study of three Australian university presses taken from a PhD thesis submitted in 2008 by Dr. Xuemei Tian who is now Senior Lecturer at Swinburne University of Technology, Melbourne, Australia. This also serves as an introduction for the reader

Example of an EAN bar code

EAN-13

- Symbol ID:]E0
- Capacity: 13 numeric
- Omnidirectional
- Supports GTIN-13
- Does not support attributes

Example of a US book bar code

From January 2007 the ISBN migrated from a 10 digit to a 13 digit code system.

The EAN-13 bar code is divided into five parts and each part is separated by a hyphen. It starts with a "978" prefix which indicates it is a book, followed by a country identifier,a publisher identifier, a title identifier and closes with a check digit that validates the number.

Example: ISBN-10 10 digits: 1234567890. Now reads as ISBN-13 / EAN: **978-1-234567-89-7**

Bookland EAN add-on code

An added 5-digit section to the EAN code is often used to designate a price. If the price is less than $100.00, the number starts with a number "5" to designate US currency.

For example Price: **$4.95 = 50495.**

Fig. 4.1 Above are examples of machine readable bar codes for books which serve as unique identifiers in both a retail and digital book manufacturing context. Examples supplied by the Book Industry Study Group (BISG).

to three different types of university presses, each of which focuses on different forms of academic literature discussed in Part 2: the academic (monograph) publisher, the textbook publisher, and the aggregator of books (Fig. 4.2).

Fig. 4.2 John Ingram, Chairman, Ingram Content Group, United States.

Interview with John Ingram, Chairman, Ingram Content Group, owner of Lightning Source Inc., now part of the Ingram Content Group, and owner of Ingram Industries Inc.

As a primary innovator, investor, and market leader of print-on-demand services, John Ingram recounts the origins of Lightning Source Inc. which started as Lightning Print in 1997.

The catalyst for offering a print-on-demand service was walking through the Ingram Book warehouse of 350k physically printed book titles with my long-time friend and then colleague Y.S. Chi who is now a Director at Elsevier. A core value of the Ingram Book Company, as a book wholesaler, was to keep lots of inventory available for retailers to purchase. We took a look at 'green bar reports' which showed which stock was moving, which stock was lingering in the warehouse, and which items were showing as back orders. We wondered: could we figure out how to store the slow moving titles electronically? **We needed a different paradigm.** Could we move to a 'print to order' approach and reduce unnecessary inventory while keeping more books available? We were seeking an elegant solution. Y.S. brought together digital workflow software, the IT development team, and IBM printing capability which was set up adjacent to the Ingram warehouse with Larry Brewster to oversee the operation.

Print-on-demand then was not mainstream. We were at the edges and the Lightning Print service appealed to the underserved or those in pain. We started with public domain titles from some aggregators, newly formed author services companies that were looking for a solution, 'micro' publishers, and later the university presses began to take an interest.

We decided to print two copies for stock: placing one in Nashville, Tennessee, and one in Rosemond, Oregon. As it turned out, having two physical copies was not a great strategy. An order for two never came in because two was of course the wrong number! However, perception of availability triggered interest and demand, which was a good and measurable result. On the premise *if some is good, more is better* [55], we realised that we had to make an important step: **move to stockless availability**.

Innovation often happens around the edges of an industry and an example of that was the front-end author services success once they were married to quick availability of printed books and e-books. iUniverse, Xlibris, AuthorHouse (later wrapped up as Author Solutions) and Lulu were all early entrants with exponential success. 'Micro' publishers, in other words very small independent publishers, also took up the service with enthusiasm.

Finally, university presses including Princeton University Press, Penn State, Cambridge University Press, and Oxford University Press embraced the paradigm as early adopters and built entire academic book publishing programmes in partnership with our developing capabilities. Web-based author services and small press services have continued to grow as the front end to Lightning Source print-on-demand services. In 2012, Ingram launched IngramSpark as a proprietary web portal frontend to manage both authors and small publishers. Our most effective and successful application of print-on-demand technology for books has been to connect digital print to the Ingram Book channel infrastructure and to achieve the economic printing of a single copy. Taking one copy to many, not many copies to one (Fig. 4.3).

Fig. 4.3 Edwin Ng, Managing Director, Markono, Singapore.

Interview with Edwin Ng, Managing Director, Markono, Singapore

Markono is a privately owned family printing business based in Singapore. As many readers may know, Singapore is a strategic distribution hub for Asia as a port for shipping containers and as an airport hub for cargo and passengers. In the mid-1990s, Markono responded to the requirements of the computer equipment manufacturing industry who implemented just-in-tlme (JIT) delivery of electronic components to manufacture and ship computers to businesses and consumers. This JIT supply chain included a requirement for printed operating manuals. Markono installed Xerox DocuTech printing technology which enabled cost-effective short-run printing JIT to assemble computers to order. Markono was therefore able to offer academic book publishing customers a printing service to supply Asia with academic books from a print and distribute hub. In the 1990s, this was not an integrated workflow. Books were ordered in batches of 100, 200, or 300 copies for shipping to libraries and customers throughout Asia. Markono was in a position to become the digital printing partner in Asia. Subsequently, Markono purchased Inkjet printing technology to their offset and digital printing capability, but it was not about the printing hardware; it was about the software which enabled them to combine the right printing solution to inventory management and demand—being able to migrate titles from many copies/high demand with warehousing down to single copy manufacturing in response to wholesale orders from across Asia. With the extension of print-on-demand into colour books, Markono acquired HP Indigo print equipment in 2007. While this solution was not effective for single copy print-on-demand supply of books, the HP Indigos worked for colour covers and small batches.

Markono has had Inkjet printers for 2 years now and has worked hard to retain academic publishers as customers. Increasingly, Markono is working with publishers in partnership for printing of books, shipping or printed book, storage of printed books—always trying to optimise the printing and distribution solution to the appropriate level of demand for book titles. Effective integration of systems has been enabled by tools like EDI for ordering, order acknowledgement and despatch notices, as well as communicating status updates and the tracking of orders. Markono has become not just a vendor but a supply chain partner for the Asia region. Printing books using digital technology and printing books using offset technology will be a balancing act in future years. Offset carries a cheaper unit cost but higher storage and distribution costs, while digital printing carries a higher unit cost and cheaper storage and distribution costs. For books that sell in volume, there will always be a place for lower-tech set-up offset printing, but for low demand books, like monographs, custom books, or specialist

Fig. 4.4 Markono, Singapore.

books, storing books on digital servers and managing the digital printing with that sophisticated technology allows publishers to align supply with demand. Markono is responsive to customers and new requirements such as custom publishing, supplying mail order services, courier track and amp; trace services and managing air/sea freight for publishers are already part of the service mix. Historically, printers ran printing companies and distributors ran warehouses and fulfilment centres; now academic publishers are increasingly outsourcing printing and shipping to a One-Stop Shop (Fig. 4.4).

Case study: What does convergence look like? The Australian University Presses Studied in 2008 by then PhD candidate Xuemei Tian [56]

Xuemei was studying at the School of Business Information Technology Business Portfolio at RMIT University writing up research results in 2008. Dr. Xuemei Tian is now Senior Lecturer at Swinburne University of Technology, Melbourne, Australia. This case is an extract from her PhD Thesis reproduced with permission. The three publishers' identities are concealed by naming them: P12, **a textbook publisher** who did not make extensive use of print-on-demand for books in 2009; P13, an **online publishing service**, Australia's only university press with 96% of its sales coming from electronic products in 2009; and P14, **the leading academic press using print-on-demand technology for books** in the Australian book publishing sector. The numbers on the section headings reference Chapter 7.

7.8 Position of university presses: Of the established (Australian) university presses (identified as) (companies, P12, P13, and P14), company P14 has been selected for a detailed description, with the other two serving as a basis for comparison. Company P14 can be characterised in terms of a cross-section of traditional and digital publishing.

7.8.1 Company background: Established in 1962, **company P12** is one of Australia's leading publishers in the fields of Australian studies and natural history. Its list also includes a wide range of titles in other scholarly and general subject areas. The company has traditionally been textbook based, although in recent times it has become more diversified. Print runs are governed by client requirements and there are cases where additional copies are printed (maybe 100 or 200) for the trade or booksellers if there is a perceived need. The company sees itself as a traditional university press, with the majority of sales derived from traditional distribution channels. Revenue (95%) comes from sales of hard copy books. They recently launched an online bookshop on behalf of the existing campus bookshop.

Company P13 has a 13-year history and has evolved from being a producer of CD-ROMs to being Australia's foremost aggregator of databases, as well as being an online publishing service. The company is Australia's only university press that is principally electronic, with 96% of its sales coming from electronic products. The company claims to be Australia's leading scholarly e-press, with online delivery of Australasia's largest collection of scholarly research material. Company P13 publishes Australasian content for the education, research, and business sectors, as well as more than 80 online indexed databases, including a range of indexed databases with links to full text documents online.

Company P14 has been at the forefront of innovative Australian publishing for more than 50 years. It has launched the careers of many great Australian novelists, published contemporary Australian poets, been a pioneering force in children's and young adult publishing, and has set the benchmark for award-winning scholarly and Black Australian writing. It is a dynamic university press known for its risk-taking philosophy and a commitment to publishing works of high quality and cultural significance. They are actively involved in the development of a digital dimension to all their activities, and intend to be major players when the digital age matures. Currently, they provide a range of packages which, depending on the needs of the purchaser, comprise the book, electronic versions of the book in PDF format and CDs, and e-books. Company P14 specialises in Print-on-Demand services, and is the leader in the use of POD technology in the Australian book-publishing sector.

7.8.2 Products, services, and value proposition: Company P13 clearly differs from companies P12 and P14, as the company derives the majority of its revenue from the sale of digital products and services. Companies P12 and P14 have similar products—Books, CDs, and DVDs, but their services and distribution channels vary, which leads to different value propositions. **Company P14, for example, has five major value propositions as follows:**

Value proposition 1: *Print-on-Demand (POD)*. The main source of revenue for the company is from POD. Their internal bookshop uses POD technology to provide a full service from printing to binding. Books or single chapters can be ordered.

Value proposition 2: *Sales of books through their own website*. The company also regards this as a communications and promotional resource, enabling downloading of images of their covers, and author information. Their website can also provide a link to other services (for example, to e-books or Mp3s) and acts as a resource for reading groups and educators.

Value proposition 3: *Self-publishing services*. The company provides a platform on its website which enables self-publishing. They believe there is potential for self-publishing via a POD model, including the reuse and repackaging of published materials to create new textbooks. The general manager indicated that some lecturers prefer to create their own teaching context. POD can be very effective in this situation.

Value proposition 4: *Strength in copyrights*. The company recognises that copyright issues are extremely important, but are difficult to deal with in a digital world. They have set up strategies to deal with *Rights* issues. They operate the DOI (Digital Object Identifier) system, which enables the identification of content in all course notes that lecturers provide, and ensure that it complies with copyright.

Value proposition 5: *Sales through collaboration with other publishers*. The company is one of seven publishers who cooperate with the Copyright Agency to provide their content for sale through CAL. They can sell their books on a chapter-by-chapter basis (as well as in their entirety), and CAL administers the platform and a search engine.

By comparison, the main source of revenue for Company P12 is through sales of hard copy books. They also have some partnership arrangements where they undertake special publishing projects for clients to whom they sell the finished product. As opposed to both Companies P12 and P14, the key value propositions for Company P13 are:

Easy search infrastructure using their bibliographic online databases. These online databases give access to fully indexed text journal articles by using a single search interface *E*-press, which is a full e-publishing service representing a cover-to-cover aggregation of journals, monographs, conference papers, reports, occasional series, and other *grey* literature published in Australia, and hitherto not widely available online. Copyrights, the agreement between Company P13 and the Copyright Agency to clear rights to these journals for inclusion on the aggregated service, marked a significant turning point in online access to scholarly content in Australia.

7.8.3 Customer base: The management teams at the three university presses were interviewed, with outcomes revealing both similarities and dissimilarities in approach, but in each case having the objective of maintaining what were remarkably stable customer bases. The majority of customers for company P14 include libraries, an internal bookshop (most sales are POD), external bookshops, Amazon, individuals (teachers, students, or others) who purchase online, and online bookshops (collaborative material, POD, and e-books).

There are considerable similarities in the make-up of the customer bases of the three firms, who are all basically involved in the academic or higher educational market. However, there are some aspects where they differ. Company P12 has developed a special niche within its customer base, involving the publication of books for local councils, who supply manuscripts for compilation, editing, and publishing, following which they are resold back to the councils. Company P13's customer base comprises libraries (notably academic, state, and corporate libraries) and small publishers, with nominal direct sales to end users via the Web. Their customer base also includes government agencies and research institutes in Australia and New Zealand, and increasingly in Asia, the United Kingdom, and North America.

7.8.4 Corporate information technology management

Use of and attitudes to technology: Whereas all three university publishers agreed that technology issues were important, they differed in respect of attitudes to its development and implementation. Companies P13 and P14 have adopted a somewhat more positive approach to the use of technology than Company 12. Although **the latter believes that book production has been revolutionised through the onset of digital printing and desktop publishing, with design and typesetting being integrated and related activities completed on a screen**, their attitude towards new technologies remains one of *wait and see*. They are enthusiastic, however, about the development of their website, which they believe to be an important tool for marketing and sales. However, at this stage, they are not directly involved in *Blogging*, although they do encourage authors to set up their own *Blog* facility, as this is potentially valuable for promotion and for obtaining customer feedback.

Companies P13 and P14 have both made extensive use of technology in order to gain market share and to obtain a competitive edge. They have both sought to market a technology-intensive value proposition. Company P13 has endorsed the potential of *many-to-many* forms of communication, including contributions from end users and the potential value of distributed content and cognition. They have developed expertise in metadata creation, file conversion, and content management. They are extensive users of XML for the management of often relatively small print runs, for the transition from source to print, and for web outputs using open standards. They are interested in the potential contained in developments involving the *Semantic Web* and *Web 2*.

Company P14 is heavily involved in the use of Print-On-Demand technology: In 2001, they initiated their own POD centre within a retail bookshop, taking advantage of the opportunity to aggregate content that was held digitally. Company P14 is interested in how to integrate digitisation with efficiency in their prepress operations, leading to sales opportunities and commercialisation of their content into different formats. They have invested in the development of their website, and believe that it is a very important resource in terms of the company's image, marketing, and sales. Currently, they are creating *MySpace*sites for the provision of high-profile books. They believe in the concept of different sites for different demographics (e.g., age and gender groups). This commitment to technological development by Companies P13 and P14 is a reflection of their continued appreciation of the value of technology to the future sustainability of their businesses. Hence, while Company P13 outsources aspects of metadata creation and file conversion, this has been done more for technical and quality reasons than simply to cut costs. **Both Companies P13 and P14 have invested in proprietary content management and workflow systems.** Key files and databases at Company P13 are based on the Terratext Foundation software developed within the company's parent institution, and for which Company P13 has a permanent licence. In the case of Company P14, all files are digitised and tagged digitally following Digital Object Identifier (DOI) guidelines to cover copyright issues. This process simplifies content management.

Digital strategy: All three companies have implemented strategies based on their belief that they are entering changing times and that preparedness is essential. Company P14's strategy involves a step-by-step process including website development, digitisation of their content, POD, and e-book development.

E-books: Company P14 believes that the new digital world and its related technologies will provide excellent opportunities to exploit backlists, POD, and e-books. They argue, however, that the marketplace for e-books is still very immature. Despite offering some e-books through their website, sales were minimal. As a traditional university press, Company P12 is currently not concerned about the development of e-books. They sell reference information through their website; for example, a law reference book (4000units of hard copy) is now available online with associated search facilities, but is not available for downloading. Access to this material is via a password and subscription fee. Compared with companies P12 and P14, Company P13 is more advanced in e-book development. The company is accepting proposals for scholarly monographs to be published in e-book format, which will be available to all their customers via the Company's websites or through third party aggregators.

7.8.5 Relationship management

Relationships with authors: Since Companies P13 and P14 are involved in POD and self-publishing, their authors can also be their customers. These authors search for suitable content, then compile and publish this content as new textbooks. Company P14 sees considerable merit in the collaborative creation of content, arguing that all links between creators (authors) and editors, and those additional external collaborative components can add to the overall result. They are in a quandary, however, over the issue of the potential sale to authors of rights for books whose shelf life has ended. They foresee continuing issues of ownership and copyright in this matter.

Relationships with suppliers: Companies P12 and P14 outsource their printing operations. Company P12 also outsources editing and technical typesetting within Australia, and minor production jobs to Mumbai. Company P12 specialises in publication projects for local councils where it compiles, edits, and publishes customised material for resale back to the client.

Relationships with partners: Although the three firms have particular relationships with higher education and scholarly communities, they differ markedly in their collaborative activities. Company P13 has the most diverse range of partners including the National Library of Australia, the Copyright Agency, and a range of government departments, various research centres in such diverse fields as family studies, criminology, agriculture, and languages, and a number of small publishing operations seeking to go digital.

Companies P12 and Company P14 are more traditional university presses who nonetheless seek to work in collaboration with external partners. One example of such collaboration is their relationship with Amazon.com. Both companies sell their books through Amazon.com. However, this occurs not through a direct relationship with Amazon, but on the basis of partnership arrangements with agents or distributors in the United States. This arrangement operates on the basis of commissions paid to the agent or distributor based on sales. The major differences in partnership and collaborative arrangements between these two university presses are as follows:

Company P12 has partnership arrangements with E-operators including US Libraries, netLibraries, and Google scholar. In many ways, these partners add value to the products and services of the case companies. Company P12 partners with Google Scholar, which provides them with exposure. Potential clients can only print out 2—3 pages and the table of contents, with normally only 20% of the content being available on the Web. These restrictions are imposed by Company P12. *Google* is allowed access to these *tasters* when people click, and also receives advertising revenue. The link between *Google* and Company P12 operates on the basis of the provision of content by the company, and the display of its material on the *Google* site, with each *click* resulting in money for *Google*.

Company P12 maintains cooperative links with other publishers, both local and overseas. If the company considers that a publication has overseas selling potential, it will seek out an overseas publisher and sell an edition. Alternatively, a common practice is where the company sells the rights to the other publishers. In such cases, the authors receive a reduced royalty of 10% of what the publisher has purchased, which is generally at an already substantial discount (sometimes up to 75%). Authors receive more from local sales than from arrangements with overseas co-publishers.

Company P14 has a strong relationship with CAL and with other publishers. These partnerships have paid dividends by giving Company P14 the ability to publish customised content, using the DOI (Digital Object Identifier) system to draw content from different sources. The DOI system enables the publisher to identify the content that individual lecturers provide, and to confirm that it complies with copyright. They tag it digitally (following DOI rules), and can subsequently assure CAL that the published material conforms to the requirements of copyright legislation. The various publishers involved all receive a royalty when the book is printed. Company P14 has a partnership agreement with an external distributor, who warehouses the company's books and is paid a fee. In addition to distribution, the firm is responsible for promotional activities, such as talking with literary agents, booksellers, and media reviewers. Company P14 only appoints publicists on rare occasions.

Relationships with customers: All three companies' customers are predominantly students and academics. Company P12 maintains relationships with customers through traditional means, which is largely through bookshops. Company P13 operates through an online environment, and Company P14 uses both methods. However, depending on their distribution channels, they have to consider various options to maintain good relationships with their customers.

7.8.6 Distribution channels: All companies offer and market their products and services through multi-distribution channels. These distribution channels include both traditional bookstores and online facilities, with the majority of sales continuing to be channelled through internal and external bookstores. Company P13 communicates with its customers mainly through online channels. Company P14's main distribution channels are as follows:

Distribution channel 1: *Internal bookstore*. Company P14 distinguishes itself from the other two companies by its heavy involvement in Print-On-Demand. This is accessed by both students and lecturers in the company's own campus bookshop, resulting in the bulk of revenue coming from the POD operation rather than from sales off-the-shelf.

Distribution channel 2: *Company website*. They have online ordering and purchasing facilities, enabling customers to purchase direct via the website, both in hard copy and electronic format. They can also download e-books. Teachers can also purchase chapters from different books.

Distribution channel 3: *Collaborative websites*. Customers can purchase through the collaborative websites, for example, those of the APA and the CAL.

Distribution channel 4: *External bookshops* via *distributors*.

Distribution channel 5: *Electronic aggregator and online bookshops*. This involves the sale of products via aggregators such as e-Book.com and e-retailers, like *Amazon*.com

Distribution channel 6: *Schools or Universities* via *representatives*. Company representatives visit schools and universities to promote their books. Normally academics who include books on their reading lists are eligible to obtain free copies, because the publishers rely on them to do this.

7.8.7 Financial respects: Company P14 derives income from various distribution channels. However, unlike other publishers, their most important income stream is from a POD service provided at the university bookshop. The company began their POD centre in 2001, and now sells 8 million pages a year (@8 cents per page, $640,000 per annum [Australian dollars]) **through this internal channel. The company believes that the initial investment for the equipment was prudent.** For the external market, the major income stream is derived from sales to bookshops via distributors in the normal way. The company's traditional profit and loss table is similar to that of other educational publishers.

7.8.8 Value chains and business models: The value chains of the three firms are all familiar in scope, although that for Company P12 is a more traditional chain of: author to publisher to printer to distributor/bookseller to reader. While in essence they are the same, the value chains for companies P13 and P14 are much more geared to the needs of a digital environment. The major stages in the value chains for Company P14 are as follows:

Stage 1: Acquiring content from authors or owners (via licensing or payment). There are two models used in this stage, the *content licensing model* and *the self-publishing model.*
Stage 2: Obtaining and converting digital files involving *PDF* and *XML* formats, the creation of metadata and databases, editing, quality assurance, and copyright confirmation (through Copyright Agency Ltd. (CAL) Australia Digital Object Identifier (DOI) system). *Content creation models, outsourcing models,* and *cooperative models* are used in this stage.
Stage 3: Printing (outsourced, black and white in Australia, colour overseas) with content held in digital repositories. *Aggregation models*, *cooperative models*, and *outsourcing models* can be used in this stage.
Stage 4: Distribution to *Amazon* through a US agent and to external bookshops via a distributor in Australia. *Aggregation models* and *cooperative models* are used in this stage.
Stage 5: Sales, marketing, promotion through representatives, print media, and virtual and physical bookshops. There are many models used in this stage, depending on their distribution channels. These include the *POD model* or *direct-to-customer model* where they sell through their own bookshop, *traditional representative sales model* where they promote their books to schools and universities, and *online-to-customers model.*

Company P12 has traditionally been textbook based, although in recent times it has become more diversified. The main parts of their value chain differ from those of Company P14, as they have their own distribution arm and **do not make extensive use of POD technology.** Their adherence to traditional methods is reflected in their business models. Their mainstream revenue is derived from sales through bookstores. Their major business model is therefore linked to bookstore selling operations. They also use an *online to customer* model, a *direct to customer* model to cater for telephone or fax requests, and *aggregated* models for collaboration with *Google* or *Amazon.* Although not firmly committed to the production of e-books, the company employs POD technology to cater for books that do not warrant a long print run. Company P13 has different value chains to the other two companies, due to its involvement with online publishing and distribution activities. Their value chain can be described in the following stages:

Stage 1: Licensing content from owners, using the services of the Copyright Agency.
Stage 2: Obtaining digital files from a number of partners, including the National Library (which provide the files by scanning them) or individual publishers (who send the material as PDF or XML). This involves extensive outsourcing. For example, metadata production is outsourced and for journal indexing, journals go direct from the journal to the indexer. However, the publisher plays a key role in quality assurance.
Stage 3: Building files and databases: This is currently performed in-house using their own software. They are investigating other arrangements including gaining a presence on corporate Intranets and Portals.

Stage 4: Sales, marketing, promotion, based on a combination of links to various consortia, licensing, and selling content.

Company P13 sees itself as having a *hybrid* business model that involves publishing and aggregating largely on a business-to-business basis. The hybrid model emerged in 1989 as a *cost-recovery* model, but since 1997 Company P13 has operated as a commercially sustainable (but not-for-profit) publisher and aggregator. Extending this perception to take a more atomic view of things, a number of component or submodels can be discerned in operation at the company.

7.8.9 Risks, opportunities, and the future

Company P12 is a successful, long-established university press. It has traditional business methods, and is comfortable in the knowledge that the business continues to display healthy growth patterns. Initially apprehensive regarding the digital revolution, they have now commenced steps to change and expand their business. Having established relationships with e-operators to expand their distribution channels, they are aware of content control and copyright issues, aspects that require constant attention. Compared with the other two university presses (Companies P13 and P14), Company P12 adopts a pragmatic attitude towards technologies, despite believing that technology has and is fundamentally affecting their business processes. The company is comfortable with its current situation and is reluctant to embrace radical change. The risk for the company is that if they do not become involved in digital change, they may lose their competitiveness in the future.

Company P13 sees very little on the horizon regarding potential risks and, in particular, nothing in the way of threats from new entrants or from developments in technology. In terms of good governance, they are focusing on keeping costs down, for instance in relation to royalty and licensing fees. The company continues to seek opportunities to improve the delivery of its infrastructure, in order to reduce the unit costs of production. There is little sign of any potential problems from, for instance, channel or supplier conflict. The company is satisfied with ongoing developments in *Open Access* publishing, regarding it as being highly domain and content-specific and where the future may lie in the publication of material that is not saleable on a commercial basis. Company P13 is currently participating in a local repository experiment, for which it is providing input on software and content management. However, they see this more as a goodwill gesture than as a commercial venture. So far as technology is concerned, they have been early adopters of digital opportunities, and foresee further opportunities in the digital publishing space, owing to their strengths in metadata creation and management and in indexing and searching. They are also intending to pursue new markets comprising library consortia and large libraries in Asia, the United Kingdom, and North America. The wider objective is to repackage and reformat existing materials for corporate and enterprise markets, and to develop new products both with regard to aggregated services and content. **Company P14 is considered a pioneer in the publishing industry through its involvement in the use of Print-On-Demand technology. The availability of POD provides an opportunity for them to establish closer business relationships with their customers, and to gain an edge over their competitors when the digital era fully matures.**

Part Two

Normalised, commoditised, and adopted, print-on-demand for books today (2015–17)

Introduction to part 2

> *Indeed until the knowledges converge, the lead time of a knowledge-based innovation usually does not even begin.* [57]
>
> –Peter Drucker, *Innovation and Entrepreneurship*

Publishers today are taking full advantage of innovation in digital publishing workflow management, digitally printed books, online bookselling, and book fulfilment. In fact, the four critical innovations that converged to enable print-on-demand to impact academic book publishing now support well-established and widely adopted business practices. Incremental product and service improvements have constantly been made over the past decade but essentially as print-on-demand markets grew, quality improved and costs decreased. More technology providers have entered the digital book printing market which has helped to commoditise print services. The digital book has established its upward trajectory including the growth of online and mobile accessible channels to market which has raised awareness of academic books and led to increased desire for print book availability and a competitive digital print service marketplace for books has become evident. Michael Jubb writes about digital printing and print-on-demand in his book *The Academic Book of the Future* (2017)

> *A key change with a major impact on the relationships between publishers, library suppliers, distributors, and wholesalers (eliding the differences between the latter two) has been the rise of digital printing. Improvements in quality, the fall in costs, and the development of systems for speedy fulfilment of print-on-demand (PoD) orders are together of particular importance for titles—like many academic books—with low unit sales; and they are profoundly changing the economics of publishing such books.* ***It is arguable that the impact to date of PoD services from companies such as Ingram and Print-on-demand has been greater than the advent of e-books****; and as Fisher and Jubb (2016) note,* ***Amazon has become a hugely important channel on both sides of the Atlantic in this context, working as producer as well as retailer.*** *For wholesalers and distributors, these developments have opened up the possibility of providing for publishers the kind of digital virtual warehouse with no physical books now operated by Ingram, fulfilling orders (which may come from booksellers, libraries, other distributors, or from publishers themselves) either as e-books or physical copies. [58]*

The creative adoption of print-on-demand technologies and services has led to book publishing innovation within the academic publishing community around the world. Integrating print-on-demand with learning environments for custom textbooks, enhancing with e-book monograph collections with a print-on-demand book service, allowing database users to compile extracts and print their own compilation book are all examples of new academic book services enabled by print-on-demand.

One key market development has been that print-on-demand for academic books has matured into a multinational 'distributed print' service. I remember seeing the BookSurge LLC exhibition stand at Frankfurt Book Fair in 2003 and the backdrop of this booth was a global map with arrows pointing at many locations of their digital book printing partners around the world. They had conceptually bought into the Xerox distributed print model where they envisioned a global network of local book printers passing book files or holding local copies of book files which would be printed on demand for the local market. Keeping local costs of printing in line with the local ability to pay. In practice it was a difficult service to execute other than for digital short-run book runs. This is because files needed to be optimised to the local print equipment, publishers had to be comfortable with their digital files sitting in repositories in territories with less robust legal infrastructure fighting piracy of books, and partnering across multiple businesses in many countries carried business risk. But the vision of truly international distributed printed books through print-on-demand was evident from the early days of print-on-demand.

Thanks to Ed Marino's international vision and John Ingram's investment support, Lightning Source opened its first operation outside the United States in Milton Keynes, United Kingdom in 2001 and grew it. By 2014 Amazon's CreateSpace POD service (built on the acquisition of BookSurge LLC) was delivering distributed print into their own facilities in the United States, United Kingdom, Germany and Japan and Ingram Content had book print and distribution facilities in the United States, United Kingdom, France and Australia as well as launching Global Connect POD services into other territories like Russia and Brazil through partnerships, and most recently China and India.

Today, in addition to single copy stockless print-on-demand services, digital printing of academic books is taking place in most countries where there is a book printing industry present as many off-set book printers have adopted digital printing and many book warehouses have installed digital print facilities. Printers in Singapore were among the earliest adopters of technical books produced print-on-demand again fuelled by orders for just-in-time computer manuals from the IT industry as this capability complemented Singapore's strategic book distribution location by air and sea. Most of the large academic publishers had operations in Singapore. Printers across Asia, Europe, Australia, and the Americas are embracing digital book printing today. The costs of the IT infrastructure and temperature control for higher quality digital book production are an inhibitor to rapid growth but enabling printed books to cross boundaries by passing files rather than cumbersome and expensive physical import/export routes has great appeal. Distributed academic book printing has come of age and will undoubtedly expand in the coming years as a complimentary service to the distributed e-book or academic e-book collection.

The next three chapters focus on current practices built on the convergence covered in part 1. The focus is on three types of academic book publishing: monographs; textbooks (including books for professional learning); and aggregated books, collections and archives. Each of these book publishing activities has been challenged by the rapid expansion of screen-based reading fuelled by the worldwide web, hypertext linking, online portals and over the past decade the advent of mobile data accessed through smartphones. When the e-book was born many expected the printed academic book to disappear. This may be true for curators of massive archives and readers wishing to search and discover books amid the myriad of published books content. But many readers prefer the printed book for a host of reasons. According to Deegan's *The Academic Book of the Future*

> *Besides the writing of academic books, we also considered how academic books are currently being read. We found that there is still a preference for print for sustained reading, and what surprised us was that this was not a generational issue: students and younger researchers expressed a preference for print, and reported finding the print format more conducive to rereading than the digital. [59]*

Most commentators today accept that we quite comfortably residing in a hybrid world of digital screen-based books and printed books.

Print-on-demand books enable choice for readers and provide profitable revenue streams to publishers because the perceived value of the printed book is simply greater than the e-book. Most commentators today accept that we quite comfortably residing in a hybrid world of digital screen-based books and printed books. Print-on-demand has been a key enabler of digital screen-based books because it provides the economic alternative for the reader to opt-out of the screen-dominated world and opt-in to a printed and bound book.

Different types of academic publishers have engaged with print-on-demand in different ways. So these chapters focus on the impact of print-on-demand upon monographs, textbooks, and archival collections and try to capture a variety of case studies that shed light on how the technology was adopted and normalised by academic publishers creating substantive book publishing programmes. These types of publishers include university presses, multinational Scientific, Technical, and Medical (STM) book publishers, academic libraries with book collections, non-profit government organisations (NGOs) with substantive grey literature in book form, social science and humanities book publishers, educational book publishing groups, and Internet database publishers with custom books. All have made print-on-demand book publishing an integral part of their publishing programmes.

Monographs on-demand

Academic monographs are undoubtedly migrating to digital e-book forms driven by academic institutional requirements of widening access, immediacy of access, the storage costs of print, and even the need for data sets and multimedia elements to be present within some monographs in some disciplines. Some argue that the very nature of the monograph is being tested and redefined in the digital arena [60–62]. While print-on-demand does not solve all the fundamental issues facing the economics of the monograph, it is playing an important role in facilitating the migration to digital by offering users the option to buy a printed and bound copy without crippling the academic book publisher who is engaged with an increasingly 'digital first' ecosystem. In recent years, there have been several surveys and studies with respect to the monograph, its uses, and economics. One significant project was undertaken in the United Kingdom where several reports came out of the project including: *The Academic Book of the Future Project Report*, A Report to the AHRC, and the British Library by Marilyn Deegan, London, June 2017, which can be found at: https://academicbookfuture.org. Another was conducted in the United States: *Reimagining the Digital Monograph*: A JSTOR Labs Report by Alex Humphreys, Christina Spencer, Laura Brown, and Ronald Snyder (June 2017). Both share the conclusion that users continue to express preference for reading long form narrative on the printed page.

Print-on-demand for books coupled with online bookselling has impacted the academic monograph in four significant ways: first, by **sustaining the availability of printed and bound monographs** to users who prefer them; second, by positively **contributing to the economics of migrating monographs to digital platforms** and services over time; third, by offering academic publishers, including university presses, **access to new markets** both geographically inside the academy but also reaching new markets outside the academy through bookselling portals; and finally by **lowering the barriers of entry for publishing printed monographs and thereby fostering the growth of new university presses,** many based in university libraries today, by generating sales revenue streams and keeping their niche books constantly available in print as well as empowering the self-publishing scholar. This chapter considers these four areas of impact and concludes with two views from a vendor of print-on-demand services and two procurement managers. The chapter concludes with three different perspectives focused on the global reach of monograph books achieved via print-on-demand today: David Taylor from the Ingram Content group, Yvette Nora from Reed-Elsevier global procurement, and Paul Major, also from global procurement at Oxford University Press.

The Impact of Print-On-Demand on Academic Books. https://doi.org/10.1016/B978-0-08-102011-1.00005-5

5.1 User preferences for print and keeping print available

Print-on-demand is supporting user preferences and printed book traditions. Academics continue to express a preference for using monographs in print format. In 2015, the Wolff et al. ITHAKA survey of academics did not observe a paper to digital format transition for monographs:

> *We observed equally in the US and the, UK that academics' preference for using scholarly monographs in various ways in print format rather than digital format has only increased since the previous cycle of the survey. The consistency of this finding across use cases and on both side of the Atlantic should give pause to the enthusiasts for a full transition to digital monographs. [63]*

Specifically, the 2012 ITHAKA survey uncovered a dichotomy:

> *The survey found that* ***scholars tend to prefer e-books over print books for basic research tasks****, such as exploring references or searching for specific topics, but* ***when it comes to more immersive reading, they prefer print books.*** *So, a scholar might use an e-book as a sort of quick finding aid before turning to a print copy of the same title to read and digest the argument. [62]*

This concurs with the more recently published 2017 Academic Book of the Future report by Marilyn Deegan:

> *...there are many new experimental partnerships between academics, libraries, and publishers to push the concept of the book beyond its covers. At the same time, there is a continuing (indeed resurging) preference for print for sustained reading and reflection. It seems that the future is likely to be a mixed economy of print, e-versions of print, and networked enhanced monographs of greater or lesser complexity. [64]*

The usage feedback regarding a mixed economy for monographs may not be that surprising, given some-deep rooted cultural preferences for the printed form throughout academic life. Many scholarly societies encourage and enable PhD students to convert their thesis into a published monograph book for an audience beyond the examiners. So it is worth considering the origins of some monographs as thesis.

The thesis has a distinguished history of being printed and bound in a handcrafted, on-demand manner. In university towns, cottage industry printer/binders for decades or even centuries performed this task of lovingly printing, binding, and embossing theses on behalf of local academic institutions. It is typically a requirement to submit PhD theses in print and even if it is not the most suitable medium. As Deegan writes in *The Academic Book of the Future*:

> ***The PhD thesis*** *is important in its own right as a long-form research output, as well as being the route to professional accreditation and a first publication for early career researchers. The British Library's EthOS online thesis service makes available*

450,000 records representing theses awarded by 139 institutions, around 200,000 of these are full text; those not available as full text can be scanned and supplied quickly, The ProQuest Dissertations and Theses Global Service includes ***3.8 million works from universities in 88 countries (1.7 million in full text) and adds around 100,000 new volumes each year. While most theses are still produced and submitted in print form,*** *this is not necessarily the most suitable format for practice-based disciplines. A research project carried out on the EthOS service by Coral Manton found a growing trend for researchers to include multimedia and non-text research outputs in their theses. Of the theses represented on EThOS, only approximately 1% is known to have multimedia or non-text elements, but some 302 different file formats are represented, including audio, image, film, data, and others (Manton, 2016). [65]*

Multiple file format and multimedia thesis submissions may be a trend to watch, but today there remains an on-demand printed book culture embedded within the thesis tradition of postgraduate dissertation. A postgraduate student thesis or dissertation traditionally requires at least two bound copies for submission to the examiners. Even in 2016, I witnessed my digital native, millennial daughter dutifully go to the appointed university printers and undertake this ritual of submitting her MA dissertation for printing and binding. Publishing a peer-reviewed monograph is one or two steps away from that ritual with the added impetus of peer recognition. It is a matter of scholarly record, evidence of original, quality work assessed by the academy peer group and made available to the academy for posterity and reference. The published monograph is also part of the academic rite of passage towards promotion, tenure, and ultimately recognition in the academy. Yes, publishing journal articles in acclaimed academic journals with distinguished editorial boards, which are subsequently highly cited by other scholars, has proved to be essential to the academy – especially in fast-moving disciplines where being first is vital for perceived success. However, long form narrative exposition of a topic continues to have an important place in many if not all fields of research. Academics are publishing all manner of digital research data and ancillary material but the writing and preparation of monographs in printed book form continues, more often than not alongside an e-book version.

5.2 Print-on-demand's positive contribution to the economics of the monograph

For The monograph, increasing numbers of publications and decreasing numbers of purchasers at the point of publication are a problem. Over time, costs may be covered but someone has to put up the cash to make that monograph if 500 libraries do not buy it on the date of publication. It is the cash flow implications of monograph origination that has everyone still in a spin. Who is going to pay up front to make all these new monographs as research output exponentially increases? How much publishing investment do they really take? How quickly is the return on investment? With digital and print there is a dual cost base, as Michael Jubb wrote in *Academic Books and Their Futures* (2017):

Reader preferences remain strongly in favour of print rather than e-books. Print therefore remains dominant, and digital printing—especially print-on-demand—has so far probably had a greater impact than e-books on the publishing landscape. Publishers therefore continue to provide both print and e-books in a range of formats; and the major sales and use of e-books are via libraries, for whom e-book packages and new procurement models offer significant advantages. ***The unresolved problems for publishers and other agents in the supply chain are that they operate with a dual cost base, and that e-book sales tend to cannibalise print sales. The result is pressure on margins and on overall revenues, and added complexity in the supply chain.*** *Preservation of e-books for the long term is also not yet fully-resolved. [66]*

Publishers are indeed managing a dual cost base in order to continue support print and e-book formats for readers, but the flip side of a dual cost base is a dual revenue stream and cost control is driving publishers towards a digital first workflow with multiple file formats being output for e-book and print-on-demand editions. It has always been the case that academic publishers clearly have to assess the commercial viability of publishing a monograph and origination of the work is a substantial proportion of the cost/investment.

This is well summarised and illustrated in 'Development of book publishing business models and finances', Frances Pinter and Laura White's contribution to **Academic and Professional Publishing** (2012). Pinter walks us through a typical monograph at the unit price/unit cost level: a 50 GBP retail priced monograph achieving 32.5 GBP in net sales receipts with origination costing 6 GBP (i.e. 18.5% of the actual sales income) [67]. This illustrates that a publisher has a substantial investment in origination before a sale can be made. Other studies show that when considering the fully loaded costs of publishing a monograph, these are substantial, typically 20,000 USD [68]. Subscriptions to e-book collections are a primary source of revenue but equally important are the print revenues enabled by print-on-demand which can be realised prior to incurring the costs of manufacture and distribution. There is certainty in the sale. For many publishers, especially those with e-book platforms or substantial e-book collections, the origination costs can be split between the e-book collection subscription value paid for by the library and print revenues typically paid for by individual researchers or students. Print-on-demand is beneficial to the publisher both in terms of cash flow (i.e., not having to pay for books held in stock awaiting a sale) and in terms of constant availability of a book over a long time frame which unlocks sales without locking up cash.

The economics and sustainability of monographs has repeatedly been called into question for decades. Is monograph publishing a service to the academic community which is writing them? Or a break-even exercise for the university press? Or a profitable publishing endeavour? Perhaps not much has changed in some respects. Back in 2001, Clifford Lynch wrote in an article: 'The Battle to Define the future of the book in the digital world'.

..for scholarly monographs digital publication and distribution helps with the inventory problem and hence with works going out of print rapidly, but has little effect on the crisis in the economics of monograph publishing. Restructuring the value chain doesn't help if the problem is first copy costs rather than distribution costs. (Clifford Lynch, June 2001) [69]

This view of the economics of monograph publishing persists even 15 years later but it underestimates the power of availability and discoverability of a book over time without the stock liability. Publishers refer to 'first copy costs' as origination costs. As we saw above, origination costs of a monograph are substantial, and in 2001 origination costs may have been an even higher proportion of the total costs due to more labour costs than today, i.e. managing the peer review process manually, undertaking sub-editing and corrections, manual indexing, designing covers and styles of text presentation, then printing, binding, and distributing the physical book.

Some origination costs have reduced since 2001, particularly with respect to the use of digital template tools associated with book composition and workflow reducing design and 'ingestion' costs as these are pushed back to the author in a self-service model. In addition, digital impact on the value chain has not only reduced distribution costs and origination costs for those with digital ingestion systems, but also improved speed of service and widened market access. The origination costs of the work can still be substantial and recouping the initial investment can be a challenge. However, print-on-demand has helped reduce the overall costs of investing cash in stock and distributing that stock to academics and institutions around the world. Origination costs might be as much as 20% of the total book costs today, so recovering those costs through as many reselling channels and markets is critical. Online search coupled with online bookselling allows the discovery and purchase of niche books around the world like never before.

Access to new markets inside the academy and outside the academy. Print-on-demand is crossing market boundaries: The academic monograph is a specialist work of writing on a single subject or particular aspect of a subject and typically is the fruit of scholarly research. If the work is too narrow, there may not be a sufficient market to sustain the book in a short period of time. This is where the traditional publisher has to consider their return on investment over time, and reaching a wider market can speed up the return on investment. Print-on-demand allows not only the lifespan of the book to be extended but also the geographic accessibility to new markets through a network of local print-on-demand services where the book can be digitally stored. The digital infrastructure today reaches a global, if privileged, audience and even the purchase price to buy your own printed copy of a niche work has potentially halved. For example, offering multiple print formats is now possible through print-on-demand: the expensive hardback at USD 50+ is still available but so is a USD 24 paperback drop-shipped within 24 h; and the e-book might cost even less for immediate download. Books on screen are everywhere and yet the printed book persists. Nearly two decades ago in 2001, Clifford Lynch wrote with an air of disappointment:

> *Digital books as literal translations of printed books, delivered via print-on-demand (perhaps supplemented with online browsing) forms an established and viable market but a small one. Print-on-demand isn't cheap and it isn't particularly convenient - it's a lot like electronically ordering a printed book for physical delivery. [69]*

Apart from the fact that print-on-demand in 2017 is the dominant facilitator of the printed academic book, the rest of his statement is still true. It is exactly like electronically ordering a book for physical delivery. And many users like that! Some of what

Lynch dreamed of in 2001 scholars now have at their fingertips: the screen based immediacy of digitally converted books and even have books created 'digital first', both of immense utility.

Is it not ironic that while the immediacy of mobile discoverability has switched users wholeheartedly to online tools (Search = 'Google it'), printing a digital book to read and reference is exactly what scholars and readers continue to want to do? For a scholar sitting in London or New York in 2017, printing and fulfilment logistics can put a quality bound paperback book ordered before 1 pm into their hands by 6 pm the same day. The 2017 'quality, time, price paradigm' for a print-on-demand book has become 'good quality, in record time at an affordable price'. The electronic copy is instantly available, which has merit, but it is only licensed to the purchaser with many restrictions on sharing, and ultimately the purchased copy is entirely dependent on the existence of the business supplying the e-book to you. These limitations sustain demand for the printed copy. While contrary to all the digital hype about solely digital collections for the scholarly to access, it seems clear that the future of the monograph is not solely digital, in an online e-book collection, downloadable e-book form, or even downloadable PDF. Scholars often print their downloads to read and review, and continue to buy printed and bound monographs. Accessible printed monographs should be available to all scholars as an option.

New geographic markets are now opening up through print-on-demand access such as China and, India which can now be more easily reached by local print-on-demand service with a digital infrastructure managing file availability. The interviews at the end of the chapter consider this in more detail.

Finally, lowering the barriers to entry for publishing has been enabled by print-on-demand and the publishing platforms it supports. The new university presses and the empowered scholar choosing to self-publish will mean new monograph publishing players enter the market. Part 3 considers some of these trends. While print-on-demand has not solved all the economic issues of the monograph, and true globalisation via print-on-demand is in its infancy, more university presses at institutions around the world are likely to be supported by print-on-demand services. Turning the University Press into a monograph service provider for academics wishing to publish monographs on the faculty is already happening at many institutions. Aligning the new university press with the library in this regard has resulted in many merging the research library with the university press or starting a university press as part of a research librarian's new role. Print-on-demand services simply lowered the barriers to entry and monographs continue to be published in both e-book and print-on-demand forms. We are likely to see this publishing activity undertaken by a more diverse publishing community using more diverse investment or funding models in support of scholarship.

Two interviews and two case studies now follow. The first interview is with a service provider responsible for taking print-on-demand around the world, David Taylor of Ingram Content, and the second interview is with Yvette Nora, Director of Central Purchasing at RELX, the parent company of Elsevier who are engaged in monograph and textbook publishing around the world. The case studies are of Oxford University Press with respect to their monographs on-demand program and finally an example of journals imitating monographs with the summary of Wiley's move to Sheridan to print their journal issues on-demand in 2012. Sheridan are an interesting example of a printer which has become a broader publisher services business, and print-on-demand is an integral part of their move (Fig. 5.1).

Fig. 5.1 David Taylor, Senior Vice President, International Content Acquisition, Ingram Content Group, based in the UK.
Photograph used by permission of the Independent Publishers Guild, UK.

Interview: David Taylor, Senior Vice President, International Content Acquisition, Ingram Content, UK

Academic publishers were one of the first movers in terms of adopting print-on-demand, especially those with a high proportion of monographs. The nature of the product – high retail price, low print run, text based, black and white, global rights – was a good fit. Publishers like CUP, OUP, Taylor and Francis, Macmillan, Springer, Bloomsbury, and Wiley-Blackwell remain very heavy users of print-on-demand for their monographs. Many now go straight to print-on-demand rather than via an initial traditional print run first. There is little doubt that the single copyprint-on-demand model, especially hardback or cased book single copy, allied to both a wholesale capability and linked to third-party distributors on an increasingly global scale, has allowed the academic monograph to survive as a viable publishing format. Advances in digital printing technologies, especially with the arrival of ink jet (which is slowly but surely replacing toner-based digital printing), affordable full colour digital printing, and improvements in finishing equipment have all improved the look and feel of the book.

The most successful publishing applications of print-on-demand books as observed at Ingram from a services supplier perspective are in six specific areas: self-publishing, micro-publishing, large print publishing, personalised publishing, content aggregation (e.g., collections of out-of-print works), and, of course, academic publishing.

Ingram's contribution to delivering print on demand for books started with developing a manufacturing and distribution workflow that enabled the delivery of single copies printed to order either as hardback and paperback books. Reselling books through Ingram's wholesale channel model and drop-shipping to end customers on behalf of publishers and distributors was a key part of that supply chain workflow. The capability to print in market rather than ship or hold local inventory was proven at Lightning Source UK (LSUK), extended to Lightning Source Australia (LSAU), and has grown through the Global Connect supply network to reach countries like India, China, Europe and, South Korea. Internationalisation of print-on-demand for books including academic books is a trend that will only continue into the future.

The development of print-on-demand services for books has brought huge positives to the publishing industry but especially academic monographs. Print-on-demand has enabled:

- titles to be published that would otherwise never have made it
- monographs to be kept in print and available for sale
- moving to sell first then print
- the reduction of speculative inventory and associated costs
- the reduction of freight costs by printing on demand in market
- out-of-print monographs to be reissued for sale and supply.

Finally and most importantly, print-on-demand has improved global availability of monograph titles by linking print-on-demand to wholesale and distribution networks.

More and more monographs will move to a print-on-demand only supply model. Increasingly, publishers will move to a market offer that provides a choice of digital and print, but more of the print option will be supported by a print-on-demand model rather than pre-printed inventory. Digital only will become increasingly unattractive and seen as a choice that makes less sense for a publisher to make for this type of publishing. Digital Print technology will continue to improve as will paper choice and case binding capabilities. Print-on-demand will become even more of a global distribution and wholesaling option with fewer monographs being printed and held in inventory and yet more and more titles being available from a virtual inventory position, increasingly printed in market with a faster supply time (Fig. 5.2).

Fig. 5.2 Yvette Nora, Director, Central Purchasing, RELX Group based in the United States.

Interview: Yvette Nora, Director, Central Purchasing, RELX Group

Elsevier is part of the RELX Group and according to their online catalogue in August 2017, there were 47,518 books and 220 major reference works available, most of which could be purchased in both e-book and print book form. Many of the printed editions will be supplied from print-on-demand printer partnerships. Yvette Nora is responsible for contributing to the short- and long-term strategies for the Global Print Program at RELX Group through collaborative relationships, shared objectives, and early engagement with business units and suppliers to ensure projects and process/workflow related opportunities are identified, evaluated, and standardised in a way that will drive efficiencies and project cost savings.

From an economic perspective, print-on-demand technology was a natural fit for Elsevier which produced highly specialised content for very specific consumers meaning order requirements would often be less than 500 copies.Elsevier has high quality standards for scientific content with critical images. Our Supplier Quality Systems team established and drove standards specific for the academic book which were first adopted through primary experience with journals to narrow the gap with the initial output by early devices and offset standards such as SWOP in the US and Fogra in Germany. (*Author's note: SWOP means Specifications for Web Offset Publications. SWOP is both a set of standards and an organisation which started in 1975 for the US print industry focused organisation which merged with Idealliance in 2005. They have affiliate organisations today in China, Korea, Mexico, and India today. See https://www.idealliance.org/swop/ for more information. ISO Fogra refers to the Fogra Graphic Technology Research Association based in Munich, Germany, which founded a Digital Printing Group in 2008).*

Elsevier developed a quality profile to validate print equipment in an impartial and methodical manner. Although we started with sheet-based toner presses, we took advantage of the introduction of roll-fed toners. Paper types were standardised to 50 lb. offset and 60 lb. matte.Trim sizes were also standardised to one each for small, medium, and large formats. Print-on-demand was introduced for books in the mid-2000s to fulfil out-of-print inventory, followed by Zero inventory for frontlist which was introduced and piloted in 2009. There were challenges to integrate file management, electronic orders to suppliers, status notifications, and fulfilment/billing to customers. The price efficiencies were much lower for books than for journals and toner limited eligibility to print runs below 300 copies and page counts generally below 600–800 pages.

The introduction of inkjet technology in 2009 allowed for short-run printing but inkjet was not conducive for single copy order fulfilment until 2014. New management software and volume batching has improved and enabled the feasibility of book-of-one printing at an acceptable price level. Elsevier has a wide spectrum of book specifications. Although we have made efforts to standardise front lists and future titles, there are still active backlist titles that deviate from the standards. In Elsevier's experience, print-on-demand lends itself to paperback and black and white books with a life of sales less than 500 copies.

Certain subject areas such as life sciences with critical content or major reference works with large page counts and thin papers are still a challenge for pricing and manufacturing.

To make print-on-demand a scalable publishing success, effective information technology is essential. IT efforts for both the printers and within Elsevier require a deep commitment and collaboration. Without only focusing on direct production and fulfilment by Elsevier, third-party sales channels are enabled to provide both self-serve print-on-demand and expanded availability of titles.

Print-on-demand technology keeps printed books viable through lower costs and faster printing to enable keeping a title available. Quality can be different so regardless of the high dpi (dots per inch applied) or ink quality, the users may be sensitive to a difference in appearance, either better or worse. Essentially, Elsevier has transitioned from being a traditional publisher to being a data provider and that change took place a few years ago. In that data provider context, print-on-demand simply allows customers to order a physical book if that is their preference.

Case study: Oxford University Press UK Monographs On-Demand

Oxford University Press (OUP) is located in Oxford, UK and is the largest university press in the world as well as the second oldest. In 2017, OUP published more than 6000 new titles of all types worldwide including dictionaries, English language teaching materials, children's books, journals, scholarly monographs, printed music, higher education textbooks, and schoolbooks. Many of these titles are created specifically for local markets and are published by OUP's regional publishing branches. Of the approximately 6000 titles the Press publishes per annum, 800–900 of those new titles would be categorised as academic monographs. This case study is written up by the author based on discussions with Paul Major, OUP's Global Senior Procurement Manager (Paper, Print, Bind and Content Creation) who is based in Oxford, England.

OUP was an early adopter circa 1999 of print-on-demand for scholarly monographs with the initiative for the program coming from the supply chain team wishing to enable just-in-time book supply around the world. The initiative developed into a significant programme driven by OUP's academic publishing division and now print-on-demand is run from corporate headquarters and can be utilized by all of its publishing divisions.

Of the 800–900 new monographs published each year, 75% are simultaneously released in hardback and paperback, providing customers with the option to choose their preferred format. It used to be that the OUP print-on-demand program was focused on end of the life books. However, now the press publishes books straight into digital print-on-demand. Hardbacks can be a challenge depending on the cover specification, for example, quality gold blocking on a cloth finishing, but OUP has overcome many issues by working closely with vendors to find solutions. Hardback binding costs are expensive and require premium pricing, while keeping paperback retail prices competitive which is important and tests the print-on-demand models. Print-on-demand for academic books has undoubtedly helped OUP's printed monograph program to survive and maintains copyright interests for the Press as well as furthering its mission of disseminating scholarly works worldwide.

OUP defines print-on-demand in terms of digital short-run books of 100 units or less and in 2016 OUP printed 28,000 books in this way in the United States and United Kingdom, in paperback and hardback.

In fact, Paul Major and the OUP team may well have been the first to apply the term 'auto replenishment' or 'auto-replen' to book inventory management, which is now widely used to describe keeping on-hand optimised forecasted demand quantities in warehouse to swiftly respond to new orders (Fig. 5.3). In 1998–2000, retail researchers coined the term 'automated replenishment programmes' (see references below). However, that was with respect to refilling retail shelves in response to consumer demand, especially for perishable food stuffs. In 2008, OUP set replenishment thresholds for books on their warehouse systems to trigger reordering of small quantities for stock. Those replenishment quantities were determined by mathematical forecasts of the anticipated demand for a book over the next few weeks and those titles automatically replenished as stock sold down. This 'managed order' logic is applied to all books whose annual forecasted demand is less than 700 units and monographs invariably fall into this category. By considering the whole cost of supply (printing, shipping to warehouse, unpacking, storing, picking, repacking, and shipping to customers) rather than only the cost of printing (i.e. the unit cost) and not tying up capital in stock, overall financial performance can be improved and waste minimised or removed.

Fig. 5.3 Paul Major, Global Senior Procurement Manager (Paper, Print, Bind & Content Creation) at Oxford University Press based in Oxford, UK.

Essentially, OUP was seeking to reduce stock in the warehouse/supply chain and eliminate waste; print-on-demand for books came along to enable that strategy. Auto replenishment can be more appropriate than stockless supply given the unit cost of a 50 copy print run with the right pricing schedule in place with a vendor. Forecasting demand takes place on OUP systems overseen by demand planners and controllers who can manipulate the sales history and troubleshoot forecasting issues. In some quarters editorial are still resistant. They have concerns because on-demand supply brings some constraints regarding formats, sizes, and papers but increasingly, the new books, for appropriate subjects, are creatively made within those constraints and more specification choices are added over time.

There are a few features of the OUP print-on-demand book program that customers may find surprising. First, lower hardback sales of monographs forced the hardback book to print-on-demand when many customers think print-on-demand for books is all about paperback books. Second, despite having warehouses in China and India as well as the United States and United Kingdom, OUP has not embraced the worldwide 'distributed print model' as originally articulated by BookSurge and implemented by many printers associated with Xerox. OUP choses to print digitally the UK and USfor stock because this is close enough to key North American and European customers and the cost of freight to other territories is not prohibitive based on the volume of longer run work still to be shipped for other divisions, such as ELT.

Third, OUP has extended print-on-demand for books beyond the monograph where they have the right specification and where the economics work. In due course as quality improves through further innovation, and the economics change further, OUP will extend the model to a wider variety of book specifications; making more types of books available print-on-demand. For example in 2017, most books with extents over 800 pages or colour books under 48 pages with a retail price of GBP 3.99 are generally not affordable through print-on-demand, but through incremental improvements this is likely to change. Inkjet technology will reduce the cost of color printing and binding technology will improve through automation and be able to accommodate very short and long extents.

Finally, OUP expects the pricing models for academic books to change in the future as customer requirements and expectations shift. Also, as more printing companies either expand their offering to other territories or traditional long run printers in those territories implement a print-on-demand offering, then the opportunity will be exploited.

Case study: Monographs in the steps of journals: Sheridan Press and John Wiley & Sons Launch Opt in printing for journals USA (2012)

This case refers to academic journals rather than books. It illustrates a commitment by a leading academic publisher, John Wiley & Sons, to 'Honoring Customer delivery choices' and 'offering the option of print'. This is an extract from a media release from November 2012. **Wiley Establishes Print on Demand Solution for Online Only Journals through The Sheridan Press.** Hoboken, NJ and Hanover, PA–2 November 2012.

John Wiley & Sons, Inc. (NYSE: JWA and JWB), a global provider of knowledge and knowledge-based services in areas of scientific, technical, medical, and scholarly research; professional practice; and global education, today announced a partnership with The Sheridan Press, print and publication services provider to the STM and scholarly journal community. Through this partnership, Wiley's online only journal titles will be available as print-on-demand (POD) copies, delivered through Sheridan's sophisticated production system. Starting in January 2013, a total of 145 online only titles will now be available in print via this solution. Over the past several years, The Sheridan Press has built state-of-the-art digital capabilities that include a proprietary interactive customer portal that generates orders for high quality digital POD journals for a growing number of STM publishers. The partnership provides Wiley customers with full order processing capability for print copies of journals. **This new service reflects Wiley's commitment to honour customer content delivery choices while providing a greater focus on digital publishing.** Craig Van Dyck, Vice President, Global Content Management, Scientific, Technical, Medical, Scholarly at Wiley, says: **"In a world which is increasingly moving to digital delivery of scholarly content we wanted to be able to continue to provide customers with the option of print if they wish.** We're delighted to be working with Sheridan to provide these Print on Demand copies for online only journals wherever and whenever they're needed." Pat Stricker, President and COO of The Sheridan Press, said, "The Sheridan Press is pleased to partner with Wiley. Outsourcing of this service takes advantage of Sheridan's sophisticated POD order intake interface and e-commerce capabilities and provides Wiley another channel through which to meet the needs of their customers."

Textbooks on-demand

6

What exactly is a textbook and how has print-on-demand had any impact on this sphere of publishing? The Oxford English Dictionary defines a textbook as: "a standard work for the study of a particular subject" and "a manual of instruction in any science or branch of study" [71]. While John B. Thompson in his book *Books in the Digital Age* (Polity, 2005) makes a distinction between what he calls 'academic books' (by which he means monographs or specialist texts) and books for 'higher education' (by which he means textbooks or books for professional development) [72]. In this book I have chosen to refer to monographs, professional development books, and books for teaching in higher education collectively as 'academic books'. However, this chapter concentrates on those academic books used in higher education and professional development which are referred to as textbooks in the sense of a standard work or manual for instruction, i.e. books typically used in undergraduate and professional development teaching. Print-on-demand has had an impact on this sphere of publishing in three ways: first the compilation of course packs where different texts by numerous authors are brought together by a lecturer or professor for teaching purposes; second the commissioning of an original textbook which might have regional variants or can be customised by the lecturers with their own notes; and finally as a printed companion to a learning environment which might be one of the above but is perhaps more integrated with software especially assessment tools. One of the key issues that textbook publishers are facing is pricing or value for money for the textbook package which is important to mention as this may drive authors to other print-on-demand solutions beyond established textbook publishers. Another issue which print-on-demand helps address is the student's preference to read and learn from textbooks off the printed page rather than screen. Print-on-demand is providing new options and solutions to textbook publishers and has the potential to empower textbook authors through self-publishing services.

Texts used in higher educational teaching pioneered the way for print-on-demand books as early as 1990 with the advent of the Primis service from McGraw-Hill. At the end of this chapter there are reproduced extracts from a Boston University management school case study c.1996 about the McGraw-Hill/Donnelly/Kodak Primis course packs/custom textbooks programme which provided the foundations for today's McGraw-Hill Create.

The Primis service started as an idea from an accounting textbook publisher supported by McGraw-Hill's corporate manufacturing manager and a systems engineer. It started with key partnerships between technology vendors, printers, publishers, and academics effectively an innovation ecosystem that worked; not the least Donnelley, the largest book printer in the world and a consistent partner with McGraw-Hill through the years and Kodak. Primis started in 1990 and by 1996 there were 1000 colleges which were using the service. Primis custom publishing products included

The Impact of Print-On-Demand on Academic Books. https://doi.org/10.1016/B978-0-08-102011-1.00006-7

locally authored stand-alone materials for sale at a specific college including core textbooks, workbooks, study guides, and software, also adapted McGraw-Hill texts and finally standard McGraw-Hill texts with a custom product or supplement. Over nearly three decades it grew and developed incrementally into Create.

Today Create is a fairly sophisticated online shop where lecturers can submit and compile new authors' textbooks and course packs from a database of textbook content published by McGraw-Hill and published by third party prepared to give license to McGraw-Hill. Here is the website address: http://create.mheducation.com. The idea of writing and compiling extracts from a variety of books and then printing them in book form was one of the fundamental principles of McGraw-Hill's Primis programme and is still popular with lecturers today through Create. It seems to be a great way to commission new textbooks too as authors are submitting their original work which might have commercial potential well beyond the local college and course for which it is written. There are some similarities with various author services self-publishing applications on the market combined with access to previously published works at least from McGraw-Hill and its publishing partners. One of the challenges for the service is that it is a closed community and there are publishers who will not contribute their copyright materials to that community. In an increasingly social digital environment textbook authors might just create alternative sharing platforms in the future, but in the meantime this remains a powerful tool for academic teaching staff.

The traditional single author printed textbook for teaching a subject, typically printed in colour and with a myriad of supplemental materials continues to be a feature of the printed textbook landscape.

Some courses have migrated to digital learning environments or are complemented by online learning environments. In this context, print-on-demand for textbooks is an emerging addition to the publisher's toolkit.

The layout of the typical colour textbook double page spread which might assist with reading comprehension is possibly at odds with the capabilities of e-books today. Today's digital composition, print technologies, and higher costs of colour book manufacturing make the print-on-demand standard textbook difficult to execute. Moreover, it seems that the added value of custom textbooks ordered in batches for classes are increasingly popular, adaptable for teaching around the world and potentially complement today's digital learning environments.

The pricing of higher education textbooks has been and continues to be a controversial issues and Joe Esposito asserted in *Scholarly Kitchen* that "...textbooks are expensive because the person mandating their use (the instructor) is not the same person who has to pay for them (the student)... If instructors had to pay for the books themselves, it would reshape the entire industry" [73]. If the lecturer would not pay, then perhaps the institution will pay as part of student fees. Apparently some institutions are keen to move to digital only 'inclusive access' models where print-on-demand might play a part for students seeking an optional print edition. Esposito continues (with the author underlining for emphasis):

> ... *Inclusive access is a reshaping tool, though of a different kind. In such an arrangement, institutions make certain commitments, and publishers respond with heavily*

discounted pricing. One form this takes is for the university to license a publisher's texts and then make them available to the students; the students pay for access through a fee. The commitments the university makes are critical; they can include a willingness to work with digital copies (with paid print-on-demand as an option) and a license that covers every student in the class (eliminating the used book and piracy markets). [73]

So far e-versions of the printed textbook have not come to completely dominate textbook purchasing and reading, but wholly integrated learning environment for students and professionals are gaining ground year on year. One example of this from as early as 2013 is a publishing partnership between edX free online classes and courses (https://www.edx.org/) and the RELX company Elsevier. In exchange for receiving anonymised usage data that will offer insights into how students use and access the content, Elsevier agreed to provide edX with science and technology book content for up to five massive open online courses (MOOC). They provide textbook content online for free as part of the course materials and offer a discount to purchase the print or electronic version of the text to those enrolled in the MOOC. This announcement follows the pilot of Elsevier textbook content as part of one edX MOOC, Circuits and Electronics taught by Anant Agarwal, edX president, and author of the Elsevier book *Foundations of Analog and Digital Electronic Circuits*. In the media release announcing the partnership Agarwal said:

We are very pleased to be using textbooks from Elsevier, a publisher with a long history of producing first-class content, ...As a result of this arrangement, students taking courses from our 29 institutions of higher education will be able to access free high-quality textbooks within the course itself. [74]

So for some types of learning and some contents predominantly digital learning has already been established and is growing. However for some textbooks, especially those with complex page formatting included in its form, a transition to digital has not yet been a success. One of the causes may be the lack of innovative product development in the e-book market which in turn holds back a full migration to digital by users. According to Joe Esposito writing for SSP's *Scholarly Kitchen* in 2017:

...it appears that Amazon's virtual monopoly on e-books has put a damper on competition and innovation. Most core college textbooks today are sold in print, and there is a reason for that. Is it a good idea to force students into digital editions when we haven't figured out how best to display text, table, charts, and graphs? [73]

Today's digital stand-alone textbook has not yet proved to be congenial to studying, learning, and retaining information. However, learning environments complete with assessment tools and multimedia components like video clips may in due course integrate print and digital resources for a better learning experience. Ken Brooks COO of Macmillan Learning refers to this in his interview which follows the Boston University Primis case study from 1996. This case is practically an ancient text in this fast moving digital age, but it is a terrific digest of college textbook history and the foundations of its 30 year transformation into an increasingly bespoke digital user experience with print on the side.

Case study: Primis Custom Publishing from McGraw-Hill Education

Before reading the 1996 case study, here is an introductory extract from the Primis website for Mechanical Engineering Design Primis textbook: [75] McGraw-Hill's Primis Custom Publishing established a standard for educational publishing when it launched its custom publishing operation in 1990. In response to the needs of changing curricula and the concern over high prices of textbooks for students, McGraw-Hill introduced the concept of making books for individual school needs and adapting books that we already publish to better fit a teacher's course content.

Our organisation has proven successful since the early years of custom publishing and we have maintained this organisational model to provide a simplified and effective basis for printing, pricing, promoting, and distributing educational products in print and electronic formats.

We are pleased to give you an overview of kind of work we can do for you:

Adaptations: An 'adaptation' simply means you can take an existing textbook and reorganise the chapters and/or abridge the contents. You may select from our vast array of McGraw-Hill College textbooks. McGraw-Hill produces thousands of products for use in college humanities, social science, languages, science, mathematics, engineering, business, and economic courses. Adaptations are generally printed in black and white, but depending on the enrolment size of your course, colour adaptations may be possible. Contact your *McGraw-Hill Sales Representative*.

Some ideas to consider are the following:

- combine chapters from more than one McGraw-Hill textbook
- delete chapters you do not cover
- include special readings or assignments with textbook chapters
- change the order of chapters to perfectly match your syllabus
- add your syllabus or lecture notes to the textbook
- add original artwork
- join the text and the student study guide together in one text

Author original: Have you written material for your course and want to have it professionally printed for your students? Original work could be a core textbook, study guide or lab manual, special exercises, etc., that you've authored. Your original project may even earn a royalty if you desire. This royalty payment can be paid directly to you, the department, or even to a special fund.

If you would like to include and/or use material that isn't your own property or the property of McGraw-Hill, we can help you research and clear permission. Permission fees can be added to the overall price of the textbook. An example of a permission item might be a famous poem you want to include in your course pack or a magazine article that is essential to your lecture.

McGraw-Hill's Primis Online gives you access to the world's best and abundant resources at your fingertips, literally. There are over 350,000 pages of content available from which you can select from our online database. With a few mouse clicks, you can create customised learning tools simply and affordable. When you adopt a Primis Online text, you decide the best medium for your students: printed black and white textbooks or electronic e-books.

McGraw-Hill has included many of our market-leading textbooks within Primis Online for eBook and print customisation as well as many licensed readings and cases. And now, Primis Online offers McGraw-Hill's PowerWeb sites! PowerWeb titles are designed to keep your course up to date using the resources of the Internet. Students log on to access continuously updated content tailored to their course – articles, weekly updates with assessment, interactive exercises, and much more! To learn more, open the PowerWeb tab on the Primis Online home page.

Case study by the Boston University, School of Management (1996)

The College Textbook Market Disruption and Transformation (only Part 1 is reproduced here with some light editing and text in bold added by the author) [76].

Introduction: The last two decades (1976–96) has seen dramatic changes in numerous industries. That industry along with all industries based on print have been forced by technology changes to radically transform every aspect of their business. Many simply did not survive, still others have but might not last much longer. Of course, the technology keeps changing. Product changes coupled with technology enable process changes and business model changes. New entrants have emerged from a variety of domains; the boundaries of the industry have blurred or disappeared. In the 1990, textbooks sales began to slump as high costs were passed along as high prices. Buyers elected to find other sources of input from notes to used books. The production process was stale, buried in the methods of the industrial revolution. Yet major publishers responded, streamlining their processes and developing new methods to get customised material into the hands of their customers...(this case study covers) the move from print to the digital economy associated with the movement from mass production to mass customisation. McGraw-Hill was one of those publishers who responded to this shift and the emerging digital economy. This era is marked by changes in the way the product was produced and distributed. It shifted market power to the data aggregators and away from traditional distribution channels.....

From mass production to mass customisation – The origins of Primis

Robert D. Lynch started his career as a sales representative in McGraw-Hill, the way most textbook editors begin their careers. He worked his way up and in 1998 became an executive editor for accounting at McGraw-Hill. As an accounting editor, he watched his books losing market share to used books and copy centres. He said to himself, "Kinko's (a national chain of copy centers which has since been acquired by FedEx) and used books clearly indicated that I must do something different to make my product more attractive to the market."[1] But what? Markets were changing and market share was being lost, but was this simply a price reaction or a more fundamental change? Textbook publishing had become more complex; textbooks were more comprehensive and included more graphics. These changes not only added to the cost but also created a better product. Nevertheless, **Accounting professors were passing up McGraw-Hill's textbooks in favour of developing their own course material – usually composed of selected chapters from texts supplemented with newspaper articles and their own writing**. Lynch realised that this was likely not just a passing phase but instead a real change in the industry. He understood the criticality of responding to this trend. Lynch's quest led him to develop a custom publishing system in the 1990s that allowed professors the flexibility to select and arrange material to suit their needs. This concept became known as **Primis Custom Publishing**. It had a very slow start, but through the years continued to grow not only in the number of universities using the services, but also in the availability of the material.

Primis as a concept appeared to have been well timed. Custom products in the college marketplace were expected to grow at around 20%–30% while the traditional textbooks were expected to grow at around 3%–5%. However, Primis also faced a number of competitors through the years. The challenge was not only to stay competitive but also to maintain their first-mover advantage.

The college textbook marketplace

The launch of Primis should be seen against the backdrop of the key characteristics of the textbook publishing marketplace in the United States during the 1990s. The college textbook marketplace

[1] Personal interview with Robert Lynch.

was the third largest publishing segment within the industry accounting for 12%–15% of net sales (the trade and professional segment are the top two segments). This market was highly concentrated due to the high investment necessary for the research, marketing, and distribution. It was also the most profitable mainly because of high textbook prices and comparatively low production costs. For example, a first-year calculus textbook retailed for as much as $77 while books for most business school courses were priced around $69 each. In the early 1990s, most industry observers believed that the total sales on the college textbook sector would be stagnant. However, by the late 1990s, sales growth neared 8%. Profit margins were a healthy 20%.[2] However, used textbooks remained a major threat to new books sales. In 1990, the used book market represented a fourth of the total test sales – up from 18% a decade ago. By 1998 they made up between 20% and 40% of total college sales. Used books were attractive to students due to the high price of new textbooks and the fact that few books were retained beyond the semester in which they were used. High costs are driven by a number of factors. At the same time, used books were being marketed more aggressively. Many large distributors had developed national computerised databases that were capable of indicating the current level of inventory of various books as well as guaranteeing delivery of the required quantity of used books at a specified time anywhere within the country. In many instances, the used books were also sold in the campus bookstores, thereby directly competing against new books. More importantly, the average profit margins for used books were about 10% higher than the new textbooks. College enrolment was also a factor for textbook sales. The National Center for Educational Statistics reported that post-secondary enrolment in degree granting institutions rose beginning in 1987 through the 2007, but with only modest changes. Going forward, from 2010 to 2020, enrolment growth was expected to be flat.[3] However, these projections are neither factor in the growth in international student populations nor do these include estimates for online educational programmes.

Key stages in producing a textbook

Traditional textbook publishing can be seen as a temporal flow of activities with seven distinct stages: acquisition, editing, manufacturing, selling, distributions, purchasing, and revising.

Acquisition stage: The first stage involves the acquisition of manuscripts. Competence in this stage was in the systematic search for potentially significant and successful manuscripts before competitors realised their value. Often, major acquisition editors could be seen in leading academic professional conferences trying to predict new topics as well as innovative pedagogical approaches. The procedures for decision-making about the acquiring manuscripts have been termed as 'guesswork, intuition and opinion'. Those responsible for acquiring manuscripts describe themselves as inhabiting a world "in which there are no formulae for finding talent… All we have to work with are probabilities and intuition."[4] Most acquisitions editors compare this phase of textbook publishing to "a poker game with the highest ante because of high costs of production." According to DC Heath, a leading publishing house, a publisher spends between $500,000 and $1 million to produce a textbook.

Editing stage: The second stage was editing the manuscript once it was received from the author. During this stage, authors worked closely with an assigned editor. Editors usually aimed to publish a particular book approximately 12 months from the time they began working on it with the author. Typically, a new book was targeted either for the fall or the winter list corresponding to most US university academic year calendars.

[2] Standard and Poors Industry Survey – Publishing, 23 April, 1998.

[3] Reported in The Chronicle of Higher Education Almanac, 29 August 1997.

[4] B. Levitt, C. Ness, The lid on the garbage can: constraints on decision making in the technical core of college-text publishers, Admin. Sci. Q. (1989) 190–207.

Manufacturing stage: Subsequently, the manuscript moved to the manufacturing state for printing and binding in lot sizes dictated by the selling department. The manufacturing stage was quite straightforward, with a particular focus on the cost and quality. Escalated costs due to poor scheduling and poor print quality could significantly damage the reputation of a publisher. The responsibility for the textbook now shifted from the editor to someone else and by the time the book was finally out, the original editor had moved on to another project. Hence, it was very common for an editor to inherit projects from former editors. This further complicates the inherently difficult prediction of success or failure of a book. So, who should be held accountable when a book failed in the market: "should the responsibility lie with the acquiring editor or someone else who inherited the manuscript along the way?"

Joseph L. Dionne (the Chairman and Chief Executive Officer of McGraw-Hill, Inc. in 1985–98) summed up typical textbook production in the following way, "Like many businesses that developed during the industrial revolution, we publishers have long been locked into an 'assembly line' approach. We would select a manuscript that we felt was worth the wider distribution. We would tell the printer how many books we wanted to print, the kind of binding desired, the number of the colours needed and so on. Then the printer would educate us on the costs involved. By the time the type was set, the plates made, the sheets fed and the cut, the pages bound, and the books distributed, assembly-line publishing became a fairly expensive propositions. As anyone here can attest, creating a textbook for a national market forces every publisher to take advantage of economies of scale. Rather than a book covering a limited range of interests, a publisher includes virtually every aspect of the topic. Which is how textbook publishers winds up with the sort of hefty tome that typifies today's textbook market."[5]

Selling and distribution stages: The next two stages were selling (including influencing the adoption decisions in leading universities) and distributing the textbook to various outlets (especially the college bookstore). Moreover, early adoption of a textbook by a prestigious university increased the chances of adoption by other universities. As an example, adoption of a textbook by the University of California, Los Angeles (UCLA) was believed to increase the likelihood of adoption by other universities within the University of California system. So, sales personnel concentrated their initial efforts at these 'lead' universities.

Purchasing stage: Purchasing was the next stage and, of course, was critical. One view **of** textbook purchase was as follow: "You have to remember that the market for textbooks is like the market for dog food because decisions are not made by the ultimate consumer."[6] Instructors made the choice of the text to be used for the course and order accordingly. However, in reality, an instructor could only recommend a book, it is the student who ultimately makes the purchasing decision. It was a decision largely based on 'value-for-money'. If some students believed that substitute products such as course notes or used books provided greater value, they simply did not buy the textbooks. According to a 1996 study[7] of over 1000 students, only 78% of the students said that they purchased books for all their courses. On average, 38% bought new textbooks, while 56% bought used textbooks and the rest borrowed books, copied books, shared books with another student, or went through courses without books. All stages are important for the final product to be best positioned in the market, but the editorial department typically enjoyed a greater status and **was more glamorous than other departments. More importantly, it was rare for all firm** employees to work on a single set of books. Therefore, there was little cohesion within a firm and no common concerns with a product across the organisation.

[5] Speech at the American Association of Publishers (College Division), 13 May 1992 at Washington, DC.
[6] Levitt and Ness (1989).
[7] Association of American Publishers (1996).

Revising stage: The final stage is revising (or updating) the textbook. This stage had been heavily influenced by the aggressiveness observed in the used book market and the author may have had little say about when to revise. The complicating factor was that this stage might either involve the same editor who worked initially on the book or another editor depending on workload in the editing department. Recent estimates indicate that the update cycle is every 1–3 years as opposed to the traditional 5-year cycle just a few years back. One author observed. "I had to ensure that my book had a 1996 date on it although the material was not substantively altered from my previous edition; if I didn't the publisher's selling staff would have found it more difficult to get my book adopted in major universities and colleges. In my view there are two overriding factors influencing the timing of revisions: the revision cycles of directly-competing books and the availability of used books; updating the content is of less importance."

Copyright issues

In 1991 Kinko's launched a product] Professor Publishing, (which) infringed on publishers' copyrights in selling photocopied course packets to students. In 1989, eight publishers had sued Kinko's for copyright infringement. The publishers argued that the copying chain was illegally using copyrighted material without making royalty payments. Kinko's attorneys countered that the firm's unpaid use for the material was for educational purposes and therefore permitted as 'fair use' under the Copyright Act of 1976. Buzzle.com provides a useful summary of the Act. The judge ruled **against Kinko's fining them $500,000 in damages and $1.3 million in legal fees**. The ruling clearly stated that commercial copiers could not make fair use determination when making multiple copies of copyrighted material for classroom use. The Kinko's ruling was reconfirmed in November 1996 when Princeton University Press, Macmillan, Inc. and St. Martin's Press, Inc. were awarded damages for the duplication of copyrighted materials. In Princeton University Press v. Michigan Document Services, it was noted that the duplication of copyrighted materials for sale by a for-profit corporation was an infringement of copyright laws and the court awarded the plaintiffs $5000 in damages per infringed work. These decisions had increased the number of requests for copyright clearances and several avenues now exist. The American Association of Publishers (AAP) president at the time, Nicholas Veliotes, commented. "Now that the courts have made clear that permission for this type of photocopying must be obtained, associate members are preparing for the expected increase in the number of permission requests. We do not anticipate any problems and are happy to hear Kinko's recent assurances of their intention to comply with the court's order." In the wake of the 1991 Kinko's decision, Copyright Clearance Center, Inc. (CCC), expanded its core photocopy licensing business from services to corporations to university course-pack licensing. Bruce Funkhouser, the then Vice President of Business Operations for CCC reported that its initial growth in course-pack licensing was 'nothing short of phenomenal' and that the course-pack licensing business would continue to grow steadily. CCC, which was located in Danvers Massachusetts, represented nearly 2 million registered titles from tens of thousands of publishers (including McGraw-Hill), authors, and other copyright owners. On its behalf, it issues licenses and permissions to make photocopies to about 10,000 businesses and nearly 3000 colleges, universities, and off-campus copy shops. CCC also had a smaller business in licensing reprints and electronic uses of tests including distance learning and licensing photographs. They developed as a 'one-stop shopping' business for all copyright permissions.

The McGraw-Hill Company

McGraw-Hill is one of the world's largest educational publishers and a major publisher of college textbooks. Headquartered in New York, they also has offices in Ohio, New Jersey, California, and Texas as well as many international locations. McGraw-Hill provided a near-perfect environment for the creation of Primis. Joseph Dionne, the CEO from 1985 until 1998, had previously served as the head of Information Systems. In the late 1980s, he envisioned McGraw-Hill as the "information turbine[8] whereby data comes into the turbine and is manipulated through a series of value-added processes to result in a portfolio of products and services". To implement his vision, he restructured the organisation around market groups such as information and publications services; educational and professional services; financial services; and, broadcasting. In 1992, the sales from these four groups totalled about $2 billion, and by 1996, sales had risen to almost $3 billion, showing a 10-year growth of 6.9% and net income reached $495.7 million, with a growth of 12.4% over the same period.[9]

Dionne directed his management team to identify opportunities and devise ways to deliver the required products and services by leveraging McGraw-Hill's vast database. He also strongly believed that **an efficient and effective IT infrastructure was central to support and shape this vision**. He remarked, "We have done a better job of mastering new technology than any other publisher and in meeting customers' needs in new and creative ways."[10] On 26 September 1996, Robert Evanson was appointed the president of McGraw-Hill's newly created 'Higher Education and Consumer group'. This group included McGraw-Hill Companies' College Division and the July acquisition of Times-Mirror Higher Education (TMHE) Group which had revenues of $228.2 million in 1995. The acquisition of TMHE Group brought the following titles into the McGraw-Hill fold: Irwin, Mosby, Brown, and Brown Benchmark. **Each unit had its own custom publishing facility**. Dionne commended, "We will be able to capitalise on our strong international presence and solid experience as the world's largest educational publisher by efficiently integrating the TMHE produce lines into our existing global marketing infrastructure upon the completion of the acquisition".[10]

The Primis concept

Primis was an electronic database publishing system that let the college instructors create a customised textbook tailored to the specific needs of a course by selecting content from a database of educational and professional information. The database was developed under the direction of McGraw-Hill editors. Professor could select core chapters and sections from existing textbooks, journals, case studies, as well as magazine articles and arrange them in their desired order and sequence. The professors also had **the flexibility to add their own materials and notes** that reflect their particular teaching approach. **There were four main types of Primis custom publishing products**. The first, **stand-alone materials** were projects usually **authored locally for sale at a specific school and which include core textbooks, workbooks, study guides, and software.** The others included **out of print titles, adapted McGraw-Hill texts, and McGraw-Hill texts with a custom product or supplement**. Primis Custom Publishing was one of the two business units within the Primis Group. The unit focused on custom textbooks produced from materials in the database – composed of McGraw-Hill's published textbooks, Business Week magazine (owned at the time by McGraw-Hill and sold to Bloomberg in 2009), and copyrighted material under license. Its key capability was assembling a custom textbook from the database on a just-in-time basis with zero inventory.

The second business unit within **Primis Group, The College Custom Publishing Series,** "took a book and published any piece of it with the same typography. Also, it published a book which the professor could not get published anywhere else, republish books out of print, or publish an individual professor's supplement to accompany a standard textbook. McGraw-Hill warehoused these products for a shelf life of about two years."[11] Separately, these two units had been

[8] Forbes, 26 November 1990; pp. 37–38.

[9] Standard and Poors Industry Survey – Publishing, 23 April 1998.

[10] McGraw-Hill Annual Report, 1990.

[11] Interview with Tom Brier and Tom Curtin, September 1996.

providing complementary services and were integrated with the goal of customising a text to suit specific instructors: their unique needs for content, their teaching technique, their style, and their pace. The name Primis was derived from the word 'prime', meaning of 'first importance' or 'the best part of anything' and 'is' for information systems. Carbone Smolan Associates, a design firm based in New York, developed the name and logotype. Robert Lynch, the then Vice President and Director of Primis at McGraw-Hill's college division, emphasised the importance of the name Primis. "We chose Primis because we wanted an easy-to-remember name that would distinguish us from other types of custom publishing. We wanted a name that communicated the attributes of electronic custom publishing-customisation, currency, and value and says that McGraw-Hill' product is the first system capable of fully customising textbooks." Lynch originally restricted his idea for a customised book to accounting which was his area of responsibility. The first book available through Primis used the contents and chapter from Meigs and Meigs Accounting: The Basics for Business Decisions, one of McGraw-Hill's most successful titles. His proposal to create a custom textbook was accepted by the Executive Vice President in 1988 since Primis was seen as part of the CEO's broad business vision.

Development of Primis

Lynch received initial seed funding for his concept, but he did not have any significant people resources, nor did he have many allies within the college division. His operational support came from two key relationships outside the divisions – the General Manager of Corporate Manufacturing Technology, who educated Lynch in the nuances of information technology needed to better understand custom publishing, and a systems designer who spent his spare time designing the systems and technology architecture for Primis. During the first 10 months, Lynch refined his concept, defined the information technology platform, and finalised the architecture for Primis. He also selected Eastman Kodak and R.R. Donnelley as partners for the Primis initiative. The partnership with Kodak created the proprietary software, while the venture with Donnelley created the manufacturing and selective-binding capabilities. At the time of signing the partnership agreements, Joseph Dionne became actively involved and approved a 1-year prototype test. Just 5 months after the prototype began, Dionne became a leading advocate for this concept and gave formal support for the full-scale venture.

Dionne remarked that "this was not technology in search of a market, quite the contrary. Because the concept was so new, we were scrambling to create a lot of the necessary technology ourselves." Lynch also shared this view, "we should accept the fact that our customers demand content first – content that is current, editorially developed, and delivered in a format that is customised to their requirements. Primis has experienced enthusiastic and extremely positive reception. In one way this is not surprising, the concept of customised material used for college courses has been part of the marketplace for many years in the form of photo-duplication."[12] Primis was officially launched in the spring of 1990 for one subject – accounting. By the end of 1990, approximately 30 colleges and universities had adopted the Primis texts. At the end of 1991, about 150 schools were using Primis books. By 1992, the Primis venture was still a lean organisational unit within the College Division with a total of 17 people – 12 professionals and 5 administrative support staff. By 1993 over 600 universities and colleges were using Primis textbooks covering 17 disciplines such as management, accounting, business law, marketing, political science, mathematics, engineering, education in English composition, and English literature. **By 1996 textbooks based on the Primis database were used in over 1000 colleges and covered over 20 disciplines.** The business

[12] Lynch's talk at Cornell University, November 1992.

relationship with Donnelly for creating the textbooks on Sun Sparc workstations linked to Donnelley printing locations was still in place. The printing capability had been enhanced beyond black and white to include halftones as well as spot colour in response to customer needs. Most textbooks were still printed at Donnelley locations and shipped to the campus bookstore or other distribution points.

How Primis worked in the 1990s

Typically, an instructor sits down with a Primis sales representative to select material from a database, which consisted of textbooks, supplements, journal and magazines articles, laboratory manuals, and case studies. Early on, McGraw-Hill decided to standardise on Adobe's PostScript. This means that all material including an instructor's own notes and material had to be converted into the PostScript language and be part of the database. According to Jeff Handen the lead manufacturing technician at Donnelley, "the average book order took between 3 to 10 minutes to build." For small lots of up to 50, the Kodak Ektaprint was used while for large orders a master was produced for use in a high-speed duplicator. Lynch pointed out, "**the appearance is not like a workbook but a high quality black and white textbook.**"[13] **The book would have the instructor's name on the cover and is paginated with a table of contents reflecting the sequence of use for the instructor's courses.**

A single examination copy could be shipped to the instructor within 48–72 h; classroom quantities were shipped from 5 to 10 days. The price of these customised books was about 50% of equivalent size of the traditional textbook. In addition, customers perceived the customised texts to be of much greater value than traditional textbooks. Dionne was pleased with the progress made. He stated, "Well, a few weeks ago we announced a new technology that cuts through the theory that customised printing will be too expensive. The new Electobook Press, using digital technology, is able to print and bind individual books in any quantity without stopping for set ups. For example, a 2000-book run can be followed by a 55-book run, which can be followed by a 450-book run, and so on, without stopping."[14]

Reactions

The reactions of authors and instructions were positive. Customised books offered the possibility of a wider audience and a new way to keep their books current. Authors could prepare less-than-book length material. Copyright permissions were handled seamlessly. Some author, however, expressed concern that selecting just parts of existing chapters might not convey the full picture the way the original author intended. Others were concerned that out of sequence material might not present the reader with the necessary prerequisite knowledge. Just prior to his departure from the company, Robert Lynch remarked, "emerging technological developments pertaining to multimedia, online databases, distance learning through the use of ISDN, data highway and others will shape and reshape how we compete in the market and deliver value to our clients. Our market is not the $2 billion textbook market, for that only represents what the textbook publishers sell, not all that students use. we see a quite different market." Dionne summarised the fundamental nature of the transformation, "the genie is out of the bottle. Whether we like it or not, a market has developed for alternatives to traditional textbooks. I want to make sure that publishers respond and retake the market. Because if we do not, its very easy to see how an IBM or an AT&T or even a Microsoft could step in and grab the market right from under our noses."[15] He may not have had the right companies in mind, but his point is well taken (Fig. 6.1).

[13] Personal interview with Mr. Lynch, December 1992.

[14] Joe Dionne's speech on 12 May 1992.

[15] Speech at the American Association of Publishers (College Division), 12 May 1992.

Fig. 6.1 Ken Brooks, Chief Operating Officer, Macmillan Learning based in the United States.

Interview with Ken Brooks, COO, Macmillan Learning

Ken has enjoyed a career across the book publishing industry as SVP, Global Supply Chain, McGraw-Hill Education; SVP, Global Production and Manufacturing Services, Cengage Learning; President, Treadwell Media Group; President, Publishing Dimensions; VP, Customer Operations, Simon & Schuster; and VP, Production, Bantam Doubleday Dell. Ken recounts some of the print-on-demand enabled projects with which he has been associated including textbook chapters supply pre-publication of a conventionally printed textbook.

While I have not been involved in academics books (monographs), I have been involved in both Trade and Educational books (textbooks). These have been used to immediately address customer needs by allowing for printing of customised materials, shortening lead times, and addressing inventory investment pressures. I have used POD/digital printing for both one-colour and four-colour printing. These projects have all been relatively successful.

At various companies, I have used a range of offshore sheet-fed, onshore web offset, short-run digital, and true print-on-demand printing applications to fulfil customer needs. The choice generally comes down to economics: how does the cost of safety stock balance against the increased unit cost of digital printing/POD in order to fulfil customer's expectation? If the quality is sufficient (and it generally is except for the very largest four-colour textbooks) then it truly is a matter of economics. There are, however, constraints driven by legacy systems: implementation of true print-on-demand requires a level of systems integration that is not always possible in legacy order management systems.

Applications of print-on-demand for book that I have been involved with include the following:

- A start-up that was doing 'build your own' cookbooks printed one-off from customer-selected recipes, but it ultimately was not successful.
- Use of print-on-demand for end-of-life titles with low demand.
- Use of print-on-demand to handle interim fulfilment until the conventionally printed inventory could come back into stock.

- Use of print-on-demand to handle early life sampling before the full print run was available.
- Use of print-on-demand to handle fulfilment of individual textbook chapters while waiting for the full book to come into the stock.
- Use of print-on-demand and variable digital printing to serialise books sent to the market for sampling and sale.

It has positively affected textbook and trade publishing by driving down the cost of publishing. Particularly, in textbook publishing where demand is shifting to digital at the rate of 15%–20% per year, both initial print runs and reprints will be done digitally. I would predict that by 2020 most use of course materials will be digital with the ability for the user to print the materials locally. The core value proposition is shifting from the content to use of material within the user's workflow, so I would actually expect the same thing to happen in Scientific Technical and Medical publishing.

To conclude Ken was interviewed in 2016 prior to speaking at Digital Book World 2017 in New York. What he said was an important indicator of the future of textbook publishing:

Success in educational publishing these days means delivering a learning experience across print and digital platforms. These offerings have to work together, but neither is yet fully self-sufficient. For example, you cannot deliver much of the adaptive assessment and interactive content in print, but students and professors in many disciplines prefer print for some uses. We are going to focus on what the customer really wants and needs, and how to deliver hybrid offerings that satisfy those needs.

The most effective print-on-demand textbook application I have observed was for A5 sized books less than 200 pages. These are typically instructional manuals or short courses in developing world markets. Delivery of draft copies can be reviewed by multiple reviewers, and returned to be edited and revised. Print-on-demand for international textbooks has positively impacted academic book publishing, in that the books become available to a wide audience for a cheaper price – especially when printed locally. Now students (particularly in developing nations) can have their own textbooks. In the developing world, there is still a high demand for the printed books. Even countries that have easy access to smart phones are still asking for the printed book. I am curious to see if the current teenagers, who have grown up with smartphones, will still want to purchase printed books, but for this generation, printed textbooks will continue.

[illegible]

[illegible] printed locally, now students (particularly in developing nations) can have their own textbooks. In the developing world, there is still a high demand for the printed book. Even countries that have easy access to smart phones are still asking for the printed book. I am curious to see if the current teenagers, who have grown up with smart phones, will still want to purchase printed books, but for this generation, printed textbooks will continue.

Book aggregators, archives and collections on-demand

7

While the publishing of new academic books either in monograph or textbook form has gradually migrated towards a digital first, if not a digital only creation process, the back catalogue of unavailable books of interest to the academy is immense. The potential for print-on-demand academic books over the next decade is therefore also immense because aggregated books, archived books, and e-book collections are growing apace. All of these databases, in languages around the world, are potentially print-on-demand books in waiting.

In recent years, there has been a tremendous growth in the number of digital collections of academic books. These have been pulled together in different ways, for example, community generated books, siloed subscription only e-book collections, and Open Access e-book collections or scanned PDFs of printed books. Different organisations have brought these collections together, for example, online communities, commercial publishers, learned societies, or libraries. These collections have been amassed for different purposes: some for profit, some for altruistic openness to scholarly communication. Where the previous two chapters focused on the creation and publication of new monographs and new textbooks with printing specifically in mind, either as original works or compilations of extracts of older works, this chapter concentrates on printed books being created as a by-product from digital collections. This is a slightly artificial perspective because, of course, when original works are pulled together into a database, especially if they are tagged into logical groupings, they form digital collections. However, these new digital collections of old books or new compilations of digital content perhaps offer the biggest potential for print-on-demand books in future. The open digital publication of old collections of academic books and new custom academic books enabled by new intermediaries and across all languages is happening today. Plugging these databases into print-on-demand book supply is an opportunity waiting to happen.

Book aggregators in this context are companies that are prepared to digitise any books into print-on-demand ready files; typically, they are working with out of copyright publications or publications without copyright restrictions. Some of these books may be academic monographs or textbooks. Two contrasting examples of aggregation are Kessinger Publishing LCC, which specialises in digitising rare or out-of-print books for profit by reselling them via internet booksellers, and WikiBooks who enable their community to assemble custom textbooks and training manuals in a copyright free environment and then purchase a printed and bound edition at cost. WikiBooks have software development partners PediaPressgmbH and the service is summarised at the end of the chapter in a case study.

By **book archives**, I mean digital conversion projects that take printed books, often in library collections, and systematically scan, tag and convert to them e-books, or print ready PDFs files. These projects are typically not-for-profit and are happening in

The Impact of Print-On-Demand on Academic Books. https://doi.org/10.1016/B978-0-08-102011-1.00007-9

academic libraries and in association with academic libraries around the world, opening up unique library collections to scholars around the world, projects like Harvard University's DASH, The Digital Public Library of America, The Digital Library of India, Canadian Electronic Library, or commercial projects such as Proquest's 18th-century collection with the British Library. All of these archival e-book collections have the potential to be print-on-demand enabled subject to copyright and licensing barriers. Local and special collections have particular value. One award winning collaboration making an archive available print-on-demand is the Bibliolabs and British Library project. Bibliolabs are an interesting example of a business working with libraries as a new intermediary, enabling community content creation, and opening up special collections. They worked with the British Library's 19th-century print book collection and there is an interview with Bibliolabs' founder Mitchell Davis at the end of the chapter.

Finally, by **book collections**, I mean books usually grouped by a publisher into their own-siloed collections, typically tagged by subject for marketing purposes, created as a by-product of routine print books and e-book publishing. In Chapter 3, Springer MyCopywas used to illustrate a service directly selling to scholars at institutions that subscribe to e-book collections and is also an example of a print-on-demand enabled e-book collection. Brill's MyBook service is also a good example of a hybrid service which is print-on-demand enabled. At the end of Chapter 5 in an interview, Emile Krankendock recounted Brill's print-on-demand for books story and this article shows how that service is being used by scholars.

Other digital collections which are fully or partially print-on-demand enabled were highlighted in *The Academic Book of the Future*:

> *Publishers too have been converting their back lists into digital collections, breathing new life into (sometimes long-) out-of-print academic books. Oxford Scholarship Online integrates over 13,000 titles published over the last 50 years, while Cambridge Core provides access to over 30,000 ebooks and 360 journals, going back as far as the beginning of the twentieth century. [77]*

The case study that the end of the chapter recounts is one of the first experimental print-on-demand and e-book hybrid digitisation projects in academic publishing focusing on history books at Cambridge University Press. Today there are a myriad of collections available underpinned by Cambridge Core.

Book collections might also be Open Access assisting like-minded smaller publishers or even like-minded authors. One example of an author-empowered initiative is Open Book Publishers. They were founded in 2008 by Dr. Alessandra Tosi and Dr. Rupert Gatti, academics at the University of Cambridge. They have become an international network of scholars committed to open access publishing. Their books are published in hardback, paperback, PDF, and e-book editions. According to their website:

> *Besides our digital and online editions, with their many advantages, such as ability to search, we also offer printed books that provide the many other traditional advantages which readers rightly value. In our experience, the two media, that are designed for*

> *the convenience of different kinds of readers, complement one another, and are able to prosper together. We use print-on-demand technology to provide top quality paperback and hardback editions of each monograph at affordable prices. Our books are printed in the UK and the USA and can be ordered from any country. Any revenue we generate goes back into publishing more high-quality monographs. [78]*

Open Book Publishers also have a free online edition that can be read via website, downloaded, reused, or embedded anywhere. According to their founder:

> *The free edition is being accessed by thousands of readers each month in over 180 countries. In addition, our digital publishing model allows us to extend our books well beyond the printed page. We are creating interactive books, and works that incorporate moving images, links, and sound into the fabric of the text. More traditional titles are equipped with digital resources freely available on our website. [79]*

Author-empowered publishing is a very interesting development and is discussed further in Chapter 10 Trends in Academic Book Publishing On-demand. Seeing print-on-demand for academic books as a natural extension of an academic e-book collection has become the new norm.

Interview: Mitchell Davis, Founder and Chief Business Officer, Bibliolabs LLC (2017) USA

Bibliolabs won the 2016 British Library Labs Award in commercial category for a project that used the British Library's 19th-century collections in a range of products, including making the collections mobile and greatly expanding the impact and audience of the works worldwide. The partnership between BL and BiblioLabs derived from a 2011 project in which BiblioLabs endeavored to make 80,000 19th-century books from the BL's collection available on the iPad. The result was a stunning and user-friendly interface that requires no technical expertise to create cost-effective,

Mitchell Davis is Founder and Chief Business Officer, Bibliolabs LLC based in Charleston, South Carolina, USA. Photograph used with permission from the Charleston Digital Corridor.

engaging digital curations. Considering that over 250,000 have used the BL app to date, it's safe to say that BiblioLabs' work with the BL makes a compelling argument for what the future role of libraries will be—and is fast becoming: places for the public to access information and create meaning in a digital environment.

Clearly, print-on-demand allows for a demand of one, so as academic research output (and other things resembling academic research) has exploded, print-on-demand has been perfectly suited to meet demand for esoteric and niche materials economically. We believe there is a massive opportunity to open up scientific research in more open 'consumer' markets and Education, Training & Development (ETD) in particular. No one can deny the power of Amazon.com to drive incremental discovery of science and research, as it is the world's largest content discovery channel. We have successfully built this bridge for specific institutions that have opted into these programmes and proven that demand for this ETD material exists in areas outside traditional academic channels.

Bibliolabs has made over 80,000 19th-century books available from the British Library, many of which had been out-of-print for over 150 years. These books are packaged intelligently by genre with a custom cover design driven by variable data.

The effect of print-on-demand on academic books has been positive, while also complicating what had been a rather traditional channel for 'real' science and humanities research. Like mainstream content going from a couple of major networks to Internet-based TV, when anyone can produce and distribute content, that flood of content can be overwhelming and discombobulating. The spectrum between good and bad research is greatly magnified in a democratised world. However, knowledge does want to be free (even if it cannot be produced and distributed for free) and these are the early days of sorting through the deluge and ensuring that curatorial layers emerge to make sense of more research output. Print-on-demand allows for this activity to leave the purely digital realm and meet the needs of those who prefer print.

In future, research will be published first and validated or evaluated second, a new group of trusted brands will emerge to help in this process, and print will remain an important distribution format for this information and research. Also, institutions will create their own Open Education Resources (OER), rather than force students to purchase from publishers. Those OER materials can be shared and modified between organisations, saving students money and winning universities political capital in lowering student educational expenses. Print-on-demand will continue to play a role in meeting the needs of students who simply prefer print.

Case study: The Cambridge University Press History Project UK (2000–04)

Written by Rufus Neal and abridged by the author. This case tells the original prepress story behind the Cambridge University Press History project. A number of history collection services available from Cambridge today benefited from lessons learnt in this experiment. Today various history collections are good examples of 'hybrid' academic book collections: digital with optional print form which is detailed at the end of the case.

In 2000, we were sent, in error, by a candidate supplier for hardback reprints, book blocks bound in a full colour paper cover—the paperback cover derived directly from the hardback jacket. This 'accident' brought home to us that a hardback-only ISBN could be set up equally easily as either a hardback reprint or as a new paperback version, or as both. The ongoing inexorable decline in monograph sales meant that we were at that time doing fewer and fewer paperbacks on first publication, and a fast decreasing percentage of books published initially in hardback-only were later moving to conventional 'first-time paperback' versions. We felt this was an opportunity to test whether producing new short-run paperback editions, where none already existed, could generate additional ongoing sales revenue from deep backlist titles. This suggestion was initially met with very little enthusiasm, but after intense lobbying the History Project was approved to test this potential.

The History Project was a major experimental project which involved taking a single subject and judiciously making some slower-selling hardbacks available in paperback and reviving some carefully selected out-of-print books. We chose History for our pilot project – we had a large and active publishing programme in history, and history books generally date relatively slowly. In all, 800 titles were selected for the project. For the purpose of financial planning, we assumed that the *average* lifetime sale of the history project titles would be 25 copies priced at a 'standard' scale price based on number of pages. We decided also that we would treat this project as a single integrated publishing project, rather than as the production of 800 individual titles. Lastly, we decided that we would try to complete the project (all 800 titles) within 12 months using the most recent revised printing processes.

Although it was crucial for us to be able to control corrections in order to make this project work at all, we were well aware of the importance of maintaining our authors' goodwill. The goodwill of authors is arguably the most important financial asset any publisher has. This no-correction policy was explained in our standard letter to authors requesting their approval to the inclusion of their book in this project. The majority of titles in the history project required scanning of text and jacket from hard copy. A very few were available in well-formed full text PDF files in our asset store. Changes were required to imprints pages, covers, spine copy,and back cover (including incorporating any legally required text from the hardback cover or jacket). An Indian supplier was selected for scanning; a local file preparation partner for typesetting, proofing, and file prep. Lightning[Ingram Content] were exceptionally helpful in working with us to streamline the process by which we set up paperbacks. Armed with the scanning partner, the typesetting and file preparation partner, and a raft of newly minted production processes, we launched into the project proper.

Some parts of the project were mostly trouble free. However, the local typesetting of blurbs and cover items was substandard and necessary remedial work too expensive in resources and money; stock management could not cope with the number of new titles with tiny initial stocks; filling the standard marketing databases was proving to be far too time consuming. We therefore put the project on hold for 5 months whilst rationalising and improving processes as needed, particularly in typesetting, stock management, warehousing, and marketing.

The history project – results and conclusions

- Number of new paperbacks published: 2002 – 492 paperbacks; 2003 – 266 paperbacks; and 2004 – 127 paperbacks.
- Average sales 25 per annum (sustained over 3 years).
- Sales, income, and profitability exceeded initial forecasts by a large margin.
- Total hardback plus paperback revenue and surplus from titles put into paperback meant in the Project invariably *increased.*
- The radically improved systems and processes required to make the History Project were crucial in ensuring high profitability for all future short-run publishing activity and [Out of Print] OP revival projects and facilitated subsequent electronic and online exploitation of deep backlist titles.

The History project was, in retrospect, a major and arguably overambitious project, [for its time] that forced us to develop completely new and innovative ways to publish and reprint short-run books. From the inception of the project, we had to eschew the 'what has always worked before' – because it would not work for us. We certainly did not get our systems close to right when we started either. We were involved in a constant process of problem solving and occasional crisis management, which ultimately led to the development of robust, completely new alternative production, publication, and stock management systems. The most valuable lesson we learnt was that time is our most important and valuable commodity, and **reducing the time overhead for short-run prepress processing at all points in the supply chain is the key determinant of a financially viable short-run printing programme.**

Postscript by Rufus Neal: Since 2006, when this case study was originally prepared, Cambridge has incorporated 'stockless publishing' (drop-ship) to further improve its distribution efficiency and reduce warehousing needs. Major revival projects followed in collaboration with the Cambridge University Library (2010–) and other major scholarly archive collections. Also of note is the rapid development of Cambridge Companions Online (2004–), Cambridge Histories Online (2007–), and Cambridge Books Online (2010–), all facilitated in part by the rights clearance and file practices introduced and developed to support the short-run programme from 2004.

Note from the author: Following on from this 2004 Cambridge History Project initiative were a raft of projects Rufus has listed above. Today the fruit of this experimentation and work is evident in the hybrid electronic plus optional print book model available.

According to the August 2017 website for one of the Cambridge collection services: **cambridge.org/cambridgehistories**: **Cambridge Histories** has become a digital collection with three digital purchasing models supplemented by print copies. **Collections purchasing:** Purchase perpetual access to the full Cambridge Histories collection, or smaller thematic or regional collections, via a one-time fee. **Title-by-title selection:** If you have previously purchased either the full Cambridge Histories archive, or one of the sub-collections, you may acquire additional titles on a pick-and-choose model. **Annual collection updates:** If you have previously purchased the Cambridge Histories archive, you can update your collection with a single annual invoice and receive access to all new Histories published in that year. **Print purchases are also available.**

Case study: Wiki Collections and the PediaPress GmbH (2007) Germany

For the past decade, Wikipedia's appointed partner delivers print-on-demand books assembled from Wikipedia articles by Wikipedia users. This partner is PediaPress in Mainz Germany. Users who wish to compile a book into a PDF and then want a printed version of that compilation can do so using the service called WikiBooks. PediaPress was founded in July 2007 as a spin-off from Brainbot Technologies AG and works with printing partners to deliver the books to consumers. Apart from providing the PediaPress.com online service, PediaPress GmbH is a software development company. They create open source software that advances the reuse of wiki content in alternative applications and media. PediaPress actively supports the MediaWiki community and formed a long-term partnership with the Wikimedia Foundation which hosts the encyclopedia Wikipedia and other free educational wikis. Here is a snapshot of the description of Wikibooks Collections from the Wikibooks website in August 2017 [80] (bold type added by author to highlight key points):

Wikibooks: Collections Preface

This book was created by volunteers at Wikibooks (http://en.wikibooks.org).

What is Wikibooks?[edit]

Started in 2003 as an offshoot of the popular Wikipedia project, Wikibooks is a free, collaborative wiki website dedicated to creating **high-quality textbooks and other educational books for students around the world.** In addition to English, Wikibooks is available in over 130 languages, a complete listing of which can be found at http://www.wikibooks.org. Wikibooks is a 'wiki', which means anybody can edit the content there at any time. If you find an error or omission in this book, you can log on to Wikibooks to make corrections and additions as necessary. All of your changes go live on the website immediately, so your effort can be enjoyed and utilised by other readers and editors without delay.

Books at Wikibooks are written by volunteers, and can be accessed and printed for free from the website. Wikibooks is operated entirely by donations, and a certain portion of the proceeds from sales is returned to the Wikimedia Foundation to help keep Wikibooks running smoothly. **Owing to the low overhead, we are able to produce and sell books for much cheaper than proprietary textbook publishers can.** This book can be edited by anybody at any time, including you. We do not make you wait 2 years to get a new edition, and we do not stop selling old versions when a new one comes out.

Note that Wikibooks is not a publisher of books, and is not responsible for the contributions of its volunteer editors. PediaPress.com is a print-on-demand publisher that is also not responsible for the content it prints. Please see our disclaimer for more information: http://en.wikibooks.org/wiki/Wikibooks:General_disclaimer.

Here is an extract from Collections Extension August 2017:

Collections Extension[edit]

Wikibooks now has a special extension for grouping individual pages together into a group called a collection. Once a collection has been created, there are three options available:

1. Download a PDF version of the collection
2. Download an ODT (OpenOffice.Org Text Document) file

3. Publish a copy by PediaPress and have it mailed to you.

If we replace the word 'Collection' with the word 'Book' in the sentences above, we can see a very clear way that this extension can be used here at Wikibooks. In addition to creating an ordinary Table of Contents and a print version, a collection can also be created that will enable PDF versions and published versions to be created quickly for your book.

There are two types of collections: **Community collections and personal collections**. Community Settings are created as subpages of Wikibooks:Collections. Each book should have only one (or a very limited number) of 'official' community versions. The community versions can be advertised using the {{collection}} template on the book itself. Sometimes, individual users prefer a slightly different reading order to the material, or like to add additional chapters from a related book, or remove a few chapters, or any number of small modifications. In this case, the user can create their own collection in their user namespace, as a subpage of Special:MyPage/Collections. Private collections can be edited and shared with other users just like a normal wiki page.

Creating a Collection[edit]

Creating a collection is easy. There are two ways to do it:

1. When you find a page you want to add, click 'Add wiki page' on the left. This will add the current page to the current collection. Continue for all pages you like. When you are happy with your collection, you can go to Special:Collection to edit, save, download, or print your collection.
2. You can create a collection on a regular page using regular wiki text. Here is an example:

```
== Title ==
=== Subtitle ===
:[[Page1]]
:[[Page2]]
;Chapter 1
:[[Page3]]
:[[Page4]]
;Chapter 2
:[[Page5]]
:[[Page6]]
[[Category:Collections]]
```

The [[Category:Collections]] at the bottom is important because it indicates to the software that the page represents an extension. To see a list of all pages in this category (and therefore all extensions), go to Category:Collections.

Here are some things that can be found in a collection, and the syntax that is used to save them:

Title and subtitle: A collection can have both a title and a subtitle. In wikitext, the title can be specified as a level-2 heading, and the subtitle can be specified as a level-3 heading. A collection may only have one of each.

Chapters and pages: In terms of collections, a 'chapter' is a large heading that precedes a group of related pages, and a 'Page' is an individual page on the wiki. Chapter names can be specified with a semicolon. Pages in a chapter can be specified as a regular absolute wikilink, with a colon in front like: [[My Book/Page 1]], not a relative link like: [[/Page 1]].

Display title: If you just use a normal link, the page will be titled 'My Book/My Page' in the generated PDF and print-on-demand book. If you use a piped link, the display name of the chapter can be changed. So: [[My Book/My Page|My First Page]] will display 'My First Page' as the display name in the generated book or PDF file.

Using Collections[edit]

Once a collection is generated, either by loading pages into your collection one at a time or by loading an existing saved collection, it can be used in a number of ways:

Downloading: A collection can be downloaded in PDF or ODT format.

Print-on-demand: A collection can be sent to our print-on-demand partner PediaPress and a copy of the book can be mailed to you.

Here is an extract from the PediaPressgmbh website:

PediaPress – Wikis in Print Customised printed books from user selected wiki content. PediaPress.com is an online service that lets you create customised books from wiki content. Simply add any articles you like into a Collection, and then click to order them as a paperback book. Covers, a table of contents, a detailed index, and a list of figures are generated automatically, and the books are printed and shipped within 2–3 business days.

The PediaPress.com web-to-print service works on all MediaWikis that have installed the free Collection Extension.

Why books? The strength of Wikipedia and other wikis is their availability for everybody, every day, and free of charge – on the Internet. However, although internet access has become near-ubiquitous in the developed world, many still prefer reading books to reading on screen, especially for longer texts.

What is PediaPress? PediaPress brings wikis to print. The service works with wikis that have deployed a special software extension. These wikis offer users the opportunity to build individual collections of articles and order them as printed books with PediaPress. Books are printed on-demand. Each produced book is unique and customised just for you.

How can I create a custom book? Go to your favorite wiki and look for a 'Create a book' box in the navigation sidebar, usually on the left side of the page. Any wiki with this link supports PediaPress. Click on the 'Books help' link to get more information about the process.

Which wikis offer the PediaPress service? The PediaPress.com web-to-print service works on all MediaWikis that have installed the free *Collection-Extension*. To check whether a wiki supports PediaPress, look for a box entitled 'Create a book' in the navigation sidebar. *Welcome* to Wikibooks, the open-content textbooks collection that *anyone can edit*. The collection contains *2957 books* with 56,618 pages. Wikibooks is hosted by the *Wikimedia Foundation* and integrated by the PediaPress service to my wiki. To integrate the PediaPressservice with your MediaWiki, simply install the open source *Collection-Extension*.

What is your relation to Wikipedia? PediaPress has established a long-term partnership with the Wikimedia Foundation which supports the development of free content on sites like Wikipedia, Wikibooks, and others. For more information, see this Wikimedia Foundation press release: Wikis Go Printable. Part of the agreement is the development of open source software with the goal to ease the reuse of wiki content in other media or applications. Software developed by PediaPress can be found at http://code.pediapress.com/.

Is PediaPress a publisher? PediaPress is not a publisher, but instead provides users with tools to order and share free or own content. Since PediaPress is not a publisher, we do not review the content of any printed books or other works offered through PediaPress tools. We expect all content to be consistent with our Terms and Conditions and reserve the right to remove content we deem to be illegal or inappropriate.

How to contact PediaPress For any question or suggestion, do not hesitate to visit our Support page. You can also try to contact us on IRC visiting the channel #pediapress on irc.freenode.net, though availability may depend on the time and day of week.

Guarantee Fast delivery Paperbacks will be produced and shipped within 2–3 business days, and colour and hardcover books within 15 business days.

High-quality typesetting and printing Your books will be manufactured in a quality indistinguishable from traditional books.

Books: How are books typeset? PediaPress uses automated typesetting software which understands wiki markup and generates printable PDF documents of high quality.

What is print-on-demand (POD)? Print-on-demand (POD) is a method of producing books one at a time using a digital file. After you have ordered your book, our print-on-demand partner produces the book based on a PDF generated by us and ships it directly to you. The whole process from placing the order to shipping the book usually takes 2–3 business days for black and white books and 15 business days for colour books.

How do your books look like? Books have dimensions of 5.5″ × 8.5″ (216 × 140 mm). Depending on the chosen option, they are perfect bound or have hardcover binding and are printed in black and white or colour.

How are book prices calculated? The cost of a book depends on the product option (binding, colour, or black and white) and the number of pages contained, in addition to a base fee.

What is the maximum size of a book? A single book has a maximum size of approximately 800 pages. If a larger book is ordered, it is automatically split up into multiple volumes.

How can I save my book?

Books are saved automatically in your browser session. If you want to finish a book you have uploaded earlier, just return to pediapress.com using the same browser and click on the Your Books tab.

Content: Are there restrictions on submitted content or shared books?

Yes, basically the contents and materials submitted or shared must not infringe German law.

- Do not upload contents that glorify violence, are demagogic or racist, discriminatory, pornographic, or otherwise considered harmful to children.
- Do not upload contents that infringe copyrights, trademark rights, or other protected rights of third persons.

Please take a look at our Terms and Conditions and read our Content Disclaimer.

How long will it take to receive an order?

Paperbacks usually are printed within 2–3 business days, and colour and hardcover books within 15 business days. You will receive an email from PediaPress when your items are shipped. Shipping takes another 2–20 business days depending on the selected shipping option and destination. **Books are manufactured and shipped from either Brazil, Germany, Sweden, the United Kingdom, or the United States, depending on your place of residence.**

Please note: Shipping and manufacturing times are estimates and not guarantees. Shipping times may be influenced by factors beyond the control of PediaPress. Examples are incorrect delivery addresses, customs delays, or falsely routed packets. Orders affected by these delays may take as long as 6 weeks to arrive.

Where in the world does PediaPress ship? We ship to every location for which an affordable shipping service is available. Books are produced either in Brazil, Germany, Sweden, the United Kingdom, or the United States, depending on your location of residence.

How can I follow up the status of my order? Currently, it is not possible to check the status of your order. If your book does not arrive within 30 days of ordering, please contact our support team.

How can I download my book as a PDF or e-Book? Currently, you can only download your created book as a PDF file directly on the Wiki. We are planning to offer e-Books later this year.

How can I add own content to my book? Currently, it is not possible to add own content to your book.

Part Three

Forecasts and trends for print-on-demand in academic book publishing

Introduction to part 3

The 'book' is a very generic term which covers a broad range of literary forms and physical formats. The 'academic book', for the purposes of this book, was discussed in Part 2 in terms of the monograph, the academic, or professional textbook and the academic book collection. The future of the book has been much discussed in recent years as e-books and online portals have opened up new possibilities as to what might be contained in a 'book'. Multimedia including audio, still images, and moving images, databases, and new functionality like adjustable font sizes to reflowable e-book text have all stretched our understanding of what a book might be.

Monographs might include digital data sets and hypertext references which supercede the confines of the printed page. Textbooks might become living documents not only including hypertext links to multimedia moving images but also regularly updated compilations of reading material for a course of study or professional development programme. Academic libraries are progressing towards being gateways to entirely digital collections accessible remotely at any time and enabling an almost incomprehensible breadth and depth of access to researchers and students. So where does the printed academic book feature in this brave new world? Surprisingly at the centre of it.

Today we are living in a hybrid world of digital and printed books each with their own utility and issues. E-books are portable in quantity on a device, can alter font sizes and be read aloud to the user. But you do need a power source and in fact when you 'buy' an e-book you are actually licensing it from the retailer who is obliged to keep it available to you (provided they are still in business when you want it). Printed books do not keep you awake all night after reading with blue light, require no power source, are sold in new form or used form and can be physically presented or passed around without the need for any licenses. Ownership of a physically printed book is clear in law. So there remains a market for the academic book in print. The questions publishers are facing vary depending on the type of academic book and the market they are targeting. For example, publishing monographs is manifestly a type of author service or institutional service and an important form of publication that enables academics to progress in their academic career. Open access funding models have taken root for these books and the costs are weighted towards the origination labour costs of peer review, revising, editing, designing, tagging rather than the digital distribution or the digital printing, binding, and physical distribution costs, which causes economic challenges for publishers unless the author, institution, or funding body pay upfront to make the book. Print-on-demand does not solve the origination problems, but it does solve the printing and distribution issues. There are in fact solutions on the horizon that could substantially reduce the origination cost and reduce the pricing for readers, researchers, and libraries. Author services designed for the peer-reviewed academic book have been launched which are open access plus reselling books through conventional online bookselling channels in e-book and on-demand printed book form with a royalty back to the author. This could revolutionise academic book publishing by removing the cost of content acquisition for institutions and barriers to entry for new authors, keeping their book in print, and digitally accessible.

Expert opinion, researchers, and students today are optimistic about the future of the physical printed academic book and that is largely down to the capability of print-on-demand.

> *There is a general view that the print book still has longevity: Fisher points out that some 80% of academic book materials are sold in print worldwide (Fisher, 2015). An Academic Book Week debate at the University of Bristol emphasised that the process of producing academic outputs needs to remain as rigorous as it ever has been—digital should not be allowed to dilute the integrity of academic research, but rather be used as a tool for assisting with its wider dissemination and engagement—a supplement as opposed to a replacement (Tether, 2015). The 2015 Ithaka surveys of UK and US academics found in both cases 'no observable trend' in a preference for digital over print; preference for print has in fact increased since the last survey cycle (3 years). [89]*

The printed version is no longer the only version, but the availability of the printed version of a book is appreciated and valued by authors and readers. The printed-and-bound academic book is an icon within the culture of the academy. It carries gravitas, it is used as a rite of passage through the academy from MA dissertation to PhD dissertation to a postdoctoral researcher's monograph. Yes, these works could entirely flip to digital forms for wide dissemination and archiving, yet for the author, the assessor and the colleague, the printed-and-bound book remains a framed, accessible, contextualised artefact, which has utility as a symbol of the research undertaking and the results it contains.

In addition, readers often find that the printed page can be easier on the eye than screen-based alternatives. Navigating an online learning environment supported by a custom printed textbook is an example of hybrid digital and digital print in action. Print-on-demand answers the need for the optional print version. Even if the digital book eventually becomes the primary version of a book, the printed-and-bound version has a market and a distinctive utility of its own. In fact without print-on-demand books, we would not necessarily feel safe enough to plunge head first into a digital dominant book world. Knowing a printed version of an e-book, properly bound with a cover, is available within a day or two, the academic or student is liberated to make the best use of each form.

With the assumption in place that there is a future for the printed academic book, Part 3 explores market and technological trends: trends in academic book publishing, trends in digital book manufacturing, and finally trends in on-demand book publishing which are about to impact the academic book.

Trends in academic book publishing that impact on-demand

8

There are many publications today dedicated to monitoring and discussing trends in academic publishing, not least the Society for Scholarly Publishing's *The Scholarly Kitchen* based in the United States and EuropaScience's *Research Information* based in the United Kingdom, both commendable. It is a full-time job to keep track of all the initiatives. There have been countless reports, white papers, power point presentations, and case studies concerning content preparation and delivery through publishing platforms, pricing and funding models from subscription to Open Access in all its variants and interactive e-learning services. However, most importantly, there have been a couple of reports from *The Academic Book of the Future* and the JISCLabs ITHIKA study published in 2017 [80a]. Clearly, we are in turbulent times in academic publishing and arguably innovative times.

One obvious and overarching trend for academic book publishing is the onward march towards original digital book publication and more digital book collections. Specifically, there are three trends taking place in academic publishing which impact the print-on-demand book. This chapter looks at these, while Chapter 10 considers On-demand Publishing Trends: more digital first print-on-demand editions, great variety of book types, more customisation, market extension across the globe, and empowered academic authors who will engage with new intermediaries – all trends in academic book publishing which point to an ongoing role for print-on-demand books for the foreseeable future.

The first trend is even more 'digital first' academic books with optional print-on-demand editions. As we will see in Chapter 9, that means more digital printing volume for the printer, whereas for the publisher and customer we are talking huge growth in the number of book titles or ISBNs. Academic research continues to grow and consequently scholarly communication is prolific. Demand for higher education and professional continuous development teaching content is also growing. The collective back catalogue of academic books output simply gets bigger and bigger. Taylor & Francis Informa alone have 145,000 print-on-demand enabled ISBNs. Gareth Jarrett in the case study below explains how they get there and some of the operational implications.

The growth in books is increasingly being fuelled by new Open Access books, new peer-reviewed author services, and more digital aggregation forming collections. All these forms present the opportunity to bolt on print capability and to create print revenue streams on top of digital subscriptions or publication fees. Michael Jubb's *Academic Books and Their Futures* (2017) highlights one Australian Open Access initiative which is using print-on-demand and is growing:

The Impact of Print-On-Demand on Academic Books. https://doi.org/10.1016/B978-0-08-102011-1.00008-0

> *Publishing OA books in any significant numbers started some 10–12 years ago. The Australian National University (ANU) E Press (now the ANU Press) founded in 2003 was one of the key pioneers. It has now published over 600 OA titles.* ***All books are peer reviewed, and are made available for sale by print-on-demand.*** *ANU Press's success has spawned the creation of new presses at other Australian universities such as Monash and Adelaide, to sit alongside the more established university presses at Melbourne, Queensland and Western Australia. European university presses with a significant record of OA books include Amsterdam and Göttingen. (ref JUBB, p. 189)*

The outlook for Open Access books is somewhat mixed compared to academic journals, but undoubtedly there will be more of them and they will be accompanied by an optional print edition.

The second trend is a more integrated book publishing ecosystem enabled by digital technologies and new publishing services. Today there is more collaboration and integration between trading partners engaged with the creation of printed academic books. The exchange of data between publishers and printers has enabled agile and prompt book fulfilment. Print-on-demand for books is now an integral part of that publishing ecosystem. Printers and publishers today work together to share data and integrate workflows to achieve successful low-inventory book publishing models. To make that happen, infrastructure and technology changes are necessary. Publishing platforms and publishing tools are also evolving. Established digital tools for publishing composition and workflow are also rapidly evolving. Publishing platforms are proliferating and joining the migration of applications to the cloud. Improvements to tools can be silently and automatically maintained and swiftly available to publishers and authors. One example driving changes in workflow for book creation in publishing houses is the migration of Adobe Acrobat software to a software as a service Adobe Acrobat Document Cloud. The user interface and utility has changed dramatically since version 11. Version 2015.0 was released in 2015 with two tracks, continuous and classic. The classic track has updates released quarterly while the continuous track has updates issued more frequently with updates performed silently and automatically. Some publishers have their own bespoke sophisticated digital composition environments which have developed with specialist academic digital content in mind, typically journal articles.

More publishing services with platforms: There has been a marked rise in the number of publishing services that specialise in technical solutions to prepare and deliver academic books in all formats and assist with continually changing publishing processes which incorporate print-on-demand as one output. Vendors such as codeMantra and Nord Comp are engaged in delivering digital first solutions to publishers. Pioneering digital publisher and learning platform O'Reilly recently divested itself of the PubFactory to the printer and publishing services provider Sheridan in 2017. Oxford University Press, IMF, De Gruyter's, Bloomsbury Academic, Brill, Edward Elgar Publishing, Harvard University Press, and Peter Lang are all PubFactory customers. There are likely to be more of these publishing services platforms in the future and many will be owned by companies that are print suppliers. Some will focus on Digital Asset Management and delivery (like Ingram's CoreSource), and will cover both e-books and print-on-demand book titles. Some publishers may even bring more software services in-house through the cloud. Publishing services will include a variety of digital publishing platforms both within the control of the academic publishing house and not in their control.

Author-centric publishing: Following the author services and self-publishing trends, it is likely that there will be more author-centric academic book publishing platforms in the future. These platforms will be selling open access services directly to academic authors and they will bypass the publishing house. Bibliolabs is active with regard to open learning and textbooks, whereas Glass Tree is active with respect to peer reviewed academic books such as monographs.

New technologies are impacting print-on-demand books and user perceptions of what can be achieved on-demand. Scholars may wish to use new services like incorporating streaming moving images on-demand in their publications: introducing 3D printed components into their publications; delivering content via mobile technology; and offering a seamless book reading experience moving from e-Books editions to print editions and back as required. Embedding Radio Frequency Identifiers (RFID) are already happening in some physical books for stock management purposes; what about embedding chips on-demand computer chips into physical books? We could reinvent the printed book as the Smart Book – all possible to print-on-demand given the right level of demand.

More custom: While traditional bulk printings of books may be decreasing, printing bespoke or variable custom books to order is on the rise. The new publishing models are fuelling print-on-demand growth: customised learning solutions complemented by printed editions; digital first Open Access books with optional printed editions; and the newly empowered academic author who no longer requires a formal relationship with a publisher to publish a book successfully, but can use a self-publishing service with peer review.

This chapter concludes with three illustrative interviews/case studies drawn from the experiences of three distinguished academic publishers who found different paths to print-on-demand and who are innovatively responding to the changing publishing environment: Taylor & Francis Group, Brill, and SAGE Publications. Not all books are suitable for print-on-demand today but more and more types of books are becoming suitable as we will explore in Chapter 10. All three cases point to the digitally driven publishing environment we are in today. From pre-press through to content delivery, the world is digital and consequently more and more stockless printed publications are being generated and marshalled by new types of publishing professionals.

Interview Gareth Jarrett, Director of Book Services, Taylor & Francis Group, an Informa Company UK (2017)

Taylor & Francis Group publishes books for all levels of academic study and professional development, across a wide range of subjects and disciplines. They publish Social Science and Humanities books under the Routledge, Psychology Press and Focal Press imprints. Science, Technology and Medical books are published by CRC Press and Garland Science. Taylor & Francis Group has three major content platforms – CRCnetBase, Taylor & Francis Online, and Taylor & Francis eBooks (http://www.tandfebooks.com) – that are built around the needs of their many varied and valued customers. As of 2017, Taylor and Francis have 145,000 print-on-demand available ISBNs and their aim is to facilitate discovery and allow users wherever they are to access relevant research and information quickly and easily.

Taylor & Francis were an early adopter of print-on-demand, and almost immediately it allowed the group to start to exploit its large and growing backlist that would previously have had to go out of stock and ultimately out of print. Though early POD was very limited in scope and application, it has grown in leaps and bounds and in the last 10 years it has been transformational to us as a business. Over a period where the number of active print ISBNs has quintupled, it has allowed us to reduce stockholdings across the globe substantially. That can only be done by creative use of on-demand printing as part of a mixed portfolio of tools to bring books to market – 'conventional' printing, short-run digital printing (automated via 'auto-stock-replenishment'), and POD itself.

It is not just about lowering stockholdings, though. In markets such as Australia, it has allowed us to massively increase the numbers of books available to order via removing the need for a long and costly supply chain from the United Kingdom. We now have close to 100,000 ISBNs live POD in Australia, and well over 100,000 in Singapore. As a result of POD, we can publish concurrently and provide a base level of availability that can be supplemented by stockholdings as required. Ultimately, this all serves to benefit consumers across the globe.

POD is at its most effective when books are relatively standardised in design. They are printed quickly, with minimal issues, and the costs are low. POD is less effective when books are more complex, which adds both cost and delay. As examples:

- CDs bound into the back of books, for example, are necessary (and essential for customers who need to access ancillary content but do not have good internet access) but do generally add an element of delay at the printer, as well as more cost.
- Scratch codes and the like are very difficult to manage and/or scale around the globe – and so we try to push for books to have e-solutions related to them that do not need such codes

We do look to our POD suppliers to offer as wide a range of formats and options as possible, so POD can run alongside conventional supply across the lifetime of a book. We do not want books to change in any way when they go POD. However, we have to be realistic about what POD suppliers can do if we want to get affordable, quick, and reliable supply. What we have therefore tried to stress is a 'design for life' attitude amongst those who commission and design books:

1. Avoid complex finishes that add cost or are not available to most printers. No spot UV. No embossing.
2. Go for 'standard' formats such as 6" × 9", R8, C4, 7" × 10" so that printers can easily batch work together, allowing quicker and cheaper production. Avoid square or landscape if at all possible
3. Avoid challenging fonts that might become spidery in faster running presses
4. Use standard papers such as 80 g offset or 90 g coated that most printers can support

Effectively, when we standardise, we keep costs in check and service levels high. The more variations to our products there are, the harder it is for our printers, putting pressure on both costs and service levels.

It is worth stating that colour printing has always been an issue in the POD space. Historically, the high click rates of toner colour has meant POD works for shorter cased titles, but the margins are tight on larger extent titles, especially if paperback, and so sold at a lower price point. The recent roll-out of inkjet printers into POD has started to change this, offering far more opportunities to support more titles in POD. Critical colour titles, for now, continue to need toner quality but we do believe that, with the new generation of inkjets now arriving, even premium titles such as architectural or medical titles will start to migrate to inkjet and therefore be supportable in POD. One thing that this will require, that said, is an additional focus on colour calibration to ensure that a book with critical colour is reproduced consistently by multiple printers across the globe every day. Experience to date has suggested that calibration standards can be spotty, and we are looking at ways to get more rigour into this process in concert with printers.

As noted earlier, what we have done is to create a mixed portfolio of tools to keep books available to readers across the globe, and POD is the base from which we now build. When books publish, they are loaded to POD printers in the United Kingdom, the United States, Singapore, Australia, and India. In some markets, they may well be POD from day 1 and stay that way throughout their life. However, in core markets, they may well have an initial print run before POD picks up the slack (such as with monographs) or they will go into auto-stock replenishment for as long as the sales levels justify it, dropping to POD as sales drop down. Others, such as key texts, may be stocked in core markets for their whole life until the next edition. However, whatever happens, POD is always there in the background to ensure that, if stock is briefly exhausted, POD can pick up the slack until the next tranche of books arrives in the warehouse. Effectively, we should always be able to supply an order.

This model cannot work for every book – not every book is suited to POD, or can at least be printed economically as POD – but it works for the vast majority of our titles and we now have over 145,000 ISBNs POD in at least one market as a result, underpinning availability across the globe.

I believe POD is hugely positive as it allows one to print books to compete against digital books in a world where stockholdings are increasingly constrained and customers expect to be able to get books the way they want it, when they want it. It allows for concurrent global publication, with books printed close to market (reducing both cash tied in up stock and carbon footprint) and for multiple formats to be supported simultaneously. Quite simply, it allows books to remain viable no matter what their sales rate, and no matter where in the world a customer is.

That said, POD is not a panacea. From a customer perspective, the biggest negative is the longer – and more variable – lead time to supply. Increasingly, POD suppliers are printing, binding, and shipping books in a 2–3 day lead time, which means it is not that much slower than picking from a warehouse. However, that 2–3 day lead time is inevitably an average, and outliers that take longer can mean customers lose faith in prompt, rapid delivery every time. That is particularly important for internet retailers who make commitments to customers based on a strict understanding of when they will receive the books. Thus, some customers remain reluctant to take POD books. The solution is nothing less than POD suppliers having to both improve their turnaround times and their controls to avoid outliers. That includes cross-trained staff, a resilient kit, and surplus capacity to handle peaks. It also means publishers being willing and able to move demand quickly between printers to help them handle sudden spikes or issues. It is a developing situation – but ensuring customers have a secure and reliable supply is critical to the continued growth of POD and the survival of print books.

There is a trend in library demand towards e-products across the globe, one that is fed by a combination of factors – the growth in the overall numbers of titles published, the changes in libraries themselves to be more 'learning environments' than mere repositories of books (which can constrain how many books they hold), and the new e-Book sales models that put readers in charge. Something that print cannot match.

However, surveys consistently show that readers still prefer print books. Academic books do not just sell to libraries – there remain strong sales through others such as Amazon in the 'retail' space. As a result, print will continue to thrive, but POD will become more and more critical. One big change will be the continued growth of 'channel' manufacturing– that is, retailers or wholesalers who take the files and print for their customer orders. As the likes of Amazon, Baker & Taylor, Ingram, and others increase the amount they print, the volume available for 'traditional' printers will likely plateau or decline. Even though more and more books are published each year, print quantities are increasingly optimized to match sales. It is increasingly likely that books will be available via print-on-demand for their entire lifecycle as so much of their demand is being printed by retailers and wholesalers.

It will be critical in such a 'channel' environment that existing printers do up their game and provide a strong and reliable service to customers. If retailers, especially insurgents, are to compete with dominant players who are now printing their own demand, they need a robust and reliable supply chain to get books to them quickly when they need it. It will therefore be critically important that all printers and warehouses (POD or otherwise) up their game to enable this to happen.

Case study Brill by Emile Krankendock, Print and Logistics Manager, Brill NL

In 2016, Brill celebrated its 333rd anniversary as an academic publisher, making it the oldest publishing house in the Netherlands and one of the oldest in the world. In May 1683, Jordaan Luchtmans established himself as a bookseller in Leiden and five generations of the Luchtmans family served as 'Printers to the University' until 1848, when Evert Jan Brill took over the firm, giving it his own name. Over the centuries, Brill has managed to adapt to changing circumstances. Brill's publications focus on the Humanities and Social Sciences, International Law, and selected areas in the Sciences. Brill publishes over 800 books per year in both print and electronic format. E-books are collated in Brill's E-Book Collection brillonline.com.

In the past, Brill Publishing sold higher quantities of printed academic monographs and other academic books. At that time, it made sense to produce high print runs using offset printing, to ensure that the costs of production per copy would be as low as possible. Unfortunately, forecasting the sales of books has been and still is extremely difficult, simply because every new publication is a new unique product. As a result, stock levels were going through the roof and a lot of stock needed to be put 'out of print' and pulped, thereby incurring additional expense due to the fact that they were not sold. Also, Brill incurred higher shipping costs than were necessary. The introduction of print-on-demand for books technology opened a door to a great new opportunity, where you can go from a 'push strategy' to a 'pull strategy'. Forecasts would be no longer necessary and it would be possible to just produce the immediate demand from the customers. Even though production cost per copy is higher with print-on-demand, the overall cost went down because the costs for production and shipment are incurred only for effective orders – which has also minimised the storage cost for such titles. Another disadvantage of the pre-print-on-demand times was that out of stock titles required careful monitoring and reprint cost calculations, which would often result in transferring those to an out of print status. Since the advent of print-on-demand, no title needs to be out of print anymore. In our business with its deep backlist, where even books from 20 to 30 years ago are still being sold today, print-on-demand has proved to be a key technology for monetising this huge revenue potential.

Brill has always been known and is known for their high-quality standards. This unfortunately collided with the introduction of the printing technology. Brill had a rough start where books supplied to customers were far below expectations of both customers and Brill. We learnt a lot from this rough start, and thereafter we selected our suppliers extremely carefully. We would not compromise on the product specifications that our customers expected and concluded that it was too soon to start printing-on-demand. Then in 2011, we found our current print-on-demand supplier Printforce, based in the Netherlands. We have been working with Printforce to develop a high-quality product that would satisfy our customers and come close to the quality of an offset printed book. Since the start of our programme in 2011, we witnessed the transformation of the print-on-demand book from what it was to what it currently is: a beautiful hardback book with round spine with high-quality print. With new technologies emerging every year, we have yet to see how this might further evolve and improve.

One trend already noticeable within the academic publishing industry is the decline in demand for printed books and the increase in demand for the digital book. I still believe the printed book has a future in academic publishing, especially thanks to the print-on-demand technology. Though digital only book will play a big role for a certain generation and in library collections, the print copy will be hard to replace for many readers and researchers. In the end, **Brill as a publisher has to provide our publications in the format that our customers want; we call this approach being 'format agnostic' in other words customers can choose hardback or paperback format on-demand.** With the ability to print one-off books, the publisher can fulfil customer demand while reducing the total cost of ownership, and therefore we are able to provide choice. Hopefully, with the rising number of high-end single copy suppliers, more and more publishers will see the use and need of this technology and will find the right balance between digital only books, print-on-demand books, and offset printed books.

The most successful application that Brill has implemented would be the **zero warehouse strategy we currently apply for print-on-demand books. This means that the majority of our front list monographs (90%) and also our journal issues (99%) are truly print-on-demand from the start and every order is produced and directly shipped to our customers.** We do not hold any stock for these titles in our warehouses. Brill has three distinctive and unique applications concerning print-on-demand. The first would be the global one-off printing for 90% of our front list monographs in high quality, the majority in hardback. The second would be that in the United States we started a collaboration with one of our biggest trade partners to use print-on-demand to lower the return rate significantly. While in the past they did a lot of advanced buying, they have now switched to real demand purchases of our print-on-demand titles. Last but not the least, we have rearranged our distribution in the United States. Brill now has its warehousing and print-on-demand activities under one roof, with the huge benefits of cost reduction, more control, and our customers receiving only one package when they place a combined stock and print-on-demand order.

Print-on-demand has positively impacted the academic book for sure! In a digital age with print runs and print sales declining, the possibility to produce on-demand for your customer is amazing and very welcome. Nowadays, you still see many digital short-run digital printers, but the single copy digital printers are increasing in number and I believe this is the future of printing. The mindset of some academic publishers, librarians, and authors may need to change in favour of print-on-demand, because undeniably the impact of print-on-demand for academic books is positive. Even in 2017, I have observed that print-on-demand for books is still not fully accepted in the academic market, possibly because it is not understood, but with the wider range of print-on-demand service providers and the advancement of technologies associated with print-on-demand for academic books and for the journal issue, print-on-demand is becoming the new norm.

Case study: Richard Fidczuk, Director of Production, SAGE Publications (2013)

SAGE is one of the world's leading independent academic and professional publishers. It was founded in 1965 by Sara Miller McCune. SAGE publishes over 800 textbooks, scholarly titles, and handbooks a year across the social sciences, health sciences, and humanities. This case is in two parts: first a write-up by Richard of how SAGE has developed its print-on-demand programmes engaging multiple print vendors and reducing waste. This is followed by an extract from the **Association of Learned and Professional Society Publishers blog** 12 June 2013 which reported on Richard's talk. This offers an insight into the future of academic book production where a flexible approach is required and changing human resources are needed to manage the changing digital content creation processes of the future.

SAGE were early adopters of digital printing technologies: in the United Kingdom, they distribute books originated by their US publishing operations (and vice versa) and they identified an opportunity to both reduce stockholdings and improve speed of delivery and availability to customers by having their titles available via Lightning Source (LSI). By loading titles into LSI's database once, books became available for printing in multiple locations internationally. Initially, only long-tail, slow-moving backlist titles were included, which required scanning of print copies as for these older titles PDF files were not available. However, as digital workflows developed and full PDFs came to be produced for all titles, scanning was eliminated and original PDFs were produced and used.

At the present time, both front list and backlist titles are loaded with an increasing number of print and distribution vendors worldwide, so that for titles where there is a higher demand than expected, books can be printed quickly to fulfil orders rather than risk losing sales by the distributor having to wait for stocks to arrive from SAGE. There are file management issues to be overcome, as files have to be sent to multiple vendors, so a good database is essential.

SAGE still prints longer runs of titles to store in their warehouse, but is continually refining their processes with printers to continue to reduce the quantity printed and hence improve stock turn. The vast majority of print orders are for digital rather than litho printing, and with inkjet technologies pushing the quantities economically feasible digitally further upwards all the time, the proportion of litho orders is continuing to reduce.

With respect to journals, in 2015, SAGE eliminated all the stockholding in their UK warehouse (they had already achieved this for their US operation) and moved to a situation where they printed enough copies to cover the initial subscription run plus a very small number of overs (held by the printer) to cover immediate back copy requests. Once these have been exhausted, all back issue requests are sent to print individually and copies printed POD and despatched. This has eliminated a significant amount of wastage; SAGE used to destroy over 10,000 excess print copies annually due to overprinting. Digital printing technologies and a workflow which allows the individual orders to be sent to the printer efficiently (including the despatch information) were essential to make this possible. There was a significant amount of technical development required between the printer and SAGE to allow this to happen, and this did take some time to set up as it was a new process for both SAGE and the printers concerned.

Extracted from the ALPSP Blog: Constant change in both journals and books businesses means the need exists to be able to adapt processes, workflows, and systems to meet changing requirements. People are needed to develop these processes, workflows, and systems. Managing resources is key. SAGE have developed an insourced approach to offshoring by establishing their Delhi office. When done well, the benefits are clear: being able to offshore staffing for production has meant reductions of 27% per page costs. Delhi handles SAGE owned journals with society contracts handled from London, due to the complexity of relationship and potential perceived (versus real) issues. Richard [Fidczuk] advises not to focus on new processes that are not ready for outsourcing as they are not stable enough. Growth has enabled SAGE to keep staff after they have offshored functions. However, it would not be large enough alone to cover all staff, so they have looked at the business to change the way they do things in order to redeploy staff. Since their business has been in a state of perpetual change, it has freed them to **think about how they can adapt processes to change.** Individual production editor tasks have evolved. They now have end to end responsibility, for online as well as print, with a shift to article based production. SAGE has created a new role – **Production Innovation Manager – which focuses on the case for improvements to production workflows, particularly around completely new products. They coordinate implementation of changes to processes/workflows and work across departments. They have also established a Global Supplier Manager who handles the relationships with all their typesetting suppliers.**

Other specialist roles have focused on XML, system specialists/super users, peer review system (using fundref and crossref), and open access expertise (e.g. managing payment interface with finance dealing with licensing issues). They have also appointed staff to support the training of teams in the Delhi office, in order to build an understanding of the processes that will enable them to work most efficiently.

Trends in book manufacturing on-demand

9

The traditional book printing fraternity and the document management brotherhood (i.e. the origins of one-off print-on-demand books) have not always made good bedfellows. They came from different places with different expectations: one from a long, distinguished, risk-averse tradition of making beautiful objects delivered in big batches for a good profit, and the other, a risk-taking upstart solving a set of problems to make 'good enough' expedient individual books for an impatient age using computer science with a profit that follows. These two extremes might sound like caricatures but there was a real cultural dissonance when on-demand books first came along. There are four trends in book manufacturing that will impact on-demand academic books over the next decade: first is the fact that printing books using digital print technology using digital workflow technologies is set to increase: so there will be more volume of digitally printed books printed and there will be more custom books within that corpus; second, there will be more standards issued by the printing research and trade organisations to ensure consistency and quality as the number of printers engaged in digital print explodes; third, there are technological developments in the wider printing industry that will come to impact on-demand book manufacturing, namely even better colour, more flexibility regarding papers, and finishing developments like inline binding and coatings for embellishments; fourth, waste reduction is increasingly important both politically and to the printing and publishing industries. Historically, there has been tremendous waste in the book industry including academic books through overprinting, storing, writing down, then writing off printed stock. Print-on-demand is reducing waste and taking cost out of the industry.

Increased volume of digitally printed academic books: A few traditional book printers were engaged with digital book printing from the start and have caught up with the order management and inventory management challenges by extending their service offerings while the document management folks have improved quality and extended the range of product offerings available.

It is important to remember the difference between short-run digitally printed books, or even ultra-short-run printed books, and one-off print-on-demand books based on receipt of an order with just-in-time supply. Digital short run is typically still printing stock in anticipation of sales, which means it needs moving into storage, storing, and picking when a sale finally comes through. This approach can dip down to ultra-short-run, maybe under 20 copies or even down to one copy, but essentially is just-in-case printing. For books with predictable demand, this can be a valid approach and we have seen many book printers partnering with book distribution

The Impact of Print-On-Demand on Academic Books. https://doi.org/10.1016/B978-0-08-102011-1.00009-2

centres like Edwards Malloy and Independent Publishing Group (IGP) in Chicago, USA; or book distributors who have extended their businesses into printing, like Marston Book Services UK, Marston Digital printing service; or book printers who extended into book distribution services such as Markono in Singapore or Clay's in the St Ives group UK. In fact, most book printing businesses incorporate digital printing in some way and that is in line with trends across the worldwide printing market segment. New innovations in binding technologies have enabled books to be bound with stronger glues which improved book durability especially useful in teaching environments (see Fig. 9.1).

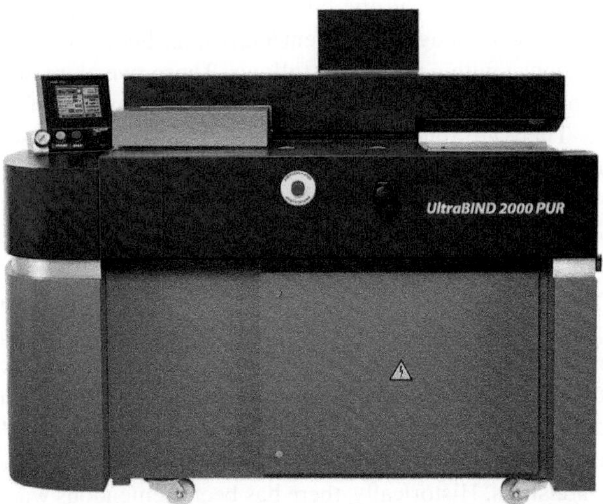

Fig. 9.1 PUR glue is a more durable glue that can replace section sewn binding with the same lie flat capability without cracking or pages falling out. The photo above is a PFI BIND 2000 PUR Image reproduced with permission from Duplo International Ltd.

According to the *4th Drupa Global Trends March 2017* report, 22% of publishing printers (which might include books, journals, magazines, and directories) reported that in 2016 > 25% of their turnover was sourced from digital print [84]. With specific reference to book printers who report their annual results to Book Business Magazine, Ellen Harvey wrote when reporting on The Digital Book Printing Conference 2017:

> *Most notably in the past several years we've seen Top 20 printers [in US book printing]increase their investment in digital book printing technology... [additionally] Webcom and Bookmasters reported that roughly 50% of their book printing revenue is from digital printing, the largest portion for any manufacturers that reported this data. [85]*

Top print technology investment plans for publishing printers reflected: 30% of the respondents planned to invest in Sheetfed offset 24% planned to invest in Digital toner cutsheet colour; and 14% were investing in Digital Inkjet cutsheet colour [86].

> *Publishing printers are having the hardest time in adjusting to digital media as evidenced throughout the report. An increasing number of titles have online editions with the consequent reduction in circulation, although the number of titles lost to online-only editions remains very low. Other means of creating added value such as personalisation, versioning, and variable content are growing but slowly (once again North America showing the way). Yet relatively few publishing printers are adding fresh added value services beyond the historic prepress, design, and storage/fulfilment options. …Publishing print is in a more defensive mode… [87]*

Printers who are serving book publishers are having to change the way they work and invest in new equipment, processes, and partnerships in order to compete. The proportion of digitally printed books is set to increase over offset printing, although there is a place for both (Fig. 9.2).

Fig. 9.2 Improved colour and workflow solutions are winning awards in 2017. Ricoh Pro C5200 is a new digital colour sheet-fed printer while Ricoh's 'TotalFlow solution' streamlines short run and on demand book production. It enables book printers to seamlessly track and efficiently complete jobs. Developed to simplify and automate many short-run digital production steps, it has a single web-based interface helping to automate production workflows, finishing operations and batch similar jobs together (Ricoh, UK).
Image reproduced with permission from Ricoh UK.

In 2014, Smithers Pira, the worldwide authority on packaging, paper, and print industry supply chains, produced an in-depth market research study *The Future of Digital Printing to 2024*, (Smithers Market Intelligence, April 2014). Now this study looks far beyond printed books into packaging but the indicative trend is clear. Their media release headlined: "Growth in Digital Printing to Remain Strong until 2024: The total digital printing market will reach 225% of the 2013 value by 2024. In 2013, the digital print market was worth $120.9 billion in constant 2012 [US] dollar values" [88]. So that would be a digital printing market worth: US$272 billion. Smithers make several points which surely apply to digital book printing:

- Digital print is growing because it allows print suppliers to improve the levels of service they offer to customers.
- Increasing versioning and personalisation helps make print more targeted to end users, which is increasingly important as the digital world continues to become more and more connected.
- Digital print will also exploit many new opportunities for high value short runs.
- [Today] electrophotography is the major contributor to the digital market. Inkjet is forecast to overtake electrophotography after 2019, and by 2024 inkjet will account for 56% of the value and 53% of the digital print volume.
- [There are] some drawbacks of digital, which tend to be associated with unit cost and productivity.
- There is also less choice of paper and substrate stocks with digital printing; however, more paper companies are now supplying suitable grades while some printers apply primers to their materials.
- Additional limitations exist in the colours that can be printed, although some equipment suppliers have introduced spot colour capability with metallic and some specialist fluorescent toner capability [88].

Thirty-two different digital print solutions manufacturers were featured in the Smithers PIRA report including the likes of Canon Oce, HP, Ricoh, Sun Automation, and Xerox. That variety of engagement is indicative of a vibrant, competitive, and innovative market segment.

The full Smithers report takes a deep dive into books and contains three tables highlighting: Electrophotographic printing output of books by geographic market, 2009–24 (million A4 prints); and Inkjet printing output of books by geographic market, 2009–24 ($ million, constant 2012 prices), which might have been interesting to review; however, the report costs $5000 USD, so we have to live without any particulars here. However, the fact that those are the metrics that they chose to report on suggests an upward trend worth highlighting. Even without Smithers' baseline data, reports of recent investments in print equipment and Drupa's global trends information suggest that books will follow the trend across printing of increasing the proportion of digital and more inkjet.

More custom publishing: The technology forecasts also point to more variable data and therefore more investment in workflow and systems. Book printers are already supplying services to textbook publishers like Pearson's Revel and McGrawHill's Create are already providing custom textbooks. These services are delivered by a number of book printers located around the world. To cope with variable print, printers offering custom publishing services need to invest in systems and workflow that can manage variable printing. According to a recent InfoTrends survey, workflow issues have increased threefold since 2013 [89]. These issues, which include planning and scheduling, managing multiple workflows, and facing large volumes of small print orders, increase the risk of error and cost inefficiency. In theory, workflow automation should be a seamless process that requires little to no human intervention. In all, 82% of print service providers have turned to cloud-based software in recent years [90]. Variable printing is becoming the norm.

More digital printing standards which will apply to books: Fogra (The Research Institute for Media Technologies in Munich, Germany) has published Process Standard Digital (PSD) which complements its well-established Process Standard Offset which lays down "guidelines ranging from data creation all the way to printing." Setting standards and then encouraging printers to meet the standards suggests that the digital print market has matured. According to their handbook for a digital printer to achieve the standard:

> *...it needs both competent staff using appropriate instruments on the one hand and the interplay of important ISO, national and de-facto standards. So it is not one standard which takes precedence. Important standards must work in concert such as ISO 3664 for image appraisal, ISO 15311 for evaluating the quality of ink on paper, ISO 13655 for the colour measurements and ISO 14861 for high quality soft proo ng. The PSD has three main objectives:*

1. **Output process control**: Achieving a repeatable print output....
2. **Colour fidelity**:... a consistent colour communication by means of faithful image reproduction...
3. **PDF/-X compliant workflow**: ... the entire workflow is subject to critical scrutiny as to its capacity for sustained achievement of consistent print quality and colour fidelity. Here PSD offers guidelines for creating, pre-flighting and processing PDF-based documents. Standardisation does not mean that materials such as substrates, inks, toner, or machinery must be limited. On the contrary, Fogra PSD aims toward a manageable facilitation of a material and process diversity in terms of rigours and consistent print quality. [91]

This might sound a bit technical for anyone who is not a printer, but what it means is that digital printing has gone mainstream. The standards and guidelines follow.

Improved colour, larger extents, and finishing solutions for digital printed books: Commercial printing (as opposed to publishing printing) has been the market where much digital printing innovation takes place and it is worth looking at a couple of innovations taking place there which could make their way to on-demand book manufacturing in due course: even better colour and more choice in finishings.

Drupa is the largest print manufacturing trade show that meets every 4 years in Dusseldorf, Germany, taking up 19 trade show halls and showcasing new innovations in the printing industry including publishing printing but also packaging and now 3D industrial printing. HP were the largest exhibitor in 2016 including their Indigo digital print solution range which is a market leading colour digital print solution. The fact that HP became the largest exhibitor for the first time suggests that digital printing has come of age. Many of today's academic book covers and colour books will have been printed on HP inkjet machines.

The last Drupa was in 2016 and there were many innovative print solutions exhibited, including digital colour presses. Following its Drupa 2016 debut, Next Generation Finishing Equipment and Colour Kodak won an award in 2017 from the European Digital Press Association whose members publish 26 colour consumer magazines using digital print technology. The KODAK NEXPRESS ZX3900 Digital Production Colour Press was the best product in the "Cutsheet printer colour up to B3 > 200,000 A4/month" category (i.e. a reasonable amount of volume and suitable for larger than typical book trim sizes). Kodak and the EDP announced:

> *The KODAK NEXPRESS ZX Platform delivers industry-leading productivity and high- quality output. Numerous print enhancement options, including* **ten specialty dry inks** *for the KODAK NEXPRESS Fifth Imaging Unit, give printers a way to set themselves apart from their competitors in the market. Furthermore, the NEXPRESS ZX Platform provides* **unprecedented flexibility** *in regards to the substrate types, thicknesses, and formats the press will work with. The standard maximum sheet length of 520 mm can be optionally extended to 1000 mm. [92]*

Without getting too technical, the variety of paper being fed through the system and the range of ink colours has been extended in this award winning solution. Today, this is a higher volume magazine appropriate digital solution offering improved depth of colour quality and accommodates a wider range of paper thicknesses, i.e. very thin papers for magazines, but the innovation may in due course transfer to book printing operations if the economics driven by the volume of demand can work. There could be potential to address the problem of large extent (over 800 pages) books requiring thin paper to be properly bound and history of art colour books requiring a level of colour unsuitable for digital printing today. Now this is just one innovation from one vendor used to illustrate the nature of the digital book manufacturing improvements heading our way over the next decade.

Drupa had literally hundreds of finishing solution companies exhibiting including binding equipment manufactures and paper coating specialists. In-line binding is where the end-to-end printing and binding process takes place within one line of equipment rather than moving between manufacturing workstations. It is a labour-reducing step because there is only one operator needed to operate the entire process. Koenig & Bauer Group (known as KBA) is the second largest press manufacturer worldwide and according to their website:

> *"...a key supplier to the global media industry. KBA's core competence is the development and manufacture of technologically innovative yet cost-effective printing systems and peripherals." [93]*

Peripherals include finishing solutions like binders. As early as 2010, CPI France was working with KBA to solve digital printing problems:

> *In response to an emerging demand from CPI's publishing customers for books – particularly thick books–that lie flat more easily when open, the new Commander CT press will even support long-grain production, where the paper fibres run parallel to the spine. [94]*

More recently, CPI France installed a KBA binder in-line in their digital printing plant and other printers are testing robotic arms for use in the binding process. Clearly more automation will come into operation in the next decade.

More embellishments: More flexible and specialist approaches to faking traditional embellishments on books are also being tried and tested. Not yet for single copy on-demand books, but already for short-run digital print runs. The economics come down to having enough demand for particular finishing requirements. Overcomplicating a document management digital workflow approach destroys the value but a number of printers have carved a niche in supplying more bespoke short-run digital finishing solutions. However, there is a demand for gold and silver edging to paper, and faked spot varnish on covers and coatings for papers that enable more papers to run through digital print equipment.

Waste reduction: Finally, it is staggering to consider the volume of wasted books that have been a feature of the publishing industry as a whole, and not least the academic book publishing industry. At the end of Chapter 8, Richard Fidczuk reported the waste saving made by SAGE from moving to journal issue printing on-demand. The traditional book supply chain allows returns to the publisher in most countries and both the high discounting, remaindering, and last resort pulping of books. Consequently, this is a very unattractive channel to market for academic publishers. Direct sales of books drop-shipped to consumers that cannot be returned or integrating with online retailers where returns are minimal has meant a much more accurate picture of true demand that is available to the publisher. Not having to deal with the financial and environmental consequences of overprinting a significant hidden benefit for publishers engaged in print-on-demand, that benefit will only increase in the coming decade.

Two interviews and a case study follow illustrating some of the trends in book manufacturing. SOS Print + Media printers offer a wide range of printing services including books in short-run and one-off in the Australian market. Laurence Bennett recounts the story of Bookmasters' entry into print-on-demand books and that is coupled with the report on Bookmasters' investment into new Inkjet printing technology to support custom digital book production using a range of new Canon OCE equipment.

Interview: Michael Schulz, CEO, SOS Print + Media, Sydney AU (2017)

SOS Print + Media Group is a privately owned company in Sydney. It was founded in 1976 and has since grown to a communications company employing more than 120 people. Turnover for SOS Sydney is approximately AUS$31 million and it is one of the largest independently owned printing companies in New South Wales. Located in two sites, they offer: offset printing; digital printing; finishing and binding; warehousing and distribution; and pre-media/IT services in-house.

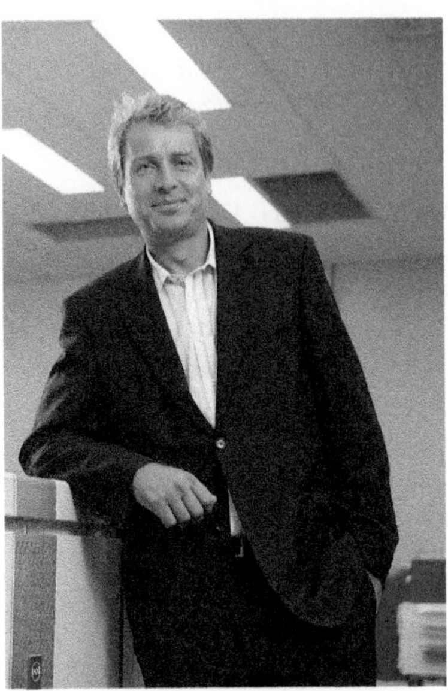

Michael Schulz, CEO, SOS Print + Media based in Sydney, Australia.

SOS Print offers two distinct services to publishers: short-run digital printing and true single copy print-on-demand coupled with shipping direct to publishers' warehouses, retailers, and consumers. Implementing a workflow solution to achieve one-off single copybook printing is critical to our success; otherwise, print-on-demand does not work economically. To do this, processes must be automated and standardised. We are significant suppliers to the higher educational and educational textbook market segment, especially to Pearson Australia.

Print-on-demand has had quite a long history in Australia. At one point, the Espresso Book Machine was installed in a bookshop in Melbourne, but it was not a success because when technical issues arose, for example, with the binding and bookshop, staff could not properly maintain or repair the equipment.

In the early 2000s, Random House reviewed their digital assets as they were using multiple storage methods and locations for native files and Acrobat pdfs. They chose to implement a distributed print model to the Australian market and moved to a workflow of fulfilling local book orders through auto-replenishment programmes and print-on-demand.

At the time, SOS had OCE and Ricoh quality short-run sheet fed printers which worked well for an inventory auto replenishment business model. Productivity of sheetfed engines became an issue so we installed a Kodak Prosper 1000 inkjet in 2010. This was an early inkjet implementation and there were several teething issues, not helped by Kodak's financial troubles at the time. Soon after, the traditional book printers Griffin Press and McPherson invested in HP inkjets with integrated binding lines. We noted that in 2009 CPI France moved to a completely inline binding solution and it is likely that more printers will move to this approach in due course, which means one operator can run the entire book production line. SOS has extended its range of sheet and web-fed printers including HP Indigo, Xerox IGen as well as black only and full colour inkjets. SOS finishes books using Hunkeler sheeting and two binding lines (EVA and PUR).

The development of **Inkjet technology has not only improved productivity and quality but has also changed the financial model for short-run digital printing.** Inkjet printing charges are based on capital investment, machine service, and ink costs, as opposed to the click charges per impression commonly used for toner machines. This means that inkjets are usually significantly more cost-effective than toner engines, especially in book runs of over 50 copies where setups and roll changes become less impactful. For covers, toner engines are still the preferred choice due to colour consistency and the wider range of stocks they can print on.

Today, SOS delivers **custom books and textbooks down to single copy** supply for customers with print-on-demand programmes. Our digital asset management database and workflow software automatically groups and sends orders to the right machine. We have enjoyed a positive shift by key customers who historically printed offshore in China and SouthEast Asia, but now have moved to print on-shore in Australia. In 2011, Pearson Australia printed 95% of their books overseas. By 2016, Pearson were printing 50% of their books on shore in Australia.

Sydney University Press uses SOS Print + Media's print-on-demand for their book-publishing programme. *[Author's note: They are the scholarly publisher of the University of Sydney and today are part of the university library. They are both a book aggregator and monograph publisher. According to their website: Sydney University Press was founded as a traditional university press and operated as such from 1962 to 1987; after a pause, it was re-established in 2003 under the management of the University of Sydney Library to meet the new challenges of scholarly communication in the networked environment. Since 2005, Sydney University Press has published over 200 new research titles in the fields of Australian literature, history, biography, public health, urban planning, social work, education, healthy ageing, Indigenous issues, and copyright. SUP's republishing programme draws on the digital library collection of the University of Sydney Library's Scholarly Text and Image Service (SETIS). SETIS is the largest collection of XML electronic texts on Australian history and literature in the world. Over 300 texts are fully searchable and readable* via *the Web. SUP provides the ability to purchase a print copy of selected texts to anyone, anywhere.]* In addition, Macquarie University uses our print-on-demand service for their student course notes and theses printing.

Digital book manufacturing is continually developing and there are several trends we have encountered that SOS Print + Media either have implemented or are considering for the near future. The perfect binding process is used in the bulk of print-on-demand manufacturing which involves hot melted glue applied to the book spine. In recent years, **PUR (reactive polyurethane) has been introduced as an alternative type of hot melt glue** which is different from the EVA and SBR (styrene butadiene rubber) hot melts. PUR glue is a more durable glue that can replace section sewn binding with the same lie flat capability without cracking or pages falling out. It is very useful for high wear and tear books used, for example, in a teaching environment. It carried a higher cost, not least because it has a longer curing time. Many of our textbook publishers are already making use of this innovation.

A second trend we have observed is **adding embellishments to digitally printed books**. Some of this can be done on digital machines in line. Xerox has clear toner which can simulate a Spot UV effect. Silver and Gold spot colour is possible, as is fake embossing on Indigo printers. Today, these are economical for short runs of 50 or even below. Foiling, embossing, and special coatings are also feasible for short runs with a minimum of 200 copies.

Finally, another key digital book manufacturing trend is the implementation of **further automation using robotics**. A robotic arm undertaking a task in book-binding today might cost as much as an operator's annual salary, but can work 24×7, 365 days of the year so that productivity over time could give a better return on investment. Robotic automation investments are likely to be made by digital printers in future.

Interview with Laurence Bennett, Executive Director, North America at Nord Comp. Headquartered in France, Nord Comp is a major supplier of prepress, digital production and design services company for publishers of books and journals, publishers headquartered in France. Laurence was previously at Baker & Taylor from 2007 through 2010 and from 2009 to 2010 he served as Vice President, Digital Print Media. Baker & Taylor (headquartered in Charlotte, North Carolina, USA) has been in business for over 180 years and is a wholesaler and library supplier of books. They supply customers in 120 countries. Yankee Book Peddler was its academic library book division. In 2011–12, Laurence was President, Distribution at BookMasters, a book distribution and printing company headquartered in Ashland, Ohio, USA. BookMasters was acquired by Baker & Taylor's owner in 2013. In 2016, the Follett Corporation, headquartered in Westchester, Illinois, USA, acquired Baker & Taylor including print-on-demand book supplier BookMasters, now known as Baker & Taylor Publishing Services.

Laurence Bennett Executive Director, North America at Nord Comp.

Prior to 2009, digital print had garnered scant attention and resources at Baker & Taylor (B&T). However, in 2008/9, the rapidly changing competitive and technological environment catapulted the digital print initiative into a high-profile, top corporate objective. In the early part of the new millennium, B&T had made a multimillion-dollar investment in a highly automated pick-n-pack system for its Bridgewater, New Jersey, USA warehouse. At that time, top-line sales were growing and the thinking was that if the automation lived up to its promise in New Jersey, it could be duplicated at other B&T warehouse facilities, greatly reducing operating costs. In 2007, the Amazon Kindle was born, ushering in the migration to e-books. In 2008, the collapse of Lehman Brothers and other financial giants precipitated the recession. In January 2010, Apple launched the iPad, adding colour to the eBook mix.The net result of these events was a slowdown in the growth of print books and sharp reductions in US public library acquisition budgets. The resulting decline in unit sales of print books extended the payback period on the automation investment and put a strain on margins overall.

At that time, the majority of company profits came from sales to public and academic/university libraries. B&T, through its Yankee Book Peddler (YBP) division, had the leading market share, followed closely by Ingram, with its Coutts library supply division. Not surprisingly, the academic libraries were among the most aggressive early adopters of e-books, which made it tempting for larger academic publishers to disintermediate their wholesalers on e-books. As unit volumes dropped, academic publishers began to rely more and more on a combination of short-run digital printing and print-on-demand. Ingram's Lightning Source (LSI) unit was by far the leading provider of those services. Thus, B&T was finding itself in the untenable position of purchasing print services, directly or indirectly, from its arch-rival.

At that point, B&T decided to make digital print a top priority. On the basis of the results of a Request for Proposals, R.R. Donnelley (RRD) was chosen as B&T's partner. In 2009, RRD built a small digital print facility inside of B&T's mammoth Momence, Illinois, USA distribution centre. At first, publishers were reluctant to go through the steps needed to set up another on-demand printer which required time spent on metadata and print file delivery. However, the prospect of faster deliveries and reduced handling costs convinced many of the academic publishers and university presses to cooperate.

Baker & Taylor successfully integrated print-on-demand capabilities with its academic sales and distribution network. Academic publishers found value in virtually eliminating returns and obsolete inventory. At the same time, the higher per unit cost of producing via print-on-demand (e.g. a 6″ × 9″, one-colour, perfect bound book) was more easily absorbed for an academic book with a list price of USD $59.95 than by a trade book with similar specifications but a list price of USD $22.95. As a result, it was harder to convince trade publishers to work with us. Also, based on the digital print technology available at the time, it was virtually impossible to provide case-bound and/or books with more than one colour on the text block at a price that would leave even a small margin for the publisher. This limited the offering to one-colour, perfect bound books.

Baker & Taylor extended the reach of its print-on-demand distribution network to multiple international markets through a series of agreements with overseas digital print partners. This enabled us to offer our client publishers a limited version of worldwide distribution with zero investment in inventory. Working through partners such as Publidisa in Spain and Books On-Demand in Germany, print-on-demand allowed us to create an incremental revenue stream for the company and our clients.

In general, print-on-demand has been an excellent tool for academic publishers in more effectively managing their businesses. It has allowed them to cost-effectively reduce their print runs, resulting in much lower returns and write-downs for obsolete inventory. The quality improvements in inkjet technology have even allowed academic publishers to use digital printing, stockless print-on-demand, or short-run digital printing for their full colour books. Similarly, advances in case-binding equipment for low quantity runs have made print-on-demand produced casebound books which are economically viable.

From my perspective when I was at Baker & Taylor, digital print technology had a generally positive impact on academic book publishing. By using print-on-demand, we were able to get new titles to customers faster. Using a combination of B&T's print-on-demand and short-run digital printing, academic publishers were able to achieve better inventory control, resulting in lower returns and less obsolete inventory. Print-on-demand was also instrumental in generating incremental revenue from previously out-of-print books. I joined BookMasters, a distributor and offset printer, in 2011, as president of distribution. Shortly thereafter, we added digital print capacity. The ability to offer on-demand print services was a strong inducement for academic publishers to use our distribution services.

In my current role with book technology firm Nord Compo, we partner with Lightning Source to create hardcover versions of softcover academic books and print versions of trade books that were created as 'digital only'. These incremental formats, sold via print-on-demand through Ingram's worldwide distribution network, greatly expand the market for an academic or trade publisher's backlist. I firmly believe that there will always be a place for printed books among the academic library community. Continued technological advances in digital print hardware will keep digital print costs stable or slightly declining, even as quality continues to improve. This will lead academic publishers to turn increasingly to print-on-demand to meet their print needs.

Case study: Bookmasters' investment in Canon OCE inkjet book manufacturing equipment (2017) USA [95]

This mini case follows on from the interview above with Laurence Bennett explaining the origins of the Bookmasters' print-on-demand service. Bookmasters, now a Follett Company, have made a multimillion dollar investment to boost digital production capacity for books, highlighting customised books. This is an illustrative case of new investment in inkjet technology being made to support digitally printing books, including academic books.

ASHLAND, Ohio – 26 April 2017 – Bookmasters, one of the largest providers of customised book publishing services in the United States, has expanded its book manufacturing services with the addition of new inkjet digital book manufacturing

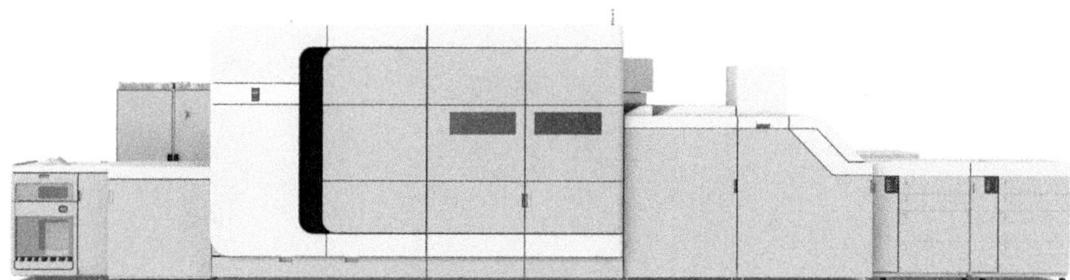

Fig. 9.3 The Océ VarioPrint i300 press.
Photograph used with permission from Canon.

equipment to its facility based here. Bookmasters has added an Océ VarioPrint i300 (with Colour Grip) colour sheetfed inkjet press. Fig. 9.3 shows a photograph of this equipment. Bookmasters is reported to be only the second US book manufacturer to offer this technology. The company has also added an Océ ColorStream 3900 monochrome inkjet press for high production one colour. In addition, Bookmasters has made an upgrade to its toner equipment with the addition of two Océ VarioPrint 6320s. Fig. 9.4 shows a photograph of this equipment. Bookmasters' investment in this digital book manufacturing equipment complements its existing digital printing capabilities for short-run digital book printing and print-on-demand (POD). This multimillion dollar investment increases Bookmasters' digital production capacity by 90%. "This improvement to our digital print platform brings us up-to-date technologically, adds capacity, improves our SLA's, and improves our service levels to our customers," says Ken Fultz, general manager at Bookmasters. "We're very proud of this expansion to our partnership with Canon Solutions America." Bookmasters was ranked No. 231 on the 2016 *Printing Impressions* 400 and reported most recent fiscal year sales of $21.00 million and 165 employees (Figs. 9.3 and 9.4 show images of the Canon print equipment like the equipment Bookmasters installed).

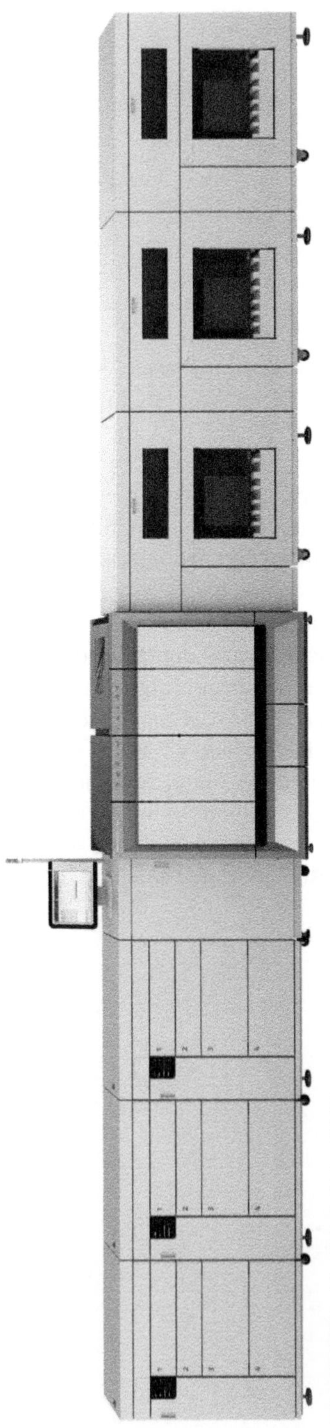

Fig. 9.4 The Océ VarioPrint 6000.
Photograph used with permission from Canon. Bookmasters. http://www.bookmasters.com/.

On-demand book publishing trends

10

The future of the academic book has been a topic of much discussion in recent years, most especially the future of the printed monograph in an open access context and the future of printed textbooks and continuous professional development books in a digital learning environment context. Both e-book monograph collections and digital learning environments challenge the need for traditional printed books. Questions abound like: Is the future digital? Is the future print? Is long-form narrative even relevant in a hyperlinked world? Are interactive data sets and moving image narratives replacing or at least competing with the book? Both e-book monograph collections and digital learning environments are growing apace. However, as the academic publishing world becomes increasingly digital, most participants are talking about a blended print and digital future for the book, sometimes referred to as hybrid. That hybrid model is digital first with print if the demand exists.

The monograph is surely following in the steps of the academic journal in two respects: moving to a **digital first** e-book with optional print book; and embracing an open access-like or author services-like publishing model. In 2012, Wiley and Sheridan Press entered a strategic relationship to print journal issues on-demand in response to customer orders rather than in print batches just-in-case for stock. The media announcement was featured as a case study at the end of Chapter 5. The most important aspect of it is a commitment by Wiley to open access and optional print versions. In the July 2017 issue of *Research Information*, David Ross, Executive Director of Open Access at Sage Publishing, indicated that Sage have spotted a rising interest in the open access Humanities and Social Science (HSS) monograph:

> *'We've seen a lot more noise around open access monographs recently, and we're going to be launching an open access monograph programme as part of SAGE Open later this year.' Ross reckons the interest partly stems from funding but also the drop in library purchases of the printed HSS monograph. 'Recently there has been no real vehicle for these types of publications, so I do see open access monographs helping to rescue this monograph field,' he says. 'This will require funding,' he adds. 'But there is quite an appetite to address this and other issues, following the collapse of the printed monograph market.' As Sage eyes the HSS monograph market, it has, without a doubt, already made huge waves in the world of open access HSS journals.* ***All of the publisher's subscriptions journals offer a hybrid option****, of which 60 per cent are social science publications. [97]*

Perhaps the monograph will follow the direction of academic journals and open access but perhaps not. In the same recent issue of *Research Information*, an article

The Impact of Print-On-Demand on Academic Books. https://doi.org/10.1016/B978-0-08-102011-1.00010-9

on the future of the monograph reported reflecting on the UK Academic Book of the Future reports:

> *Perhaps not surprisingly, the researchers discovered that* ***many welcome open access, but confusion exists around its benefits for books,*** *with few ready to move to Gold open access anytime soon. But anxieties aside,* ***research also indicated that the academic monograph is still highly valued in scholarly circles and can look forward to a bright future in a mixed print-electronic, network-enhanced format.*** *[98]*

This study, and others, concur that the future of the book form is hybrid. The wider issues about the nature of the book or open access business models are beyond the scope of this book, but it seems safe to assume that there will be (even if in diminishing numbers) an ongoing need in a hybrid environment for printed books for the academic and scholarly community, at least for some disciplines if not for all. So, what are the notable key trends in on-demand book publishing? There are five unmistakable trends worth noting.

First, **more digital book collections sold on subscription or in open access with a purchasable print-on-demand edition** for specific books in the collections. We have seen the beginnings of these services in Springer's MyCopy, Brill's MyCopy, Cambridge Core, and Oxford Scholar Online, but as collections increase in size and depth and user awareness grows, more publishing will increases to create print books like facsimiles from digital products, large specialist research collections like Gale's Eighteenth Century Collection from the British Library or Google Books be enhanced with print-on-demand book ordering capability. Or what about Google Books' vast collection of scans from research libraries around the world? Might the copyright issues be overcome to enable all those books to be printed on-demand from those sources? Overcoming the rights restrictions through Open Access or other business models may be a challenge but undoubtedly these obstacles will be addressed and solutions found.

Some specialist collections in libraries may have exclusive rights to a range of books or out of copyright books which can be reproduced through on-demand publishing. Print-on-demand is enabling the university library to become a university press offering not only reproduction and distribution of books through print-on-demand services but also full publishing services (also known as author services) for members of their academic community.

Second, more **variety in the types of books available on-demand** both in terms of types of literature form (including monographs, learning resources, grey literature, reference works, illustrated textbooks, and bound journal issues) and the variety of physical attributes of the printed and bound volume (paperback, hardcover, long extents, decorative embellishments). Different types of literature including more complex colour illustrated books will be published on-demand as inkjet technology takes over from toner and the cost of colour reduces. In the past, print-on-demand books were dominated by paperbacks with hardback books being the exception. In future, formats will become increasingly flexible and variable, with hardback binding costs reducing while the quality of hardbacks is improved through technical developments like PUR glue. In Chapter 8, academic book publisher Brill offered an insight into their experience of holding out for high-quality hardbacks on-demand which has revolutionised their approach to supplying books. Spiral binding for lay flat learning books, saddle stitch for booklets and pamphlets, enhanced books with other media like audio CD or DVDs, and even books that might benefit from 3D digital printing with parts to assemble, for example, kits of chemical models; all these forms might in due course find vendors prepared to offer on-demand solutions for the right price.

Third, **customisation of individual books** becomes increasingly commonplace and affordable. Custom coursepacks pioneered the commercial custom book, but managing variable data for individual custom books has primarily been a consumer or trade book service so far, for example, Put Me in the Story (custom gift books for children), Student Treasures (custom book service for classroom teachers in the United States), or photobooks (uploading your own photographic images and printing them on high-quality paper with quality bindings). Perhaps customised books using more sophisticated variable data might play a part in generating printed resources for tailor-made courses targeting individual students engaged in continuous learning in the future.

The fourth trend in academic on-demand book publishing is the **globalisation and diversification of languages available print-on-demand** enabling new academic book markets to be effectively reached around the world. Multilingual publishing, publishing versions of books for specific markets, reducing the time to market in difficult to reach territories, and enabling academic institutions anywhere in the world to access books thorough sharing files and then locally printing on digital equipment all become possible.

Globalisation of print-on-demand books, through distributed systems into more locations, even remote locations, is a significant opportunity for academic books. There may be new copyright issues, new piracy issues, and scalability issues to overcome but the publishing opportunities generated could be considerable and of significant monetary value to the academic publishing industry. In Chapter 5, David Taylor from the Ingram Content group presented an alternative model of internationalisation of print-on-demand books through the integration of their services with other printers around the world.

The fifth and final book publishing trend may in fact be the most significant. The revolution that is **academic author services** has only just started to target university presses and begun to incorporate reputable peer review as part of the author services experience, coupled with on-demand book printing solutions. The rise of author services targeting consumers has considerably increased book publishing output and grown the book publishing industry. The market leader in 2017 is a venture capital owned company. Author Solutions LLC (which includes AuthorHouse, iUniverse, Xlibris, Hay House, and other imprints) has changed ownership on several occasions since its inception as 1stBooks/AuthorHouse in 1997. Most notably, Pearson, the then owner of Penguin, acquired them in 2012 but later Penguin Random House group divested of them in 2016. In 2015, AuthorHouse partnered with the first university press to be supported by a self-publishing or author services provider: Alliant University's Alliant Press supported by Author House. [97] Alliant is a relatively new university established in 2001 in southern California with several campuses focusing on psychology, health, business studies, and law. The partnership is to support publications from its faculty and student community.

The past 20 years have seen an author services revolution where traditional book publishers have not been the beneficiaries. Authors, illustrators, small publishers, services providers of author services, particularly online author services solutions, have benefited and grown. Organisations like Author Solutions, Books On-demand Germany (bod.de supplies consumer author services solutions in German [catering for Euro & Swiss Francs], Danish, Finnish, and Swedish), and Lulu.com who provide author services in English to four distinct markets/currencies: USA, Canada, UK, and Australia, in German to two distinct markets/currencies: Germany and Switzerland, in French to France and a French language version on the Canadian dollar site, in Spanish to Spain and a Spanish version on the US site, as well as Dutch and Italian. These multilingual services are well thought through allowing the appropriate currency transactions to take place with authors in the corresponding language. These publishing platforms are mature enough now to take on not just consumer books but academic books provided services like the peer review process and referencing are addressed. In 2015, Lulu launched Glasstree to do just that and it is a very exciting development indeed.

The rise of academic author services might in due course address some of the issues around excessively high-priced Open Access publishing fees and the domination of commercial academic book publishers, particularly if funding bodies underpinning research activity assume responsibility for disseminating research results. That could disintermediate the traditional publishers, and lead to an even bigger explosion of published research in digital and printed book form.

The following three case studies are drawn from recently published sources and are indicative of on-demand publishing trends. The first addresses the predicted growth in Open Access books at Springer Nature, the second is an example of print-on-demand technology for biblical scholars' bible translations taken to remote communities around the world by Wycliffe Associates, and the third is an interview with a leader in the emergent world of academic author services, Glass Tree Academic Publishing.

Interview with Harmen van Paradijs, Vice President of Human Sciences Publishing at Springer Nature, NL (2017)

Highlighting the growth in Open Access supported by print-on-demand, this extract from 'A Monograph for Tomorrow' by Rebecca Pool (21 July 2017, *Research Information*, a Europa Sciences publication) [98] asserts that Open Access looks set to shake up the humanities and social sciences book landscape for the better. Palgrave Macmillan, Macmillan Education, Nature Publishing Group, and Springer Science+Business Media, Springer Nature merged to create the industry's leading Humanities and Social Science (HSS) publishers, publishing around 4000 books in the fields of humanities and social sciences.

According to van Paradijs, journals are clearly ahead of books when it comes to open access publishing, partly thanks to promotion from the likes of Springer Nature and BioMed Central. However, for him, right now, the real action lies in books. "In total, last year [2016] we published just over 100 books as open access out of our 4000-strong collection, which is a very small percentage," he says. "But the growth rate is absolutely staggering, and I am seeing a momentum in this market now; it is really taking off. I would expect the number of HSS books that are open access to double over the next two to three years." As van Paradijs points out, Palgrave Macmillan, just one of Springer Nature's HSS imprints, currently offer authors and their funders the option to publish open access research across all publication formats via Palgrave Open. The imprint is claimed to be one of the first to offer an open access option from humanities and social sciences and aims to develop sustainable business models for these disciplines.

Paradijs reckons the appetite for the open access monograph has been helped by cash, now coming from a host of national funding agencies across Europe as well as Canada and the United States. Austria's national research council, for example, was one of the first to provide funds for open access HSS monographs via its Austrian Science Fund. Meanwhile, myriad organisations from the European Research Council and Humanities in the European Research Area, to Canada's Federation for the Humanities and Social Sciences and the UK Department for International Development have built funds to cover costs associated with open access book publications. "We have seen broad acceptance of open access with all the national science funds and funding agencies, especially in Europe," highlights van Paradijs. However, it is not just national funding agencies that have made a difference. As the Springer Nature vice president highlights, non-governmental organisations have also been instrumental in taking open access to the humanities and social sciences. Many NGOs aim to distribute information either through their own operations or long-term local partnerships, and marrying traditional book publications with open access has been beneficial. Indeed, as van Paradijs asserts: "I'd be hard-pressed to name a major NGO that is not pushing open access to the humanities and social sciences." Thanks to the rise in funds, Palgrave Macmillan now publishes entire monographs and individual chapters as open access. "This depends on the funding and the funder, but if the funds are available, it is our duty to ensure both are technically possible," says van Paradijs, adding open access tends to be particularly strong in what he calls the 'hard side' of HSS, with sectors such as educational and economic development leading the way. "We work with the International Labour Organisation – an UN agency – and they fund an entire series of open access books on human geography..."

Case study

Bible Translations On-demand – two projects: The American Bible Society and Wycliffe Associates (2017) USA plus an anonymous set of observations about print-on-demand for textbooks in developing countries. Below are two examples where print-on-demand for books is making specialist books available to new markets: the first enables indigenous minority language speakers within the United States to access Biblical texts translated by Biblical scholars into their language. The second enables remote communities to have access to books immediately in their locations. Biblical scholars and translators have created Bible translations (part of the Bible or even the complete Bible) and then manufacture them on the spot using low-tech print-on-demand for books.

According to their website, the American Bible Society offers diverse language translations using print-on-demand:

> **Print-On-Demand:** *Scripture resources in languages for your church or ministry. As the American Bible Society pursues its strategic direction to see 100 million people residing in the United States actively engaged with God's Word by 2025, we are pleased to be able to offer this powerful and exciting aspect of our ministry:Print-on-Demand.* ***This print-on-demand service provides churches and ministries with Bibles and New Testaments in languages for their diverse communities.*** *Now it is easier to get Scriptures in the language you need when you need them. Languages now available:* ***Apache, Chinese*** *(simplified and traditional),* ***English, French, Hawaiian, Hmong, Italian, Jarai (Vietnamese), Korean, Russian, Spanish, Tagalog,*** *and* ***Yupik.*** *[99]*

Wycliffe Associates are actively translating the Bible into all languages of the world and have a programme which enables an entire print-on-demand print shop to be set up for on-demand supply of copies to local markets. This low-tech approach to remote areas revolutionises access to texts. According to their website: "**PRINT-ON-DEMAND: Three letters that are revolutionising Bible Translation: POD**." [100] They go on to describe how providing end to end print-on-demand low-tech system set-up is working:

> The world of Bible translation is being permanently transformed by Print-On-Demand technology. With a POD system, national Bible translators can finish their work – and have printed Bibles in people's hands within hours. ... There are thousands of languages in the world – some of them spoken by isolated people groups. Providing a printed copy of God's Word for all of these people groups would have seemed like an impossible task. Until now. As word of this revolutionary technology has spread, and people see its results in neighboring groups, they want it for themselves. ... Right now we're hoping to provide 29 new POD systems for groups that desperately need them. [101]

These projects are delivering the fruits of academic biblical scholarship and translation into communities. In addition to these projects, there is a printer in Germany who is working on solving the thin paper and large extent issues around printing complete **Bibles** on-demand. The inability to run very thin papers through digital printing heat processes with success and the limitations of spine widths have meant that large extent book (e.g. in excess of 800 pages) are difficult to print and bind on-demand. This has been a technical limitation of print-on-demand books to date. I would expect a viable solution to be in place which will assist all academic publishers with high-extent books within the next couple of years (Fig. 10.1).

Finally, here are some observations regarding globalisation of print-on-demand textbooks from an anonymous provider of educational literature to students in developing countries. UK (2016) The most effective print-on-demand textbook application I have observed was for A5-sized books smaller than 200 pages. These are typically instructional manuals or short courses in developing world markets. Delivery of draft-copies can be reviewed by multiple reviewers, and returned to be edited and revised. Print-on-demand for international textbooks has positively impacted academic book publishing, in that the books become available to a wide audience for a cheaper price, especially when printed locally. Now students (particularly in developing nations) can own their

Step 1: Computer

Step 2: Printer (2 shown)

Step 3: Laminator

Step 4: Creaser

Steps 5 and 6: Stack Cutter (right) and perfect binder

Print-on-demand–Entire system

Fig. 10.1 Wycliffe Associates print-on-demand solution for bible translation in remote locations. Six steps using six pieces of equipment: (1) computer, (2) printer, (3) cutter, (4) binder,(5) laminator, and (6) creaser.
Photographs used with the permission of Wycliffe Associates.

own textbooks. In the developing world, there is still a high demand for the printed books. Even countries that have easy access to smartphones are still asking for the printed book. I am curious to see if the current teenagers, who have grown up with smartphones, will still want to purchase printed books, but for this generation, printed textbooks will continue.

Case Study: Daniel Berze, Senior Vice President, GlassTree Academic Publishing/Lulu Press

Since 2002, Lulu has enabled authors in more than 225 countries and territories to self-publish nearly two million publications. Lulu has developed industry-leading tools and its global community helps authors hone their craft and publish printed books or e-Books for free, then sell them around the world via multiple channels. At Lulu, authors are in control, owning the rights to their works, setting their own price, and keeping up to 90% of their book profits. In 2015, Lulu launched Glasstree Academic Publishing, which enables academic authors to publish books with a managed peer review service as part of the package. Daniel Berze, Senior Vice President at Glasstree Academic Publishing, was interviewed by **Research Information** who first published this interview in December 2016 entitled **Independent publishing: the next big thing?** and reissued it in February/March 2017 entitled: **Independent publishing: breaking the mold? Broken pact in scholarly communication motivates shifting locus of control.** The original version of the article is reproduced here with their permission. [102]

Broken pact in scholarly communication motivates shifting locus of control, writes Daniel Berze In decades past, there existed a tacit 'pact' between the academic community and academic publishers; namely that the academics would conduct the research, create the content, perform peer review to ensure quality and the publishers would disseminate it. This sounds like a sensible arrangement. The advantage to the academics is that they do not have to invest their precious time and money in an area that is not their core raison d'être. The obvious advantage for the publishers is that they receive quality content that they can then disseminate to the appropriate academic audience.

So what went wrong?

1. **Pricing**: The price of academic content has increased disproportionately to the costs associated with its dissemination. One of the arguments for introducing digital technology into the dissemination process is that it would make the entire process cheaper and faster. In fact, it has become much more expensive for users (ask any librarian), and looking at submission to dissemination times, the speed of dissemination can also be questioned. Publishers would argue that the tremendous increase in volume accounts for the increased costs and slowness of the system, but the entire principle of technology is that it can handle large volumes of content without significantly impacting costs. Does it really cost more to process 1000 digital manuscripts than it used to take to process 100 hard copy manuscripts? The cost of computing memory, hardware, and software has reduced dramatically in the last decade. What is the justification for these massive price increases? In my previous career at a learned society, I would receive letters from publishers announcing that "we have restricted price increases this year to 15 per cent" when inflation was less than 2%.
2. **Division of profits**: In the aforementioned 'pact' between academics and publishers, it was tacitly agreed that academics would submit their articles for nothing (or their book manuscripts for roughly 9% of royalties), and conduct their peer reviews for nothing, and the publishers would support the dissemination process over time to ensure sustainability and that content would reach intended user communities. It was expected that a profit would be charged in order to support the process and to allow for the investment in new technologies, adding value and increasing the user experience. However, no one expected the disproportionate, almost extortionate profit taking that many (but not all) publishers had realised. The academic community felt betrayed, their excellent content being used to spike publishers' share prices instead of being used to further the goals of science. Academics felt betrayed.

3. **Status grab:** In the original pact, it was clearly understood who was to receive the credit for high-quality content – namely the content generator. It takes years of high-quality education, innate ability, and hard 'roll up your sleeves' work in order to create a successful academic researcher. Yet publishers seem to have turned the tables, basking in the limelight of 'their' excellent content. Publishers take credit for high-quality content, while they are mere facilitators. Both the editorial process, as well as the content generation process is a product of the academic community. Not that this facilitation process is unimportant, but the publisher does not deserve the status that it often projects to the international community for the operational role it plays. Also, content users now typically search for content according to subject relevance and individual bibliometric indicators and do not care about the so-called 'status' of the journal or publisher.

While one could focus on many more reasons as to why this pact has been disturbed, let us restrict matters to these three.

Being responsible for the operational processes and magnetisation of academic content dissemination, academic publishers often took advantage of their privileged position. Irrespective of the complaints issued by the academic community, they enjoyed total control of the model and have used their considerable financial resources to defend themselves from alternative competing models (via legal actions or buy-outs, for example).

When editorial boards walked out, they have been replaced. When academic societies have legal ownership of the journal, they typically have moved to another publisher, or publish themselves, or in partnerships with other like-minded bodies, taking care that the new financial model ensures sustainability but does not support an unrealistic profit-making model. Book authors have turned to self-publishing en masse (fed up of having to self-finance expensive book buybacks), making certain that the dissemination of their content is facilitated, while ensuring that they obtain the majority of the royalties in order to support further research instead of padding the pockets of academic publishing company shareholders. Several academics are so frustrated with the traditional model, that they have issued formal public pledges not to participate with some traditional publishers (e.g. www.thecostofknowledge.com).

Open Access is one model that was created to circumnavigate the control of traditional academic publishers. However, many academic publishers have pivoted quickly, ensuring that income flows have shifted from content users (OA content is free for users) to content generators (the very academics that publishers were supposed to serve)! To realise the sustainability of their financial model, academic publishers have charged academics (via 'article processing charges', or 'book processing charges') prices that have essentially broken the 'pact' between publishers and academics.

As providers of both content and the financial resources necessary to support the entire model, there is a shift in locus of control back to the academics, who are not willing to underwrite the expensive traditional publishing model for the benefit of the Publishers and who understand that it is they who control the financing and the creation of academic content.

What's next? I anticipate that after open access, the next biggest surge that academic publishing will witness is 'independent publishing' (otherwise known as 'self-publishing'). If academics are financing the content and creating it, why should not they control pricing, determine and benefit by a division of profits that is skewed in their direction, and receive the resulting status which their work might generate? This is the future we are preparing for.

Appendix 1

Survey results from Library Juice (Litwin Press) survey March 2017

Type of library (only academic shown here)	Role in library	Words associated with print-on-demand
Questions asked	*What is your job role or department? (i.e. acquisitions, technical services, reference, etc.)*	*What are some words you associate with print-on-demand?*
Academic	Technical services	Expensive
Academic	Cataloguing	Vanity works, unedited, poor quality, reprints
Academic	Instruction	Non-publishable
Academic	Reference	Low quality, errors, hard-to-find, specialty
Academic	Technical services (cataloguing)	Becoming the norm
Academic	Reference/instruction/ILL	Alternative, DIY, self-published, questionable, public domain
Academic	Access services	Self-published items, cheap, OER
Academic	Assessment, reference, management	e-Books, vanity books
Academic	Instruction/information literacy/ reference	Availability/patron-driven
Academic	Cataloguing/metadata	Cheap, copyright, fast
Academic	Subject librarian/reference	Bad dissertations; public domain
Academic	e-Book cataloguer	Money-saving, hard to catalo, time delay

How does print-on-demand affect your thinking about a book?	**How do you find out if a book is print-on-demand?**
In the context of your job, if a book is print-on-demand, how does that affect your thinking about it or your treatment of it, if at all?	***In the context of your job, do you know if a book is print-on-demand, and if so, how do you find out?***
Hesitant	No
I am reluctant to order a print-on-demand title until I have read some reviews. If I am cataloguing something we have already purchased, its usually more challenging because authors who use print-on-demand do not often adhere to the same conventions as those who go through traditional publishers. I still have a higher opinion of traditional publishers	I know of some print-on-demand publishers, so I often recognise them. I will sometimes visit a publisher's website if I am curious
I would probably not use without reading reviews by others	I would start with an internet search of the title, author, publisher, followed by reviews of the title in library journals
Probably would not buy unless germane to our collection	Yes, via amazon or our wholesaler
I need to refer to catalogue examples to ensure that dates and relationships are recorded correctly	There can be a statement on the reverse of the title page or at the end of the book
I think of a print-on-demand book as inherently of lower quality as an object, but not necessarily as lower-quality content. For example, we are using POD copies of The Wind in the Willows for a book discussion group this semester, and though the novel is one of my favourites, I am finding it difficult to read because the text is small, the margins are unjustified, the print is too close to the gutter, etc. In my former position as a public librarian, I would occasionally see POD self-published books come in as donations, and I automatically assumed they were unedited	In my experience, it is easy to tell a POD book by the quality of the printing and binding and the absence of the usual publishing hallmarks such as copyright information
Never really see these except certain OER textbooks	Students mention it
At the moment, I do not often interact with books that are print-on-demand	Only Springer books through MyCopy. Otherwise, I do not know and have no idea how to find out
Because I was introduced to it in a way that was very positive, I have no problem downloading or acquiring something I may want or need or a student may need in order to fulfil a research request. Its much faster and easier than a request	Yes, I have figured it out based on a couple of extra steps one must seemingly do to download something
I wonder about copyright issues. I might think the book is cheaper or lower quality (physically and intellectually)	Usually rely on publication statements on cover or interior of book
I would look twice at it before purchasing but would not count it out	No
It complicates cataloguing, mostly due to our rules; it complicates shelf-ready and approval plans	I have not had to deal with any

Continued

Type of library (only academic shown here)	Role in library	Words associated with print-on-demand
Questions asked	***What is your job role or department? (i.e. acquisitions, technical services, reference, etc.)***	***What are some words you associate with print-on-demand?***
Academic	Reference and instruction	Low quality; vanity
Academic	Faculty – coll. Dev., reference and teaching	Cheap, typos, photocopy, public domain
Academic	Cataloguing	Varies in quality, often incomplete
Academic	Administration	Fast, easy, convenient, timely, aiding scholarship
Academic	Instruction	Espresso, convenience, out of print
Academic	Collections coordinator	PRN [as needed], self-publishing, niches, granular, cost-effective
Academic	Cataloguer	Annoying
Academic	Technical services, reference	Poor quality, scam
Academic	Director of Library Services	Timely, esoteric
Academic	Repositories/reference	Efficient
Academic	Cataloguer	Unpredictable quality
Academic	Reference	Self-publish
Academic	Technical services	Time-consuming
Academic	Public services	Interesting idea
Academic	Assistant Director – Technical Services	Fast, out of print, self-service, low quality, espresso book machine

How does print-on-demand affect your thinking about a book?	How do you find out if a book is print-on-demand?
In the context of your job, if a book is print-on-demand, how does that affect your thinking about it or your treatment of it, if at all?	***In the context of your job, do you know if a book is print-on-demand, and if so, how do you find out?***
Not relevant to my job	No clue
Well I suppose I would look more closely before ordering it (to see if a better copy was available if it was a reprint or to make sure it is something we want if its newly published). I know it is also a bit of a pain for the acquisitions department	Yes, because I select titles so I need the publishing info. I look
It requires extra time, especially if the agency that does the reprinting is sloppy or unfamiliar with what a library wants and needs	The colophon often indicates if it is POD. Sometimes, verso of the title page or prefatory information
Have not encountered this. If a really necessary book is only available as print-on-demand, and the price was not outrageous, I would acquire it. If it were only of marginal use, I would not, p-o-d or not	Truthfully, I do not know. I imagine that a description of a p-o-d book would indicate that it is. If such is *Not* indicated, I assume it is a regularly published and available title
Not at all – we do not have any print-on-demand machines	No idea
Due to limited people-power and funds, we simply avoid PODs	By looking at the descriptors and by consulting with acquisitions librarian
The problem for me is figuring out the publisher, place of publication, and date of publication; often have to use a combination of information and numerous 264 fields, which is now allowable in RDA	I am not generally looking for that information, but the final page usually has a date and place of manufacture in POD books
Lowest priority	Yes, by the binding, publisher name and location, that it is obviously a scan
We check to make sure it is within copyright compliance	It can be hard to tell, but some ordering systems give that information
Less quality	?
Depends on the publisher	Books in print usually states print-on-demand, as do some booksellers
I have received mail in the past from authors (especially scholars) who do their own advertising by sending letters to librarians to promote their work. Subject matter is of utmost importance and the potential demand for such works	No
Not at all	No
Really no affect since our budget is so limited	Yes – but have never considered
I would not want my library to spend materials funds on a print-on-demand book unless it was absolutely necessary. I feel patrons themselves should come up with the funds for printing a book that is not readily available through traditional library acquisitions	I pay attention to the source of the book. Most of our purchases come from trusted library vendors. Those that come from amazon may include some print-on-demand titles, but I am not personally aware of a method to recognise these

Continued

Type of library (only academic shown here)	Role in library	Words associated with print-on-demand
Questions asked	*What is your job role or department? (i.e. acquisitions, technical services, reference, etc.)*	*What are some words you associate with print-on-demand?*
Academic	Cataloguing	Dubious
Academic	Cataloguing	Paper, ink, strain on library resources if we have people printing books out or have to purchase/lease a dedicated printer, not certain about quality of finished product, relatively new concept – not sure how it fits in with our workflow, cheaper for consumer?
Academic	Cataloguing	Useful, freeing, enjoyable, creative
Academic	Reference and user experience	Cost effective
Academic	Director of Library Services	Cost effectiveness, monograph printing, publishing style
Academic	Cataloguing and metadata	Varying quality, local authors, alumni authors, ISBN problems
Academic	Technical services	Mysterious, ambiguous
Academic	Technical Services	Rare
Academic	Head of cataloguing	Fast, available, paperback, usually no colour
Academic	Cataloguing	Saving; time consuming

How does print-on-demand affect your thinking about a book?	**How do you find out if a book is print-on-demand?**
In the context of your job, if a book is print-on-demand, how does that affect your thinking about it or your treatment of it, if at all?	***In the context of your job, do you know if a book is print-on-demand, and if so, how do you find out?***
Did we really do this? Is the (physical) quality up to mark?	As an experienced cataloguer, it is generally easy for me to tell if a book did not come from a traditional publisher, although I might not know that it is print-on-demand vs. vanity press vs. locally "published" item (e.g. local histories)
If I had to catalo the item, it might require a bit more work	I would hope it would be indicated on the item. I am guessing I could tell by the books construction. I have never dealt with a print-on-demand item
No difference, except I wish POD authors would remember to put publishing information on the book	I catalogue books, so can recognise the features of a POD book – they often leave off the publishing details, ISBNs, and other parts that are included in a book published by a traditional publisher. In fact, I have created several POD books myself
Wonder if students find it easy to use	I do not know
Does not change my thinking of it, or treatment of it	I do the book ordering and cataloguing, so I would know if it was POD
Depends on how hard it is to catalo. If the bibliographic information I need is there and if the quality is good, often I might not even notice if something is self-published. When the print quality is poor or the nature of the content makes it difficult to summarise/analyse for subject headings, then I notice	Knowing the signs (the information on the back that suggests it went through Amazon), bibliographic cues, ISBN issues
It is all the same	It is pretty obvious when there is no clear identification of a publisher or its not the product of the defunct publisher appearing on the title page
It is generally rare as I deal with non-Roman language material and print-on-demand is apparently rare for such materials. I treat it differently only because I must then go look up the cataloguing rules/guidelines about how to treat such material when cataloguing them, so it generally takes more time than I would prefer to spend cataloguing such items	You can generally tell based on the formatting; some "publishers" you recognise the names of
Require a publishing date	Usually a reprint of an out-of-copyright book, printing info at end of book
I think it might not be available and search for something else	I do not know

Continued

Type of library (only academic shown here)	**Role in library**	**Words associated with print-on-demand**
Questions asked	***What is your job role or department? (i.e. acquisitions, technical services, reference, etc.)***	***What are some words you associate with print-on-demand?***
Academic	Instructional technology	Economical, flimsy, black-and-white, flexible
Academic	Reference	Espresso book machine
Academic	Interim Dept. Head Collection and Resource Services	Cost effective, innovative, demand driven
Academic	Reference, instruction	Customised, self-publishing, customer-driven, costs
Academic	User experience (a blend of IT and public services); subject librarian/ liaison	Fast, inexpensive, innovative, new publishing methods
Academic	Technical Services	Pod
Academic	Technical services (acquisitions and cataloguing)	Low-quality
Academic	Reference	Interesting; helpful; cost-effective; need special equipment if you want a bound text
Academic	Reference, special collections	e-Books, collection development, books (may be wrong)
Academic	Public services and instruction	Quick, poor quality, cheap, cutting-edge
Academic	Reference	Vanity press

How does print-on-demand affect your thinking about a book?	How do you find out if a book is print-on-demand?
In the context of your job, if a book is print-on-demand, how does that affect your thinking about it or your treatment of it, if at all?	***In the context of your job, do you know if a book is print-on-demand, and if so, how do you find out?***
It is not the kind of book we had hope/expect to keep forever. Its going to have a limited shelf-life, and that is okay	I do not deal with print-on-demand titles directly. As far as I know, the only ones we have are in our reserves collection. I think there may be mixed opinions among the library faculty and staff about whether the library should be purchasing print-on-demand titles. I am in favour of it, but I would also want to hear about the circulation staff's experiences (and possibly issues) with them
Need to refer patron to area where such printing is available	If it is not clear, we have a database to look up available titles
No special treatment. If someone requests, we buy it	There is a link in the catalo offering opportunity to request book purchase
Where it was printed, for what reason (research, recreational, curiosity, etc.), how does it affect other non-print-on-demand books (circulation, purchasing, etc.)	Probably not. At least, if I have encountered one already, I have not known about it. I would probably be able to tell if I took a closer look at it and examined the materials, binding, subject matter, and did some additional research on the title itself
Depends on publisher – in some cases, I might think of it as lower quality; in other cases, I think of it as smart and efficient	In many cases, I am likely not aware; in some cases, its obvious in the book jobber/selection platform we use (GOBI) that the book is print-on-demand
Price must be higher	Via Binding
I avoid if possible and think twice about purchasing print-on-demand books because they are often of lower quality and have generic covers and lack information regarding the reprinting/republishing	I often recognise print-on-demand companies by name and some ordering systems identify books as print-on-demand
Would probably try to find an alternative	Have not seen one, but it might show up in our discovery tool
No difference	Sorry, I do not. I have not dealt with print-on-demand ever, so I have forgotten what it is
This has never come up in my job. However, my thinking about/treatment of it would probably depend on how relevant the subject was to my library's collection and how well the author was regarded	I do not know if a book is print-on-demand or how to find out
I think e-books are a much more environmental-friendly option	Google it

Continued

Type of library (only academic shown here)	Role in library	Words associated with print-on-demand
Questions asked	*What is your job role or department? (i.e. acquisitions, technical services, reference, etc.)*	*What are some words you associate with print-on-demand?*
Academic	Outreach/Public Services	Textbooks
Academic	Cataloguer-technical services	Fast
Academic	Access Services	Just-in-time, speedy, costly
Academic	Administration	Not here
Academic	Access services	Just-in-time, self-publish, economical
Academic	Digital collections metadata and reference	Easy, service
Academic	Cataloguing	New print publishing business model
Academic	Archives/special collections	Last minute request
Academic	Reference and instruction	Apple Books
Academic	Scholarly Communications, Collection Development	Efficiency, timing, delay, technology
Academic	Library director and reference/ instruction librarian	Self-published, out-of-print, questionable physical quality
Academic	Administrative—facilities	Fee-for-service, scanner/copier/printer (reprographic appliance), espresso machine
Academic	Reference and instruction	Print the book as needed
Academic	Collection development	Inaccurate, cheap, missing pages

How does print-on-demand affect your thinking about a book?	**How do you find out if a book is print-on-demand?**
In the context of your job, if a book is print-on-demand, how does that affect your thinking about it or your treatment of it, if at all?	***In the context of your job, do you know if a book is print-on-demand, and if so, how do you find out?***
Is it page-by-page, whole chapters, or whole book? If its page by page (like many ebsco materials) I probably would not print because its time consuming	I have not really thought about this. All I know is its based off of copyrights and what certain databases will allow
It does not	No, I do not know
Might not be the best-quality binding	Do not know, check Amazon
I would think it has nothing to do with me.	NA
It would depend on the book and the reason it is print-on-demand. My thinking would be swayed by other factors than whether it is POD	I do not know that I have encountered POD books in the context of my job, so I do not know how I would find out. Maybe Amazon
Not at all	A faculty member or library staff person will typically let the reference desk know to anticipate questions from students about a print-on-demand book
LC-PCC PS 1.11 notwithstanding, we've found that most POD items are NOT reproductions and should be treated just like any other print volume	If it contains an indication, e.g. the POD "bug" in the back ("LVOW11*1448171014", etc.); we do not do research outside the item itself for this determination
Not at all; this department does not lend materials	Do not generally know if its print-on-demand
Never deal with this	Has never come up
It depends on the publisher, and whether I have used print-on-demand services with them before. Some publishers are using this process to lower overall costs of production, but the 'on-demand' component does not seem accurate – I have waited up to 8 weeks for a book to arrive. It would have been faster to find a used copy for the collection instead. If the print-on-demand copy if from a local bookstore or a vendor that has faster turn-around then I think its a great option	Typically, the publisher or bookstore indicates this at point of order
I likely would not purchase it unless it is the only way to replace an out of print book that we need	It can be difficult to tell, to be honest
One less book to find a place for on fixed-capacity shelving, if for me, then fine another way	In the online catalogue
It is probably out of print, rare, or does not have enough of a demand to print a certain number of copies	I probably would not know off-hand unless I specifically asked about it or purchased it
Makes me sceptical about the book for purchase	Yes, by investigating the title as I would any title for purchase via publisher, availability, etc.

Continued

Type of library (only academic shown here)	Role in library	Words associated with print-on-demand
Questions asked	*What is your job role or department? (i.e. acquisitions, technical services, reference, etc.)*	*What are some words you associate with print-on-demand?*
Academic	Public Services Librarian	Self-publishing, small print runs
Academic	Reference	Custom, niche, vanity, low quality
Academic	Web services/reference	On the fly
Academic	Acquisitions	Self-published, non-returnable, expensive machines
Academic	Reference	Vanity, scam, poor quality, not vetted
Academic	Instruction	Cheap quality, disreputable… I hate that I subconsciously associate these words with it! Also, convenient!
Academic	Subject specialist	Vanity, quick, cheap, low quality
Academic	Administration	Fast, economic, cost-effective, patron-centric
Academic	Instruction	Fast, amateur, made-in-the-USA
Academic	Acquisitions Librarian	Poor quality!
Academic	Collection development and acquisitions	Hardware, paper
Academic	Reference	Convenience – may be lower quality binding
Academic	Digital projects	Cost-effectiveness; low-overhead; efficient
Academic	Collection development	It means books are never out of print

How does print-on-demand affect your thinking about a book?	**How do you find out if a book is print-on-demand?**
In the context of your job, if a book is print-on-demand, how does that affect your thinking about it or your treatment of it, if at all?	***In the context of your job, do you know if a book is print-on-demand, and if so, how do you find out?***
This is difficult, as we have worked with several self-published titles (I collect for a very specific discipline), and the quality has varied so wildly its really hard to assess the potential value of titles	We use a variety of tools for collection development, and generally, I find out when I am looking at Amazon. Amazon's CreateSpace is the platform I am most familiar with
While there is a negative connotation to print-on-demand titles, especially from my faculty, I think the reality is that some projects make sense for that route. For instance, I just had a professor purchase a book that is being handled as POD. The author is a professor at a university and the books is about a very specific banking topic. I think all academics need to be a little more flexible when it comes to changes in publishing, but we also need strong peer review of those titles to ensure they have academic merit	I make too many assumptions, probably. If its only for sale from an author website, then I figure it is a POD book
It feels less permanent. Not sure why…maybe because it can just be made as needed rather than a tome on the shelf	We do not have that at our library
Depends how much my students need the book or how much is available on the topic	It is usually listed on the vendor site during the purchasing process
Would likely dismiss it as a credible source	It depends, when performing collection development duties, I would know, by examining the publisher
If it is a book I am excited about, it does not affect it much. I just bought a PoD book and its one of the best I have read this year	Rarely. I am not in collections
Tends to put me off	Acquisitions has a list of vanity presses- also research online if not sure
Makes me less likely to buy a "real" copy of the book if it could be printed by someone with the need for it in the future	I am not really sure about this. Need more info
I anticipate it will require more processing	Vendor interfaces will tell you
We order print-on-demand because it is the only option for many new titles	We can tell in the Oasis ordering system, its marked as Lightening Source
I want to know who the publisher is, what the author's credentials are and why it did not get a traditional publisher	Idk
Possibly needs more preservation	No idea
It does not affect my thinking about it	Check for typical POD printer marks (Lightning Source, e.g. has identifiable information, usually on the last page of the book)
Concern about the binding	Frequently not until it arrives

Continued

Type of library (only academic shown here)	Role in library	Words associated with print-on-demand
Questions asked	*What is your job role or department? (i.e. acquisitions, technical services, reference, etc.)*	*What are some words you associate with print-on-demand?*
Academic	Instruction	Automated, patron driven, cheap paper quality
Academic	Technical services	Vanity publishing
Academic	Technical services	Cheaper, reprints
Academic	Reference	Textbooks
Academic	Cataloguer	Unusual; Meaningful
Academic	Cataloguer (technical Services Department)	Cheaper quality; lower cost; NOT backordered
Academic	Reference	n/a
Academic	Acquisitions/collection development	Non-standard, marginal, low volume
Academic	Lib manager in a solo library	Uses a lot of paper;- > Quality of photocopy is crap - i.e. am thinking dissertations here
Academic	Reference	Obsolete, specific, not applicable
Academic	Technical services	Convenience, costs
Academic	Reference	Order what patrons want
Academic	Library director	Expensive poor quality
Academic	Public services, business liaison, reference, distance learning	Self-published, dissertations, conference publications

How does print-on-demand affect your thinking about a book?	**How do you find out if a book is print-on-demand?**
In the context of your job, if a book is print-on-demand, how does that affect your thinking about it or your treatment of it, if at all?	***In the context of your job, do you know if a book is print-on-demand, and if so, how do you find out?***
Not much	Not really
I mostly work with archival collections so this has not come up	n/a
Its a bit harder to catalogue, as publishing information is often non-existent on the item	I catalogue, so I figure it out while I am cataloguing it
My experience is that they appear to be similar to course packets, and often do not have ISBNs, which makes it a bit more difficult to locate them in our collection. However, there is likely much I do not know, as I have not investigated the topic, and would certainly expect this technology to evolve in the coming years, since it is such a good way to provide content without storing it 'just in case'.	A professor has put it on reserve.
I try to treat it with greater attention and care because I know how few copies of it may exist – cannot rely on hundreds of copy-catalogue records to be in OCLC. I also think of it as meaningful because somebody cared enough to write a book and get it into my hands	I only know based on things like publisher's statement, cover art, [or overall book design]. Either I recognise the publisher as a print-on-demand publisher or it ends with 'LLC' – book design/art, sad to say, is usually sub-par or pixelated so I can tell that way
Makes no difference to me to catalogue an expensive art book with plates, or a POD book	Generally, I can tell by the publisher (also we purchase POD DVDs of films and there is never any added value
I have never considered it	I do not encounter this
If we want the book it does not make a difference	We do not know unless it obviously states it
We do not deal with them, we use our overall Univ. library for E-book access instead, or interlibrary loan (students do it themselves)	No
Poorly worded question/unclear	Poorly worded question/unclear
Not really, just catalogue it like any other item	Sometimes I can tell, sometimes I do not know and I do not have time to find out
We just started a print-on-demand project, so I do not know yet what the impact on reference services will be	Cannot answer
Will order it if that is the only source and faculty asked for it	It is noted on our vendor websites
It depends on *why* it is print-on-demand. Even some self-published books will be considered if the author is a scholar. Some of our faculty chooses to self-publish so they can keep the book in print longer	When selecting materials for the library, we generally use Amazon (sometimes GOBI/YBP), so it is easy to tell there

Continued

Type of library (only academic shown here)	Role in library	Words associated with print-on-demand
Questions asked	***What is your job role or department? (i.e. acquisitions, technical services, reference, etc.)***	***What are some words you associate with print-on-demand?***
Academic	Associate dean	Quick, convenient, user friendly
Academic	Scholarly communication and emerging technology	Access
Academic	Assistant director	Not permanent, pricey, convenient, wasteful
Academic	Cataloguing	Futuristic, conserving
Academic	Reference (although I am doing a lot of web services right now)	OER, self-publishing
Academic	Public services	Hassle; suspect; ignore
Academic	General librarian	Ease, expense, costly
Academic	Digital collections/special collections	Collections, patrons, services
Academic	User services	Low-quality, non-reliable
Academic	Reference	Savings, oversight
Academic	Access services	Pay per use
Academic	Scholarly communications	Possible solution, open educational resources
Academic	Director of the Library	May take a few days longer to receive the book
Academic	E-resources, reference	Either self-published or limited availability

How does print-on-demand affect your thinking about a book?	How do you find out if a book is print-on-demand?
In the context of your job, if a book is print-on-demand, how does that affect your thinking about it or your treatment of it, if at all?	***In the context of your job, do you know if a book is print-on-demand, and if so, how do you find out?***
Guess it depends – if its pod only, like a vanity press, then maybe we look twice. We have a set of parameters for coll dev though and will order just about anything a patron needs	This is outside the scope of my job
Time to print, is printing worth the cost?	Unsure
I have never used print-on-demand in print. There are some that also have pdf options and I do use those	Most are labelled that way in catalogues
Figuring out its material type is a challenge	Either I do not know, or have not dealt with any
I have never encountered it. I expect that it will become part of our reserves as faculty move to OERs but it has not come up yet	Again, I have not encountered it
Usually disregard	Do not usually encounter
Would not purchase	The quality is generally lower, though some print-on-demand titles look like any trade paper back
Possibly newer, less established, less scholarly	Not always, but I can find out through additional research
I would initially look for something else	n/a
It makes me feel the book is sought after	No
I would double check its authenticity	It would say on the order form/page
I think about it from the perspective of open educational resources, in which case I see it as a positive as it allows students and other users to read a book in print should they not want to read it online	Not currently
Well-known publishers, including scholarly ones, are using print-on-demand, especially for backlist titles or those with limited sales potential, so I have no problem with that. We purchase local history materials that are sometimes print-on-demand, and those are ok. If it is a "self-published" book, such as what would have been published by a 'vanity press' in the past, then we would need some compelling reason to purchase it – local history is one example, but others would be a publication by one of our faculty members or one that was reviewed favourably	I used to be the collection development librarian before I was director of the library, so still do some ordering of books for the library and try to stay up-to-date on acquisitions and collection development. We purchase from Amazon and the imprint sometimes notes if it is print-on-demand. In addition, certain publishers are known to be print-on-demand, such as Lulu or CreateSpace. So I do know sometimes, but not all the time
Might give more thought to its reliability—is it print-on-demand or is it self-published?	Not really since we order everything through YBP, all we see is available or unavailable

Continued

Type of library (only academic shown here)	Role in library	Words associated with print-on-demand
Questions asked	*What is your job role or department? (i.e. acquisitions, technical services, reference, etc.)*	*What are some words you associate with print-on-demand?*
Academic	Technical services	Grief
Academic	Reference/instruction	Hassle; expensive; questionable
Academic	Technical services	Copyright, poor info, poor formatting
Academic	Technical services	Vanity publishers, low-demand
Academic	Metadata, Cataloguing	Ephemera, local, low quality
Academic	Department head	Neat, expensive for the printer, cheap for the end-user
Academic	liaison	Black and white, quick, cheap, possibly low quality
Academic	Library liaison to three departments (Collections), and Open Education, Copyright and scholarly communication librarian	Lulu Press, softcover, ExpressoBook machine, OER
Academic	All technical services	Problems cataloguing, finding information, OCLC records, hate them, misinformation
Academic	Technical services	Quick, low quality, expensive
Academic	Instruction	PDF Collection Books ILL
Academic	Administration	Espresso, self-publishing, machine
Academic	Cataloguing	Print as needed, one at a time
Academic	Digital scholarship	Cost-saving, Amazon, publishing

How does print-on-demand affect your thinking about a book?	How do you find out if a book is print-on-demand?
In the context of your job, if a book is print-on-demand, how does that affect your thinking about it or your treatment of it, if at all?	***In the context of your job, do you know if a book is print-on-demand, and if so, how do you find out?***
Grief and also leads to questions of validity of content	Most often, yes. Sometimes pre-order and other times quality of binding as well as print, imprint within publication or lack thereof as well as the lack of bibliographic record in OCLC
May consider not purchasing due to questionable quality, both physical and content	Not always sure how to determine this; would be nice to have a standard way of knowing that – a specific designation in the ISBN??
Print-on-demand books are much harder to catalogue because contributors and publishing information is usually missing. It makes it hard to distinguish this edition from others. I wish we did not allow print-on-demand titles to be purchased, as has been a rule at other institutions where I have worked	I find print-on-demand books very obvious because of the poor formatting and lack of title page, etc.
I have to admit I am a little leery of PoD books; I am more likely to purchase books from a University Press or well-known academic source	Its on the title page verso, often, and there are certain publishers – like CreateSpace – who are known for it
It does not affect my treatment of it as most go into our local history section	Yes, by looking at the lack of publication information
Does not affect my thinking of it	I do not think I could tell
Might make sure the library copy is NOT print-on-demand	Cannot necessarily tell. Would count on vendor, or book jobber to let me know
I rarely run across these mentioned explicitly in the systems I use for purchasing	Not usually, until I hold it in my hand or unless it is not available via the regular channels (Gobi)
Takes me longer to catalogue, need to set aside not busy days (when I have little reference duty time)	Usually only after another librarian has ordered, I try not to order if I see I know that the publisher is on print-on-demand and I can acquire books on the topic somewhere else
Quite a bit harder to catalogue, sometimes (due to poor binding, etc.) additional worries about preservation	Generally some sort of visual clue when it arrives on my desk for cataloguing
None	Publisher
It does not change my thinking	Usually do not know
It presents cataloguing challenges, though I haven't done many yet	I work closely with the librarian who orders, so might know
It does not	Occasionally; if I know the Press it's coming from or if it comes from Createspace or a similar area

Continued

Type of library (only academic shown here)	Role in library	Words associated with print-on-demand
Questions asked	*What is your job role or department? (i.e. acquisitions, technical services, reference, etc.)*	*What are some words you associate with print-on-demand?*
Academic	Director	Inexpensive, paper waste
Academic	Instruction	Self-publishing, niche books, more expensive for the consumer
Academic	Reference and instruction	Quick, easy, affordable, variable quality, accessible, targeted
Academic	Reference, instruction, collections (all)	Publishers
Academic	Technical Services	Self-published, vanity press
Academic	Administration	Sketchy, unvetted, occasional gems, local
Academic	Archivist and digital Preservation librarian	Less printed waste
Academic	Collections and acquisitions	None
Academic	Subject librarian in collection dev./ management	POD
Academic	Reference librarian	Cost-effective
Academic	Reference	What people want
Academic	Space and stacks management	Get it when I need it
Academic	Special collections	Quick, cheap, as needed, reprints
Academic	Collection development	Unknown
Academic	Distance services and reference	Cost-savings, efficient, possibly not a lot of publisher backing, could be a self-published book
Academic	Systems and cataloguing	Amazon.com, self-published

How does print-on-demand affect your thinking about a book?	How do you find out if a book is print-on-demand?
In the context of your job, if a book is print-on-demand, how does that affect your thinking about it or your treatment of it, if at all?	***In the context of your job, do you know if a book is print-on-demand, and if so, how do you find out?***
Students would appreciate it	I would need some indication from the publisher or through the vendor
It might make me suspicious at the author is self-publishing so I would work harder to investigate who is publishing the book	This does not come up a lot unless I am helping students evaluating resources
I would want to see a sample of the print-on-demand work to determine quality prior to purchase. If the quality was high enough I would have on issue purchasing a print-on-demand book for our library collection	Overall, I do not know if a book is print-on-demand unless a publisher or book vendor specifically states this. However, it is very possible that I have come across books printed-on-demand and did not realise it
It depends on how badly it is needed, but really - not at all	Only if I place an order for it (or am asked about POD by a colleague)
We scrutinise greater before adding to collection	Knowing specific print-on-demand houses, familiarity with look and feel of print-on-demand items, googling publisher info
Likely not a purchase, unless topic/author is locally related	Research publisher
No change	I have no idea
We do not perform print-on-demand	n/a
When I am looking for second-hand books I try not to buy these	Sometimes. sometimes abebooks.com says
Not sure	No – I do not know
It does not affect it at all	No I do not
Not at all unless the library binds it and it now needs to be shelved with the rest of the printed materials	No but I can find out by searching our materials via our LMS
Is it available in original text; would this be better in the general collection	Vendors, websites
We have a small collection, so if I see something that is print-on-demand I think twice about purchasing it, though I have bought public domain works in a print-on-demand format	I recognised some publishers that are print-on-demand. I do not specifically look for that information, but I always check the publisher as part of my evaluation process
If it is from Springer, that's fine – at least eversions can be previewed thoroughly, the print is a great cheap alternative; if the only format option is PoD, I might question the publisher's backing of the text, look into the author, etc.	I think GOBI may make it clear, and other databases (like Springer), but if there are folks that do it and its not clear from point-of-purchase. I do not know, what I do not know, I guess
Likely to need original cataloguing; sometimes collection development staff ordered it by mistake	Typically I will find out if I have to create an original catalogue record for it

Continued

Type of library (only academic shown here)	Role in library	Words associated with print-on-demand
Questions asked	*What is your job role or department? (i.e. acquisitions, technical services, reference, etc.)*	*What are some words you associate with print-on-demand?*
Academic	Archivist	Access; e-resources; printer jams
Academic	Public services	Cheaper, quick, same quality
Academic	Reference and instruction	Unfamiliar
Academic	Instruction and Assessment	Patron-driven, point of need, electronic first
Academic	Technical services	Difficult to catalogue
Academic	Cataloguing	Cheaper, lower quality design, mixed quality of content
Academic	User services	Online, Small run, Out of print, Out of copyright, Fair use, Instruction
Academic	Reference	cumbersome, delay in acquisition, unnecessary
Academic	Public services	Low cost, digital technology, self-publish
Academic	Assessment and virtual reference	Unknown
Academic	Director of Library Services	Low-cost, low-quality, quick, self-published
Academic	Technical services and reference	Self-published, questionable worth
Academic	Cataloguing	Cheaply printed/bound; publisher info often unclear
Academic	Digital projects	Shifted overhead. Questionable quality. Easier access
Academic	Admin	Ease of access, patron driven, printing equipment

How does print-on-demand affect your thinking about a book?	How do you find out if a book is print-on-demand?
In the context of your job, if a book is print-on-demand, how does that affect your thinking about it or your treatment of it, if at all?	***In the context of your job, do you know if a book is print-on-demand, and if so, how do you find out?***
Logistical differences only	The catalogue tells me
I would feel more comfortable marking it up, if I own it	I rarely use print-on-demand books, but as far as I know there is no way to know unless the quality is not as professional. Though, I have seen professional publisher books with lesser quality printing than some print-on-demand
Think less highly of it	We do not have any print-on-demand books
I am probably more likely to think about its likelihood of being used by our patrons	I do not think this shows up in the part of the ordering/selection process that I see
Put aside for when there's time to put a lot more work on it	There is little information printed information about the book and no Versa page
As a cataloguer, I tend to catalogue what has been selected, but in ordering we tend to be careful of print-on-demand	In cataloguing print-on-demand is fairly easy to spot through the publication information, in ordering we keep track of some names
It depends on its context. I look to see if there is an online option, if it is out of copyright, or if it is out of print. In general, I avoid print-on-demand and look instead to other options	This is a good question! We often do not know this. It takes additional research to determine if it is available elsewhere or in another format
I typically try to find an alternate title to purchase	I rely on the company that I purchase the title from to let me know in the product description
It depends, if it's non-scholarly	Yes
No idea	No idea
It makes me less likely to purchase it because it means it isn't a priority for publishers, meaning it is likely low-quality or old	Some publishers mark print-on-demand titles, or Amazon does, in some cases
Harder to find OCLC record match	We see particular publishers doing it. Also, recent book with no copyright date is a red flag
I would rather buy from a "real" publisher first. PoD is a last resort	Easy to tell on Amazon if it's their PoD. Otherwise I might not know until it arrives
Not at all	I usually check the publisher's site, if it comes up at all
No affect	I would not know

Continued

Type of library (only academic shown here)	Role in library	Words associated with print-on-demand
Questions asked	*What is your job role or department? (i.e. acquisitions, technical services, reference, etc.)*	*What are some words you associate with print-on-demand?*
Academic	Technical services	Expresso machine
Academic	Subject librarian	Annoying, spam
Academic	Reference	Easy
Academic	Acquisitions, ill	Unpublished, machines, ad hoc, economical
Academic	Systems	Expensive, convenient
Academic	Technical services/Cataloguing	Shoddy, vanity, low-quality
Academic	Academic services	PDF, cost
Academic	Public services – research support (ILL and reference)	OER, OTN, download, WEPA, copier, copy centre, open source
Academic	Instruction Librarian	lower quality printing and binding
Academic	Outreach librarian	Economic, unavailable, unpopular

How does print-on-demand affect your thinking about a book?	How do you find out if a book is print-on-demand?
In the context of your job, if a book is print-on-demand, how does that affect your thinking about it or your treatment of it, if at all?	***In the context of your job, do you know if a book is print-on-demand, and if so, how do you find out?***
Question is not clear	Has not come up in my library
Unlikely to acquire or recommend	It is rare that I miss a print-on-demand book. An examination of its attributes such as cover image, table of contents, and content coverage. Most of these are reprints of government documents (which I am familiar with), so it is easier for me to notice them
Lots of printing costs; have to wait a long time in line for next print job	We block book printing – too costly; too much paper; too much toner; we encourage reading online
Anticipate it taking longer to obtain, would feel the need to scruntinise the quality more closely	Book jobbers, vendors supply the info, or through the publisher webpage, or by email from publisher that a (serial) publication is moving to print-on-demand
Not at all	I assume that a book is not print-on-demand by default
Sceptical of the quality of research and content	Typically notice lack of comprehensive/ recognisable publisher information and 'erratic' content type
doesn't affect thinking about it	Catalogue
Does not affect really – cost is transferred to student	OER network, Open Textbooks, Open source sites
I would need to know a LOT about it, the author, scholarship, etc. before adding it to the collection. If it was reviewed in all of the typical sources then this might not be an issue… if not I might hesitate	No I do not think I would be able to spot one if the printing and binding were done well… again most of our materials are chosen by librarians after consulting faculty and/or reviews in many of the mainstream sources
It tells me that the publisher has little faith in the item	I never know if a book is print-on-demand unless technical services tells me because it delays arrival

Continued

Type of library (only academic shown here)	Role in library	Words associated with print-on-demand
Questions asked	*What is your job role or department? (i.e. acquisitions, technical services, reference, etc.)*	*What are some words you associate with print-on-demand?*
Academic	Technical Services	Dubious; vanity press; equal opportunity
Academic	Reference and instruction services	Higher costs, less access, fees
Academic	Bibliographic instruction	Efficient
Academic	Systems, technical services, reference, instruction, electronic resource acquisitions	Convenient
Academic	Administration	Cost, flexibility
Academic	Technical services	Available
Academic	Reference and instruction	Convenience, economical
Academic	Technical Services	Lower-quality paper, poorly reproduced illustrations
Academic	Instruction	Cheap, low-quality
Academic	Associate Dept. Head (manage campus library)	Lack of quality, not very in-demand, self-publishing
Academic	Technical services/cataloguing	Difficult to catalogue

How does print-on-demand affect your thinking about a book?	**How do you find out if a book is print-on-demand?**
In the context of your job, if a book is print-on-demand, how does that affect your thinking about it or your treatment of it, if at all?	***In the context of your job, do you know if a book is print-on-demand, and if so, how do you find out?***
Normally we buy whatever faculty asks for. If it is a POD title, I examine the record in Amazon closely. I read the reviews, try to analyze if they are real or written by family members of the author, try to verify that the book is not just a reprint of a free website (we have bought some Wikipedia and other printouts), that the book is well-edited. If its a reproduction of an out-of-print title, I check to see if its available for free in digital format and try to get a sense if the quality of the reproduction is clear. We certainly buy POD titles – fiction, poetry, student, and alumni publications. I am more cautious about titles that appear academic. If I think the POD is problematic, I will email the faculty requestor and lay out the reasons for my scepticism and make sure that s/he is aware of the potential issues. If the faculty member still wants the title, we get it	I am familiar with the most common POD publishers available from Amazon (Create Space, Xlibris, Kessinger Reprints, etc.) If I am not sure, I google the publisher. Its usually pretty obvious from the website
Not preferred. Will turn to a different resource	It is spelled out in the library catalogue or database if there
Maybe less rigorous	No
Would use a lot of copy paper and student's copy/print quota for the semester	I assume it would say so
Only how the book could be purchased and offered to patrons	Not sure
Does not affect my thinking – just another way of publishing	Assume it is print-on-demand if book has publisher Xlibris, Createspace, etc.
Not at all	I would look at a vendor site but I do not always notice for each and every book
Would consider purchasing it if were my only option to have a copy of that title	I do not do a lot of the ordering, but in my limited experiences, I would locate a title on Amazon and see that it was available as print-on-demand when searching for a print copy
Would not buy it unless specifically cited, or authored by a student or faculty	Not after it has been purchased, but when placing orders there is often an indication from the publisher or distributor
I look at reviews, etc. a little more carefully before ordering	Usually it will say in GOBI (where we actually order) or Amazon (where I sometimes look for more information than I find in GOBI or Library Journal
Presents difficulties in finding information to catalogue material or to know how to catalogue material	No – I probably never find out, but fall back on the 'unknown' defaults for publication information

Continued

Type of library (only academic shown here)	Role in library	Words associated with print-on-demand
Questions asked	*What is your job role or department? (i.e. acquisitions, technical services, reference, etc.)*	*What are some words you associate with print-on-demand?*
Academic	Technical Services	Sloppy, no ISBN, badly edited
Academic	Electronic resources	Immediate need
Academic	Library Director	Accessibility
Academic	technology and technical services	Public domain, out-of-print, indie author, small press
Academic	Technical Services	Convenient, customisable
Academic	Collection development	Low-quality binding
Academic	technical services	Printer, online, local, e-book, single copy, personal use
Academic	Technical services	Out-of-print, questionable quality, overpriced, vanity publishing
Academic	Public services	Convenient, expensive equipment
Academic	Reference and Instruction	Cost, printing, flexibility, institutional repository
Academic	Technical services	Poor quality, convenient, flexible, headache
Academic	Director of Library Services	Convenience, expensive, availability
Academic	Access services	Self-published, scam, copyright
Academic	Administration	Self-publishing, cost effective for the author
Academic	Technical services	Old style dissertations
Academic	Reference/interlibrary loan/ collection development	Efficient, costly
Academic	Reference and instruction	Economical
Academic	Acquisitions	Expensive, may lack quality
Academic	Reference, instruction, collections	Amateur, convenient, inexpensive
Academic	Reference/instruction/circulation	Potentially low-quality (why did not they get a run from a publisher?)

How does print-on-demand affect your thinking about a book?	**How do you find out if a book is print-on-demand?**
In the context of your job, if a book is print-on-demand, how does that affect your thinking about it or your treatment of it, if at all?	***In the context of your job, do you know if a book is print-on-demand, and if so, how do you find out?***
Much of the time, there is no cataloguing record, so I have to put it aside until I have time to catalogue it	Usually, the only date I find is the print date, not copyright or publication. Very frustrating!
Do not encounter	No
Accessibility	We do not have any that I am aware of
Depends; If it is a copy of a scanned text, I mostly worry about the readability of the text	I am familiar with many/most of the major POD imprints, such as CreateSpace, AuthorHouse, iUniverse, Lulu, etc.
It means we cannot order it and add it to our collection unless it is part of an agreement with a publisher	We find out when we go to purchase it and see the available options
I am less likely to purchase it	I order books…so it is in the record from the jobber
No change in thinking	Check with electronic media acquisitions
Generally we avoid POD as it typically costs significantly more than a conventionally published book and it may be of questionable quality both aesthetically and editorially. In the case of vanity publishers we use previews on Amazon to determine a book's quality and suitability for the collection. We purchase very few vanity published books	Yes, I do know. I check for specific editions on Amazon and request that only these editions are ordered. If said editions are not available we do not purchase
We are so far from a place where we could print-on-demand that it is irrelevant	No
I do not really work with print-on-demand books very often	We only have print-on-demand books in our institutional repository as far as I know
May need more work to accurately describe	Only if it tells me (I have the book in hand)
It is not something that we offer or usually spend funds on to acquire	It does not matter, we decide on purchases based on price and utility
I would be more sceptical of the contents	I would not know unless I happened to notice a difference with print quality or an unknown publisher
Probably would not add it to the collection, but would make a special purchase for a patron	Usually explained on Amazon or publisher's page
Harder to catalogue	I think you can get them at Amazon
Can we support the print technology required?	None of our books are, so NA
I do not think I have ever noticed it	It might be in our ordering system, but I don't think I've ever noticed it
I will look for other alternatives before purchasing it	Discover it when I go to purchase it
I would assume it was a self-published item	Publisher
It makes me think it may not be very widely needed/read at this point in time	No; I would have to ask my director who handles collection development

Continued

Type of library (only academic shown here)	Role in library	Words associated with print-on-demand
Questions asked	*What is your job role or department? (i.e. acquisitions, technical services, reference, etc.)*	*What are some words you associate with print-on-demand?*
Academic	Director, cataloguer, reference, instruction, etc.	Quick, timely
Academic	Administration	Convenience speed flexibility cost
Academic	Reference Librarian	Expensive
Academic	Technical services	Poorly edited, often poorly written
Academic	Manager	Clueless
Academic	Head of a department (teaching and learning)	Low cost
Academic	Faculty librarian	Difficult to assess the source
Academic	Technical services and acquisitions	Cheap, smelly, public domain
academic—Community college	Technical service, and reference	I am not clear about how long it would take to get them
Academic—community college	Operations Manager	Print-on-demand, pay per page, PDF, self-published
Academic—community college	Outreach/technical services	Technology, access, Wi-Fi
Academic	Technical services – catalogue librarian	Quick-out–of-copyright—historical
Academic	Special collections – but Instruction, Reference, Collection Dev too	Not authoritative
Academic (community college)	Cataloguing	Self-published, uncertain, poor quality of publication data, sometimes poor physical quality
Academic (community college/college)	Electronic resources, circ, reference, collection development	Not sure, sorry if not helpful
Academic/Medical	Cataloguing	Fast, expensive, postage

How does print-on-demand affect your thinking about a book?	**How do you find out if a book is print-on-demand?**
In the context of your job, if a book is print-on-demand, how does that affect your thinking about it or your treatment of it, if at all?	***In the context of your job, do you know if a book is print-on-demand, and if so, how do you find out?***
Does not really affect my thinking or treatment of it	I am not sure I could tell if something in POD
Would look at it as a space saving or economy measure with convenience for patron	Ask collections librarian for assistance
It depends on the content and how it was put together.	Check with the publisher
I find them difficult and annoying to catalogue. They almost always require original cataloguing or extensive copy cataloguing	I can recognise the publishers by now and they also have a less professional look to them
???	???
It does not at all	I do not think I have been in this situation
How to determine the source, the validity of the author	Only can find out on amazon if you search around
POD manifestations are the reason why field 264 can be so ugly in RDA. POD is also generally a poor quality incarnation of something that is less complicated delivered electronically. Something that needs a reproduction note	In hand the paper quality is awful. There is also a distinct odour to the item. Creately and other POD services are on amazon, the cover art is strange or non-existant. There are a few records in OCLC that identify these publishers
We are told not to order POD to stick with available titles because they are ordered faster	I see in the Gobi ordering form that it is listed as POD
If Purchasing can make a PO with the publisher, it is probably fine	I would hope the publisher site would make that information plain
Cost and personnel are significant issues; equipment needed to print–on-demand; training of librarians to help patrons print-on-demand	Research if not immediately apparent
It is hard to catalogue – requires original OCLC cataloguing	You can easily tell by the publisher name – and by the way it looks
Probably would not consider it	By the publisher
If it is a POD reprint of some classic thing, librarians are often asked to reconsider whether we still want to add it to the collection in favour of a more conventional edition of a title. Self-published POD are more likely to be kept, depending on the subject, but frequently means the title needs original descriptive and subject cataloguing and being assigned a call number by librarian (i.e. copy cataloguer cannot handle alone)	It is often easy to tell once the book is in hand. It apparently can sometimes be difficult to tell from the vendor's website (but I am not in acquisitions, so I do not know what our vendor interface looks like)
I am not sure	I do not know
The books we need, reading list books, are not currently published this way. Payment would be an issue but my boss has a company credit card	The person who orders them sits next to me and I know where each comes from and how

Continued

Type of library (only academic shown here)	Role in library	Words associated with print-on-demand
Questions asked	***What is your job role or department? (i.e. acquisitions, technical services, reference, etc.)***	***What are some words you associate with print-on-demand?***
Academic 2 year college	Acquisitions	Convenient, expensive, questionable
Academic but my library is joint use with a public library system	Reference Librarian	Consumer-driven
Academic consortium office	Technical support	PDF, facsimile, limited run, independent publisher
Academic health sciences library in an academic medical centre	Associate Director but mostly education/instruction	Expensive
Academic library (R1 institution)	Director of publishing	e-Book, digital, Lulu
Academic- community college	Public service	Cost, quality of product, home publishing
Academic-community college	Reference	Expensive, hassle, lower quality
Academic, community college	Access services	Economical, limited audience
Academic, 2 year	Reference, instruction, collection development	Cheesy
Academic/Research Library	Metadata (aka cataloguing)	Variable quality; ecological; innovation
Academic	Librarian and student success coordinator	What is it.
Academic	Acquisitions/cataloguing	Poor quality, cheap

How does print-on-demand affect your thinking about a book?	**How do you find out if a book is print-on-demand?**
In the context of your job, if a book is print-on-demand, how does that affect your thinking about it or your treatment of it, if at all?	***In the context of your job, do you know if a book is print-on-demand, and if so, how do you find out?***
I have been burned a few times. Cheap, fuzzy looking duplication that looked like it had been made on a copy machine in someone's garage. No binding	I see it as part of the record in Gobi, TitleSource, Oasis, etc.
I probably would not be aware the title exists	I have never come across this issue and I select for several collections
I have to be aware that the rules for describing a particular on-demand copy might mean that my description might not exactly match earlier or later on-demand copies, which could lead to union catalogue duplication and questions from cataloguers on how to proceed	In the context of my present job, I do not know that. When I worked in an acquisitions setting, I relied on vendor information, such as from YBP, Amazon, or the publisher's details, to identify on-demand options
I cannot get it because we do not offer it? I do not know much about it. The only thing I know about POD is from when they were available from kiosks. I do not know how they do it nowadays	I suppose I would look on something like GOBI from YBP or in publishers catalogues/websites
it does not have an effect	Most of the time, I know whether a book is print-on-demand because only open access e-books can be freely printed. Any e-books in our collections that have traditional copyright and licensing usually do not allow printing of more than a few pages
I am often leary of these titles unless they are already well established or well-known authors/publishers	Occasionally the vendor may note that it is a print-on-demand title
Tend not to purchase	Usually it will be stated on our vendors site if it is a print-on-demand book
We have never ordered a print-on-demand book at out library	All of the books that we order come through YBP or Amazon. They are more mass market appeal as we are a community college looking for more general resources. We do not order self-published materials either
I am less likely to buy it	It is usually reprints of public domain works, and I Google the publisher.
	Those we have bought have been low quality and not attractive to students. I will often buy a different edition of that book. My concern is quality
Good to know it would not go out of print; does not affect treatment	No—I do not acquire the materials, just describe them
Sounds like a book store publisher rip off	No
Prefer not to purchase	Book description online

Appendix 2

Questionnaire for interviewees

During October 2016 and July 2017, the author asked each of the expert opinion interviewees five questions and they responded either in person, on the phone, or in writing. The responses were then edited and returned to the interviewee for comment with a permission to publish request. Two respondents did not want their organisation names or their names used in the book but were prepared to answer the questions and have the answers published. Several interviews became longer case studies either based on interview or supplemented by the interviewee's contribution. Here is the basic questionnaire.

Questionnaire from Suzanne Wilson-Higgins

What is this book project?

The Book Title: The Impact of Print-on-demand on Academic Books
Author: Suzanne Wilson-Higgins
Subject category: Media Technology
Publisher: Chandos Publishing, an imprint of Elsevier
Expected publication year: 2017
Target market: Publishing & Information Professionals – especially in academia and libraries

Thesis: Looking back over 20 years at the conflation of print-on-demand technology for books, online bookselling to readers and cost-effective small packet logistics, this has positively enabled academic book publishing including the publishing of monographs and access to them. However looking forward, print-on-demand for academic books may only be a transitional media technology to be supplanted in due course by the digital monograph held in digital archives.

How can you assist? I would very much appreciate your expert opinion either to quote explicitly and credit as a case study or to quote anonymously as an industry expert. Please indicate your preference in the permissions of use section below.

Here are the five questions:

Question (1) Looking back over 20 years, what has been your personal experience and/or your organisation's experience in the innovation or application of print-on-demand media technology for the benefit of the academic book, especially the academic monograph?
Question (2) Please state and contrast the most effective/successful application of print-on-demand technology for books by you/your organisation with the least effective/unsuccessful application of print-on-demand technology for book by you/your organisation.

Question (3) In what distinctive or unique applications of print-on-demand technology or on-demand publishing strategies have you or your organisation been engaged? For example 'one-off printing'/delivery of monographs around the world OR offering monographs to library patrons directly through your own portal OR creating a unique repository of books and making them available
Question (4) In your experience, has print-on-demand media technology positively or negatively impacted academic book publishing and academic monograph publishing and in what ways?
Question (5) Looking forward to 2020, what is your prediction regarding the future of the printed-on-demand academic books/monographs versus digital-only academic books/ monographs?

Bibliography

[1] R. Adner, Match your innovation strategy to your innovation ecosystem, Harv. Bus. Rev. 84 (April 2006) 98–101.

[2] R. Adner, The Wide Lens: What Successful Innovators See That Others Miss, Portfolio, 2013. Revised edition June 25, 2013.

[3] R. Anderson, The good, the bad, and the sexy: our espresso book machine experience, The Scholarly Kitchen (2011). August 2, 2011. https://scholarlykitchen.sspnet.org/2011/08/02/the-good-the-bad-and-the-sexy-our-espresso-book-machine-experience/.

[4] Aries Systems, Editorial Manager website accessed August 2017: http://www.ariessys.com/software/editorial-manager/.

[5] AAUP (Association of American University Presses), Annual Statistics 2016, AAUP, New York, 2017.

[6] AAUP (Association of American University Presses), Annual Statistics, 2013 Through 2016, AAUP, New York, 2017.

[7] Association of Research Libraries, Graph 2: monograph and serial costs in ARL libraries, 1986–2000, ARL Statistics (30 July 2002). 1 August 2002 http://www.arl.org/stats/arlstat/graphs/2000t2.html.

[8] C. Anderson, The long tail, Wired Magazine (2004). 1 October 2004. https://www.wired.com/2004/10/tail/.

[9] C. Anderson, The Long Tail, Hyperion, New York, 2006.

[10] M. Anderson, Joint Funding Councils Library Review: Report of the Group on a National/Regional Strategy for Library Provision for Researchers, 1996. http://www.ukoln.ac.uk/services/elib/papers/other/anderson/.

[11] R. Anderson, Is a rational discussion of open access possible? Discussing Open Access (2014). https://discussingoa.wordpress.com/.

[12] R. Anderson, How important are library sales to the university press? One case study, Scholarly Kitchen (2014). https://scholarlykitchen.sspnet.org/2014/06/23/how-important-are-library-sales-to-the-university-press-one-case-study/.

[13] R. Anderson, Library publishing redux: an unprecedented example of a scholar /library/publisher partnership, Scholarly Kitchen (2015). https://scholarlykitchen.sspnet.org/2015/09/15/library-publishing-redux-an-unprecedented-example-of-a-scholarlibrary publisher-partnership/.

[14] M. Armstrong, We're all in this together: supporting the dissemination of university research through library services, in: B. Bernhardt, L.H. Hinds, K.P. Strauch (Eds.), 2011 Charleston Conference Proceedings, Purdue University Press, West Lafayette, IN, 2011.

[15] J. Atkinson, Quality and the Academic Library, Chandos, Amsterdam, 2016.

[16] A. Baverstock, et al., How the role of the independent editor is changing in relation to traditional and self-publishing, Learned Publishing 28 (2015) 2. http://onlinelibrary.wiley.com/doi/10.1087/20150206/full.

[17] Berlin Declaration on Open Access (2003), https://openaccess.mpg.de/Berlin-Declaration.

[18] D. Berze, Independent publishing: the next big thing? Res. Inform. (2016). 13 December 2016 and Independent publishing: breaking the mould? February/March 2017. https://www.researchinformation.info/news/analysis-opinion/independent-publishing-next-big-thing.

[19] Bethesda Statement on Open Access Publishing (2003), http://www.earlham.edu/~peters/fos/bethesda.htm.

[20] M. Bide, How much can improved metadata help sell? Publ. Perspect. (2016). 12 October 2016.

[21] A. Bourke-Waite, Innovations in Scholarly Peer Review at Nature Publishing Group and Palgrave Macmillan, Insight 28 (2015) 2. http://insights.uksg.org/articles/10.1629/uksg.243/.

[22] J.L. Bower, C.M. Christensen, Disruptive technologies: catching the waves, Harv. Bus. Rev. (January–February 1995). https://hbr.org/1995/01/disruptive-technologies-catching-the-wave.

[23] British Academy and Publishers Association, Joint Guidelines on Copyright and Academic Research, 2008. . http://www.gla.ac.uk/media/media_237747_en.pdf.

[24] R. Broekmeulen, K. van Donselaar, et al., Automated store ordering: an enabler for new inventory replenishment strategies in supermarkets, 2004. Report of the Faculteit Technologie Management, Eindhoven, Germany.

[25] Budapest Open Access Initiative, N. Canty, Altmetrics and the humanities, in: The Academic Book of the Future, UCL Press, London, 2002. http://www.budapestopenaccessinitiative.org/.

[26] Buffett, Jimmy and Lee, Amy. Fruitcakes Margaritaville Records/MCA/ MCAD-11043 (U.S.CD).

[27] L. Campbell, Self-published titles '22% of UK e-book market', 2016. March 23, 2016. http://www.thebookseller.com/news/self-published-titles-22-e-book-market-325152.

[28] R. Campbell, E. Pentz, I. Borthwick, Academic and Professional Publishing, Chandos Publishing, Elsevier, Oxford, 2012.

[29] M.M. Case, Principles for emerging systems of scholarly publishing, ARL: A Bimonthly Report 210 (2000) 1–4.

[30] Chodorow, Stanley. "The once and future monograph." Specialized Scholarly Monograph. 11 September 1997, http://www.arl.org/scomm/epub/papers/chodorow.html.

[31] M. Christopher, Logistics & Supply Chain Management, fifth ed., FT Press, London, 2016.

[32] D.J. Closs, A.S. Roath, et al., An empirical comparison of anticipatory and response-based supply chain strategies, Int. J. Logist. Manag. 9 (2) (1998) 21–34.

[33] E. Collins, et al., OAPEN UK Final Report, 2016. http://oapen-uk.jiscebooks.org/files/2016/01/OAPEN-UK-final-report-single-page-view.pdf.

[34] L.Y. Conrad, The Ebook R/evolution – not as easy as it seems, The Scholarly Kitchen (2017). 24 April 2017. https://scholarlykitchen.sspnet.org/2017/04/24/ebook-revolution-not-easy-seems/.

[35] A. Cope, et al., Supplemental materials for 'A study of direct author subvention for publishing humanities books at two universities', 2015. https://scholarworks.iu.edu/dspace/handle/2022/20358.

[36] L. Cox, Scholarly Book Publishing Practice: the ALPSP Survey Findings, 2009. http://www.alpsp.org/write/MediaUploads/SBPP1003FAB_Cox_for_web.pdf.

[37] G. Crossick, Monographs and Open Access: A Report to HEFCE, 2015. http://www.hefce.ac.uk/media/hefce/content/pubs/indirreports/2015/Monographs,and,open,access/2014_monographs.pdf.

[38] D. Crotty, Ask the chefs: "When do we stop printing?", The Scholarly Kitchen (2014). 31 July 2014, https://scholarlykitchen.sspnet.org/2014/07/31/ask-the-chefs-when-do-we-stop-printing/.

[39] R. Crow, A Rational System for Funding Scholarly Monographs, Association of Research Libraries, 2012. http://www.arl.org/storage/documents/publications/aau-arl-white-paper-, rational-system-for-funding-scholarly-monographs-2012.pdf.

[40] R. Crow, Prospectus for an Institutionally-Funded First-Book Subvention, Association of American Universities and Association of Research Libraries, 2014. http://www.arl.org/storage/documents/publications/aau-arl-prospectus-for-institutionally-funded-first-book-subvention-june2014.pdf.

[41] R. Darnton, The state of the libraries, Harv. Mag. (2015). 14 May, 2015, http://harvard-magazine.com/2015/05/state-of-harvard-libraries.

[42] P.J. Daugherty, M.B. Myers, et al., Automatic replenishment programs: an empirical examination, J. Bus. Logist. 20 (2) (1999) 63–72.

[43] M. Deegan, The Academic Book of the Future: A Report to the AHRC and British Library, 2017. London (June 2017), https://academicbookfuture.org/end-of-project-reports-2/.

[44] R.J. Deibert, Parchment, Printing and Hypermedia: Communication in World Order Transformation, Columbia University Press, New York, 1997.

[45] W.T. Dennis, Parcel and Small Package Delivery Industry, CreateSpace, North Charleston, SC, 2011.

[46] P.F. Drucker, Innovation and Entrepreneurship, reissued 1999, Butterworth-Heinemann, Oxford, UK, 1985.

[47] Drupa, Post Show Report, 2016. Dusseldorf, Germany. www.drupa.com.

[48] M. Elliott, The Future of the Monograph in the Digital Era: A Report to the Andrew W. Mellon Foundation, USA: Journal of Electronic Publishing Vol.18 No. 4, University of Michigan Press, Ann Arbor, MI, 2016. https://pid.emory.edu/ark:/25593/q4fd0.

[49] Ekman, Richard. Economics of Scholarly Communication. New Challenges for Scholarly Communication in the Digital Era: Changing Roles and Expectations in the Academic Community. ARL Scholarly Communications, 8 April 1999, http://www.arl.org/scomm/ncsc/ekman.html.

[50] A.E. Ellinger, J.C. Taylor, et al., Automatic replenishment programs and level of involvement: performance implications, Int. J. Logist. Manag. 10 (1) (1999) 25–36.

[51] M. Enis, U. Minnesota Press, CUNY Grad Center Develop Hybrid Publishing Platform, Libr. J. (2015). 18 May 2015, http://lj.libraryjournal.com/2015/05/publishing/u-minnesota-press-cuny-grad-center-develop-hybrid-publishing-platform/.

[52] J. Epstein, Book Business Publishing Past, Present and Future, WW Norton, New York, 2002 edition.

[53] J. Esposito, Having relations with the library: a guide for university presses, The Scholarly Kitchen (2013). https://scholarlykitchen.sspnet.org/2013/07/16/having-relations-with-the-library-a-guide-for-university-presses/.

[54] J. Esposito, How to reduce the cost of college textbooks, The Scholarly Kitchen (2017). 27 March 2017, https://scholarlykitchen.sspnet.org/2017/03/27/reduce-cost-college-textbooks/.

[55] J. Esposito, Monograph Output of American University Presses, 2009-2013: A Report Prepared for the Andrew W. Mellon Foundation, 2017. https://3spxpi1radr22mzge33bla91-wpengine.netdna-ssl.com/wp-content/uploads/2017/02/Monograph-Output-of-University-Presses.pdf.

[56] M. Eve, Some of the Arguments, Counter-Arguments, and Political Alignments for and Against Open Access, 2016. https://www.martineve.com/2016/11/04/arguments-counter-arguments-and-political-alignments-for-and-against-open-access/.

[57] A. Faherty, Academic Book Discovery, Evaluation and Access, Report for Academic Book of the Future Project, 2016. https://academicbookfuture.org/academic-book-discovery-report/.

[58] Faherty, Robert L. Response to Richard Ekman. New Challenges for Scholarly Communication in the Digital Era: Changing Roles and Expectations in the Academic Community, ARL Scholarly Communications. 17 May 1999. http://www.arl.org/scomm/ncsc/faherty.html.

[59] H.M. Fenton, F.J. Romano, On-Demand Printing; The Revolution in Digital and Customized Printing, second ed., Graphic Arts Technical Foundation (GAFT), Pittsburg, PA, 1997.

[60] H.M. Fenton, F.J. Romano, On-Demand Printing; The Revolution in Digital and Customized Printing, second ed., Graphic Arts Technical Foundation (GAFT), Prentice Hall, Upper Saddle River, NJ, 1998.

[61] E. Ferwerda, et al., A Project Exploring Open-Access Monographs in the Netherlands: Final Report, OAPEN-NL, 2013. http://www.oapen.org/download?type=export&export=oapen-nl-final-report.

[62] S. Kavanagh, ALPSP Blog covering a talk by Richard Fidczuk, 2013. http://blog.alpsp.org/2013/06/outsourcing-good-bad-and-ugly-richard.html.

[63] J. Finch, Accessibility, Sustainability, Excellence: How to Expand Access to Research Publications, 2012. https://www.acu.ac.uk/research-information-network/finch-report-final.

[64] R. Fisher, in: Academic books of the future: something misunderstood, Panel Presentation, Futurebook Conference, London, 2015. https://academicbookfuture.files.wordpress.com/2016/08/richard_fisher.pdf.

[65] R. Fisher, The monograph: keep on keeping on, part one, Scholarly Kitchen (2015). 10 November 2015, https://scholarlykitchen.sspnet.org/2015/11/10/guest-post-richard-fisher-on-the-monograph-keep-on-keepin-on-part-one/.

[66] R. Fisher, M. Jubb, Discoverability, Demand and Access: The Role of Intermediaries in the UK Supply Chain for Academic Books, Academic Book of the Future, London, 2016. https://academicbookfuture.org/discoverability-demand-and-access-the-role-of-intermediaries-in-the-uk-supply-chain-for-academic-books-richard-fisher-and-michael-jubb/.

[67] K. Fitzpatrick, Planned Obsolescence: Publishing, Technology, and the Future of the Academy, NYU Press, New York, 2011.

[68] Franklin, D (2015) An Earthquake in the Petrified Forest: How Digital Publishing is Evolving in the Book Industry, talk at the Royal College of Art, 23 November 2015. https://medium.com/digital-matters/an-earthquake-in-the-petrified-forest-86f6ffa5c85d.

[69] Fogra in Brief 2017, Fogra, Munich, 2017. www.forgra.org.

[70] Fogra Digital Printing Handbook from 2014.

[71] Fogra News 48, Fogra, Munich, June 2017. www.forgra.org.

[72] Fogra Annual Report 2015, Fogra, Munich, June 2016. www.forgra.org.

[73] E. Gadd, UK "University policy approaches towards the copyright ownership of scholarly works and the future of open access", Aslib J. Inform. Manage. 69 (Jan 2017) 95–114.

[74] R. Gatti, Introducing Some Data to the Open Access Debate: OBP's Business Model (Part One), Open Book Publishers Blog, 2015. 15 October 2015, http://blogs.openbookpublishers.com/introducing-some-data-to-the-open-access-debate-obps-business-model-part-one/.

[75] M.K. Gold, The Digital Humanities Moment, 2012. http://dhdebates.gc.cuny.edu/debates/1.

[76] S. Goldsworthy, The Future of Scholarly Publishing, OUP Blog, 2015. 10 November 2015, http://blog.oup.com/2015/11/future-scholarly-publishing/.

[77] Gomez, Print is Dead: Books in Our Digital Age, Macmillan, London, 2008.

[78] A.N. Greco, The general reader market for university press books in the United States, 1990–99, with projections for the years 2000 through 2004, J. Sch. Publ. 32 (2) (2001) 61–86.

[79] A.N. Greco, et al., The Culture and Commerce of Publishing in the 21st Century, Stanford Business Books, Stanford, CA, 2007.

[80] Greco, Albert N. et al. (2014), The Book Publishing Industry, third ed. New York, Routledge.
[81] A.N. Greco, et al., University presses in the twenty-first century: the potential impact of big data and predictive analytics on scholarly book marketing, J. Sch. Publ. 46 (2) (2015). http://www.utpjournals.press/doi/full/10.3138/jsp.46.2.01.
[82] S. Greenberg, et al., Creative writing and open access. The Bookseller blog, 2016. 11 November 2016, http://www.thebookseller.com/blogs/creative-writing-and-open-access-, 429851.
[83] R. Guthrie, Publishing Principles and Practice, Sage, London, 2011.
[84] F. Hall, G. Harper, The changing role of the editor: editors past, present and future, in: A Companion to Creative Writing, Wiley Online Library, 2013.
[85] M.H. Hugos, Essentials of Supply Chain Management, third ed., John Wiley & Sons, Hoboken, NJ, 2001.
[86] Humanities and Arts on the Information Highways. Project report. Getty Art History Information Program, Coalition for Networked Information, and American Council of Learned Societies. September 1994. http://www.cni.org/projects/humartiway/humartiway.html.
[87] R.S. Humphreys, Why do we write stuff that even our colleagues don't want to read? Specialized Scholarly Monograph (11 September 1997). http://www.arl.org/scomm/epub/papers/humphreys.html.
[88] J. Hammersley, J. Lees-Miller, H. Oswald, J. Allen, Exciting News – ShareLaTeX is joining Overleaf, 2017. Overleaf website. August 2017. https://www.overleaf.com/blog/518-exciting-news-sharelatex-is-joining-overleaf#.WZtBVq2ZOFg.
[89] Hansell, Saul, (1998) "Amazon.com Is Expanding Beyond Books". The New York Times. 5 August 1998. (Retrieved 10 January 2016).
[90] Hargreaves, I (2011), Digital Opportunity: a Review of Intellectual Property and Growth, http://webarchive.nationalarchives.gov.uk/20140603093549/http://www.ipo.gov.uk/ipreview.html.
[91] Hastings, Max (2016), The UK—Edging Ever Closer to Open Access to Research Publications, Universities UK, http://www.universitiesuk.ac.uk/blog/Pages/the-uk-edging-ever-closer-to-open-access-to-research-publications.aspx.
[92] H.T. Keh, Evolution of the book publishing industry: structural changes and strategic implications, J. Manag. Hist. 4 (2) (1998) 104–123. https://doi.org/10.1108/13552529810219593.
[93] Higher Education Funding Council for England, Open Access Research: Policy Guide, 2015 and updated. http://www.hefce.ac.uk/rsrch/oa/Policy/.
[94] S. Hill, Making the future of scholarly communications, Learned Publishing 29 (2016) S1. http://onlinelibrary.wiley.com/doi/10.1002/leap.1052/full.
[95] Hilton, J et al. (2015), A Study of Direct Author Subvention for Publishing Humanities Books at Two Universities: A Report to the Andrew W. Mellon Foundation by Indiana University and University of Michigan, https://deepblue.lib.umich.edu/handle/2027.42/113671.
[96] Hole, B (2016), New Models for Open Access Monograph Funding: Presentation to Books, Libraries and Open Access Seminar, Helsinki, August 2016, http://www.slideshare.net/brianhole/new-models-for-open-access-monograph-funding.
[97] The Internet Bookshop (Oxford) Limited, (1998) Full accounts made up to 31 December 1997. Companies House, UK. 1998-11-23. [(Retrieved 17 July 2015)].
[98] Jisc, Investigating OA Monograph Services: Final Report, 2016. https://www.jisc-collections.ac.uk/Global/Investigating%20OA%20Monograph%20Services/Jisc-OAPEN%20pilot%20Final%20report.pdf.

[99] Jisc and OAPEN, Report of 'Green OA for Books', 2016. https://www.jisc-collections.ac.uk/Global/Investigating%20OA%20Monograph%20Services/Jisc-OAPEN%20green%20OA%20for%20books%20report.pdf.

[100] Jisc (2016), Digital Access to Monographs: Call for Participation, https://monographs.jiscinvolve.org/wp/files/2015/11/digital_access_to_monographs_CFP.pdf.

[101] Jisc (2016), Monograph Solutions: Working on Bibliographic Data and Digital Access to Books, https://monographs.jiscinvolve.org/wp/.

[102] K. Johansson, P. Lundberg, R. Ryberg, A Guide to Graphic Print Production, third ed., John Wiley & Sons, Hoboken, NJ, 2011.

[103] Jones, A (2015), OAPEN-UK: 5 Things We Learnt About Open Access Monographs, http://blog.oup.com/2015/11/oapen-uk-open-access-monographs/.

[104] J.S.T.O.R. Labs, Reimagining the Digital Monograph: Design Thinking to Build New Tools for Researchers, 2017. A JSTOR Labs Report. http://labs.jstor.org/monograph/.

[105] Jubb, Michael. (2017) Academic Books and Their Futures (June, 2017): A Report to the AHRC and British Library, London (June 2017), https://academicbookfuture.org/end-of-project-reports-2/.

[106] M. Jubb, Peer Review: the Current Landscape and Future Trends, Learned Publishing 29 (2016) 13–21. http://onlinelibrary.wiley.com/doi/10.1002/leap.1008/full.

[107] Kahn, M et al. (2015), Supplemental Materials for 'A Study of Direct Author Subvention for Publishing Humanities Books at Two Universities,' https://deepblue.lib.umich.edu/handle/2027.42/113093.

[108] C. Kamposiori, Five librarians discuss the future of the academic book, Brit. Acad. Rev. 29 (2017). http://www.britac.ac.uk/node/5491/.

[109] M. Karatas, et al., #AcBookWeek: The Manchester Great Debate, 2016. https://academicbookfuture.org/2015/11/26/manchester-great-debate/.

[110] W.E. Kasdorf, The Columbia Guide to Digital Publishing, Columbia University Press, New York, NY, 2013.

[111] J. Kay, Clearing a path through the copyright jungle, Brit. Acad. Rev. 11 (2008). http://www.britac.ac.uk/sites/default/files/15-kay.pdf.

[112] KBA Media Release April 20, 2010 KBA Commander CT for market leader in mono book printing: CPI group in France opts for innovative KBA technology. Website (Accessed 22 August 2017), http://www2.kba.com/gb/news/detail/article/cpi-group-in-france-opts-for-innovative-kba-technology/.

[113] C. Keene, et al., in: The rise of the new university press: the current landscape and future directions, Paper Presented at LIBER Conference, June 2016, 2016. http://eprints.hud.ac.uk/28989.

[114] M.L. Kelper, The Handbook of Digital Publishing Volume II: The Definitive Guide to Digital Publishing, Prentice Hall, Princeton, NJ, 2001.

[115] Kitchen, S (2016) The Academic Book in the South: Conference Report. https://academicbookfuture.files.wordpress.com/2016/06/the-academic-book-in-the-south-conference-report-180416-md_sk_final.pdf.

[116] Knight Higher Education Collaborative, Op. Cit, Policy Perspect. 10 (3) (2001) 1–11.

[117] C. Lehmann, Commercial presses: burning down the house, Lingua Franca (September 1997) 48–52.

[118] M. Knöchelmann, Open Access Book Publishing and the Prisoner's Dilemma: A Theoretical Approach to a Description of the Slow Scalability of Open Access Book Publishing, forthcoming, UCL Press, London, 2016.

[119] LaTeX, Wikipedia online, August 2017. https://en.wikipedia.org/wiki/LaTeX.

[120] R. Lewis, Musical Scholarship and the Future of Academic Publishing, 2016. Blog Post, 16 May 2016. https://academicbookfuture.org/2016/05/16/musical-scholarship-and-the-future-of-academic-publishing/.
[121] Library Journal, Ebook Usage in US Academic Libraries 2016, 2016. http://lj.libraryjournal.com/downloads/2016academicebooksurvey.
[122] S. Lippincott, Library Publishing Directory, Library Publishing Coalition, 2016.
[123] LISU (2015), Public and Academic Library Statistics, http://www.lboro.ac.uk/micro-sites/infosci/lisu/lisu-statistics/expenditure.xls.
[124] Litwin, Rory, "Librarians' knowledge and attitudes about print-on-demand: an informal study" Library Juice: On the Intersection of Libraries, Politics and Culture, 11 March 2017, https://libraryjuicepress.com/blog/?p=5498.
[125] A. Lockett, et al., New university presses in the UK: accessing a mission, Learned Publishing 29 (1) (2016).
[126] C. Lynch, The Battle to Define the Future of the Book in the Digital World, 13 May 2001. http://www.firstmonday.dk/issues/issue6_6/lynch/index.html.
[127] C. Malpas, L. Brian, Strength in Numbers: The Research Libraries UK (RLUK) Collective Collection, OCLC Research, Dublin, OH, 2016.
[128] C. Marden, in: Open Access and the Wellcome Trust, University Press Redux Conference 17, March 2016, 2016. https://cdn.shopify.com/s/files/1/0791/4263/files/Marden.pptx?17890079848606959522.
[129] N. Maron, et al., The Costs of Publishing Monographs: Toward a Transparent Methodology, Ihaka S+R, 2016. https://doi.org/10.18665/sr.276785.
[130] J. Maxwell, et al., Reassembling scholarly communications: an evaluation of the Andrew W Mellon Foundation's monograph initiative, J. Electron. Publ. 20 (2017).
[131] H. McGuire, B. O'Leary, Book: A Futurist's Manifesto: A Collection of Essays From the Bleeding Edge of Publishing, O'Reilly Media, Boston, MA, 2012.
[132] The McGraw-Hill Companies, Annual Report 2005. Originally Retrieved 15 January 2006, from: http://www.mcgraw-hill.com; Now stored at: http://www.annualreports.co.uk/HostedData/AnnualReportArchive/t/NYSE_MHP_2005.pdf.
[133] The McGraw-Hill Companies, Inc., Annual Report 2004 Originally Retrieved 8 February 2006, from McGraw-Hill 2004 Annual Report Web site from: http://www.mcgraw-hill.com.
[134] McGraw-Hill Create website accessed 22 August 2017: http://create.mheducation.com/createonline/index.html.
[135] J. Milliot, As E-book sales decline, digital fatigue grows, Publishers Weekly (2016). http://www.publishersweekly.com/pw/by-topic/digital/retailing/article/70696-as-e-book-sales-decline-digital-fatigue-grows.html.
[136] Milloy, C et al. (2016) Investigating OA monograph services: Final report Jisc and OAPEN, https://www.jisc-collections.ac.uk/Global/Investigating%20OA%20Monograph%20Services/Jisc-OAPEN%20pilot%20Final%20report.pdf.
[137] M.B. Myers, P.J. Daugherty, et al., The effectiveness of automatic inventory replenishment in supply chain operations: antecedents and outcomes, J. Retail. 76 (4) (2000) 455–481.
[138] K. Nedo, What's driving the surge in art books? Artnet News (2016). 4 November 2016, https://news.artnet.com/opinion/whats-driving-the-surge-in-art-book-publications-732641.
[139] H. Newton, et al., Experiment in Open Peer Review for Books Suggests Increased Fairness and Transparency in Feedback Process, 2014. LSE Impact blog, 28 February 2014, http://blogs.lse.ac.uk/impactofsocialsciences/2014/02/28/palgrave-macmillan-open-peer-review-for-book-proposals/.
[140] S. Nias, CPI co-founder Bovard in surprise departure from company, Print Week (2008). 9 October 2008.

[141] Nielsen (2016) Nielsen Book Research: 2015 in Review https://quantum.londonbookfair.co.uk/RXUK/RXUK_PDMC/documents/9928_Nielsen_Book_Research_In_Review_2015_The_London_Book_Fair_Quantum_Conference_2016_DIGITAL_FINAL.pdf?v=635995987941118341.

[142] Nielsen (2016), Students' Information Sources in the Digital World 2015/16. OAPEN UK (2014), Researcher Survey 2014, http://oapen-uk.jiscebooks.org/research-findings/researcher-survey-2014/.

[143] A. Okerson, With Feathers: Effects of Ownership on Scholarly Publishing, September 1991. http://www.library.yale.edu/~okerson/feathers.html.

[144] Okerson, Ann and A Holzman (2015), The Once and Future Publishing Library, Council on Library and Information Resources, https://www.clir.org/pubs/reports/pub166.

[145] Open Book Publishers (n.d.), Author's Guide, https://www.openbookpublishers.com/shopimages/resources/OBP%20Authors'%20Guide.pdf.

[146] R. Osborne, Open access publishing, academic research and scholarly communication, Online Inf. Rev. 39 (2015) 637–648. https://doi.org/10.1108/OIR-03-2015-0083.

[147] Pearson Revel website accessed 22 August 2017, http://www.pearsoned.com/pearson-community/revel/.

[148] A. Perrin, Book Reading 2016, Pew Research Center, 2016.

[149] F. Pinter, The academic 'book' of the future and its function, in: R. Lyons, S. Rayner (Eds.), The Academic Book of the Future, Palgrave, London, 2015.

[150] F. Pinter, Open access for scholarly books? Publ. Res. Q. 28 (2012) 183. Springer Science+Business Media. https://doi.org/10.1007/s12109-012-9285-0.

[151] P. Pochoda. Universities Press On. Nation 29 December 1997. Dept. of English. Brock U. 1 Aug. 2002, http://www.brocku.ca/english/courses/4F70/univpresses.html.

[152] R. Pool, A monograph for tomorrow, Res. Inform. (2017). August/September 2017, Cambridge, UK. https://www.researchinformation.info/feature/monograph-tomorrow.

[153] A. Prescott, Are we doomed to a world of PDFs? Digital Riffs (2015). 22 November 2015, https://medium.com/digital-riffs/are-we-doomed-to-a-word-of-pdfs-11f57edaf926#.cr3rl1s4x.

[154] Primis website for Mechanical Engineering Design, seventh ed., 2004 (Accessed 22 August 2017), http://highered.mheducation.com/sites/0072520361/information_center_view0/primis_online.html.

[155] The Publishers' Association, Statistical Yearbook 2015, The Publishers' Association, London, 2016.

[156] Publishers Communication Group, Increasing the Value of Scholarly Books, 2016. http://www.pcgplus.com/wp-content/uploads/2016/11/Increasing-the-value-of-scholarly-books.pdf.

[157] K. Reeve, The Role of the Editor: Publisher Perspectives, UCL Press, London, 2015.

[158] F.J. Romano, H. Fenton, On-Demand Printing: The Revolution in Digital and Customized Printing (Graphic Arts Technical Foundation), GATF Press, Pennsylvania, 1998.

[159] F.J. Romano, The Typencyclopedia, R.R. Bowker Company, New York, 1984.

[160] F.J. Romano, Digital Media Publishing Technologies for the 21st Century, Micro Publishing Press, Torrance, CA, 1996.

[161] F.J. Romano (Ed.), Delmar's Dictionary of Digital Printing & Publishing, Delmar Publishers, Albany, NY, 1997.

[162] F.J. Romano, M.B. Cary, Pocket Guide to Digital Pre-Press, Delmar Cengage Learning, New York, 1995.

[163] F.J. Romano, Digital Printing Pocket Primer: Mastering On-Demand and Variable Data Printing for Profit, Windsor Professional Information, San Diego, CA, 2000.

[164] R.M. Romano, F.J. Romano, The GATF Encyclopedia of Graphic Communications, GATF Press, Pennsylvania, 1998.

[165] M. Rosenthal, Print On Demand Book Publishing: A New Approach to Printing and Marketing Books for Publishers and Authors, Foner Books, New York, 2004.

[166] Ruark, Jennifer K. "University presses suffer bleak financial year." Top Education News. U of Houston. 12 July 2001. 1 August 2002, http://www.uh.edu/admin/media/topstories/chron_712b.html.

[167] A. Schiffrin, Payback Time: University Presses as Profit Centers, Chron. High. Educ. 18 (June 1999) B4.

[168] Scholarly Editions in Jeopardy. Editorial, New York Times (21 October 2000) A28.

[169] A. Shepard, Aiming at Amazon: The NEW Business of Self Publishing, or A Successful Self Publisher's Secrets of How to Publish Books for Profit with Print on Demand and Book Marketing on Amazon.com, Shepard Publications, New York, 2006.

[170] A. Shepard, POD for Profit: More on the NEW Business of Self Publishing, or How to Publish Your Books With Online Book Marketing and Print on Demand by Lightning Source, Shepard Publications, New York, 2010.

[171] Shifflett, Crandall. "Scholarly Exchange: Electronic Publication and Scholarship in the Humanities." Address. Virginia Polytechnic Inst. and State Univ. 23 February. 1998, http://www.rgs.vt.edu/resmag/Randy.html.

[172] R.M. Solow, F. Oakley, P. Franklin, J. D'Arms, C. Jones, Making the Humanities Count: The Importance of Data, Amer. Acad. of Arts and Sciences, Cambridge, 2002.

[173] The Specialized Scholarly Monograph in Crisis; or, How Can I Get Tenure If You Won't Publish My Book? Conf. sponsored by the Amer. Council of Learned Societies, the Assn. of Amer. Univ. Presses, and the Assn. of Research Libraries. Washington, DC. 11–12 September 1997. 11 September 1997, http://www.arl.org/scomm/epub/papers/index.html.

[174] T. Sullivan, The future of the genre, Specialized Scholarly Monograph (12 September 1997). http://www.arl.org/scomm/epub/papers/sullivan.html.

[175] Summerfield, Mary, Carol Mandel, and Paul Kantor. The Potential of Online Books in the Scholarly World. Online Books Project. Columbia U. December 1999. 1 Augugust 2002, http://www.columbia.edu/cu/libraries/digital/texts/about.html.

[176] Schonfeld, R (2015a) Meeting Researchers Where They Start: Streamlining Access to Scholarly Resources, Ithaka S + R, http://www.sr.ithaka.org/publications/meetingresearchers-where-they-start-streamlining-access-toscholarly-resources.

[177] R.Schonfeld,Dismantlingthestumblingblocksthatimpederesearcheraccesstoe-resources, Scholarly Kitchen (2015). 13 November, http://scholarlykitchen.sspnet.org/2015/11/13/dismantling-the-stumbling-blocksthat-impede-researcher-access-to-e-resources/.

[178] R. Schonfeld, Grab and go and the gravitational pull of discovery, Scholarly Kitchen (2015). 14 May, http://scholarlykitchen.sspnet.org/2015/05/14/grab-andgo/.

[179] R. Schonfeld, Open Ebooks coming to Project MUSE: an interview with Wendy Queen, Scholarly Kitchen (2016). https://scholarlykitchen.sspnet.org/2016/08/11/open-ebooks-coming-to-project-muse-an-interview-with-wendy-queen/.

[180] R.C. Schoenfeld, Will the monograph experience a transition to E-only? The Scholarly Kitchen (2016). April 4, 2016, https://scholarlykitchen.sspnet.org/2016/04/04/an-e-only-monograph/.

[181] SCONUL, 2015, SCONUL Annual Statistics 2013–14. SCONUL, 2016, SCONUL Annual Statistics 2014–15.

[182] A. Shaw, Vision, mission, passion and luck: the creation of a university press, Learned Publishing 29 (1) (2016). http://onlinelibrary.wiley.com/doi/10.1002/leap.1051/full.

[183] Shullaw, M (2016) "What's the Point of the Academic Book? Part Two: Mari Shullaw" https://academicbookfuture.org/2016/01/26/the-point-of-the-academic-book-part-two/.

[184] Simba Information, in: Simba (Eds.), Global Social Science and Humanities Publishing 2013-2014, 2014. Open Access Book Publishing 2016-2020, 2016. http://www.simbainformation.com/about/release.asp?id=4026#.WCcWflrhLjQ.twitter.

[185] SmithersPira, Growth in Digital Printing to Remain Strong Until 2024, in: The Future of Digital Printing to 2024, SmithersPira, Surrey, UK, 2014. www.smitherspira.com/news/2014/april/digital-printing-to-remain-strong-until-2024.

[186] Speicher, Lara. Open Access Monographs: Current UK University Press Landscape, https://www.interscriptjournal.com/online-magazine/open-access-monographs.

[187] Springer Nature website accessed 22 August 2017. MyCopy printed ebooks service. http://www.springernature.com/gp/librarians/products/product-types/books/my-copy.

[188] Springer Nature website accessed 22 August 2017. Ebook Collection Overview. http://www.springernature.com/gp/librarians/products/product-types/books/ebook-collect?countryChanged=true.

[189] Stack Exchange Inc., TeX and LaTeX entries (July 2017). https://tex.stackexchange.com.

[190] C. Straumsheim, Pressing Challenges: Amid Declining Book Sales, University Presses Search for New Ways to Measure Success, 2016. Inside Higher Ed, 1 August 2016, https://www.insidehighered.com/news/2016/08/01/amid-declining-book-sales-university-presses-search-new-ways-measure-success.

[191] B. Stone, The Everything Store: Jeff Bezos and the Age of Amazon, Little Brown and Co., New York, 2013.

[192] P. Suber, Open Access, MIT Press, Boston, MA, 2012.

[193] K. Sutherland, How should we read a monograph? Brit. Acad. Rev. 29 (2017). January 2017, http://www.britac.ac.uk/node/5490/.

[194] S. Tanner, An Analysis of the Arts and Humanities Submitted Research Outputs to the REF2014 with a Focus on Academic Books: An Academic Book of the Future Report, King's College London, 2016. November 2016, http://doi.org/http://dx.doi.org/10.18742/RDM01-76.

[195] TeX, Wikipedia online, August 2017. https://en.wikipedia.org/wiki/TeX.

[196] J.B. Thompson, Merchants of Culture: The Publishing Business in the Twenty First Century, first ed., Polity Press, Cambridge, UK, 2010.

[197] J.B. Thompson, Merchants of Culture: The Publishing Business in the Twenty First Century, second ed., Polity Press, Cambridge, UK, 2012.

[198] J.B. Thompson, Books in the Digital Age: The Transformation of Academic and Higher Education Publishing in Britain and the United States, Polity Press, Cambridge, 2005.

[199] C. Tenopir, R. Volentine, D.W. King, Article and book reading patterns of scholars: findings for publishers, Learned Publishing 25 (4) (2012) 279–291. http://libvalue.cci.utk.edu/content/article-and-book-reading-patterns-scholars-findings-publishers.

[200] S.G. Thatcher, Thinking systematically about the crisis in scholarly communication, Specialized Scholarly Monograph (11 September 1997). https://www.arl.org/scomm/epub/papers/thatcher.htm.

[201] X. Tian, B. Martin, Business models in digital book publishing: some insights from Australia, Publ. Res. Q. 25 (2) (1 June 2009) 73–88.

[202] United States Court of Appeals for the Federal Circuit 05-1074, -1075, -1100 On Demand Machine Corporation, Plaintiff-Cross Appellant, v.Ingram Industries, Inc. and Lightning Source, Inc., Defendants-Appellants, and Amazon.com, Inc., Defendant-Appellant. http://www.finnegan.com/files/Publication/67c79514-405d-4a6a-8aff-ff646d2f2ad9/Presentation/PublicationAttachment/f54c42f8-8c01-411e-a28f-0025992db7c3/05-1074%203-31-06.pdf.

[203] N. Venkatraman, J. Strock, Part 1: From Mass Production to Mass Customization: The Origins of Primis, Boston University Management School, Boston, MA, 2012. http://smg.bu.edu/exec/elc/documents/Primis%20PLI%20(2).pdf.

[204] C. Walters, J. Hilton, A Study of Direct Author Subvention for Publishing Humanities Books at Two Universities, 2015. https://deepblue.lib.umich.edu/bitstream/handle/2027.42/113671/IU%20Michigan%20White%20Paper%2009-15-2015.pdf.

[205] M. Wasserman, How much does it cost to publish a monograph and why? Specialized Scholarly Monograph (11 September 1997). http://www.arl.org/scomm/epub/papers/wasserman.html.

[206] L. Waters, Are university presses producing too many series for their own good? Chron. High. Educ. 27 (October 2000) B7–B9.

[207] Watkinson, A (2016), The Academic Book in North America, https://academicbookfuture.org/academic-book-north-america-watkinson/.

[208] C. Watkinson, Why marriage matters: a North American perspective on press/library partnerships, Learned Publishing 29 (1) (2016). https://cdn.shopify.com/s/files/1/0791/4263/files/UP_Redux_Watkinson_031616.pptx?17890079848606959522.

[209] C. Watkinson, C. Murray-Rust, D. Nesdill, A. Mower, in: B. Bernhardt, L.H. Hinds, K.P. Strauch (Eds.), Library publishing services: strategies for success, 2011 Charleston Conference Proceedings, Purdue University Press, West Lafayette, IN, 2011.

[210] B. Webster, S. Bogas, How to Self-Publish Your Book the CreateSpace Way: A Step-by-Step Guide To Writing, Printing and Selling Your Own Book Using Print On Demand, CreateSpace, Charleston, SC, 2010.

[211] Wikipedia, Adobe Systems website accessed August 2017: https://en.wikipedia.org/wiki/Adobe_Systems.

[212] P. Williams, I. Stevenson, D. Nicholas, A. Watkinson, I. Rowlands, The role and future of the monograph in arts and humanities research, ASLIB Proc. 61 (2009) 67.

[213] WIPO (n.d.) Managing Intellectual Property in the Book Publishing Industry: A business-oriented Information Booklet, http://www.wipo.int/edocs/pubdocs/en/copyright/868/wipo_pub_868.pdf.

[214] WIPO (2017), Standing Committee on Copyright and Related Rights, http://www.wipo.int/policy/en/sccr/.

[215] L. Withey, et al., Sustaining Scholarly Publishing: New Business Models for University Presses, Association of American University Presses, New York, NY, 2011.

[216] Wolff, Christine, Rod, Alisa B., Schonfeld, Roger C. (2016) Ithaka S+R, Jisc, RLUK UK Survey of Academics 2015 (15 June 2016) ITHAKA. http://dx.doi.org/10.18665/sr.277685.

[217] Wycliffe Associates website accessed 22 August 2017: Resources Print-on-demand, https://resources.wycliffeassociates.org/translation-tools/print-on-demand-pod/.

[218] Wycliffe Associates website accessed 22 August 2017, Donate: Three Letters that are Revolutionizing Bible Translation - POD. https://give.wycliffeassociates.org/p-1472-print-on-demand.aspx.

[219] Academic Book of the Future, About the Project, 2017. Available from: https://academicbookfuture.org/about-the-project/ (accessed August 22, 2017).

[220] The Economist, A fable concerning ambition Would Britain's leading on-line bookseller have done better in the United States?, June 19, 1997. Available from: http://www.economist.com/node/597845.

[221] L. Waters, A modest proposal for preventing the books of the members of the MLA from being a burden to their authors, publishers, or audiences, PMLA 115 3 (2000) 315–317.

[222] L. Waters, Rescue tenure from the tyranny of the monograph, Chron. High. Educ. 20 (2001) B7.

[223] C.A. Lynch, The scholarly monograph's descendants, Specialized Scholarly Monograph, September 12, 1997. Available from: http://www.arl.org/scomm/epub/papers/cliff.html.

[224] P. Givler, Scholarly books, the coin of the realm of knowledge, Chron. High. Educ. 12 (1999) A76.

[225] S. Wilson-Higgins, Interview with publishing services provider based in Chennai, India, (2017).

[226] Research Information, "A Broken Model" interview with Nigel Lee, Glass Tree Academic Publishing, July 2017, Available from: https://www.researchinformation/info/interview/broken-model.

[227] Ingram, Case Study of Lightning Source Inc. and John Wiley & Sons, Ingram Book Company, La Vergne, TN, 2009. Available from: http://www.stm-assoc.org/2009_12_03_Eproduction_Lightning_Source_Wiley_%20Case_Study.pdf.

[228] Lightning Source Inc., Media release, Ingram Book Company, La Vergne, TN, April 2008.

[229] John Wiley & Sons, Annual Report (2015), Available from: http://www.wiley.com/legacy/about/corpnews/fy15_10kFINAL.pdf.

[230] John Wiley & Sons, Annual Report 2016, 2016. Available from: http://www.wiley.com/legacy/about/corpnews/FY16-10K.pdf.

[231] The McGraw-Hill Companies, Global Market Information Database, in: The Market for Books and Publishing. Company Profile, May 1, 2004. Available from: http://www.gmid.euromonitor.com/Tree.aspx (retrieved February 4, 2006).

[232] M. McMahon, Elsevier Provides Textbooks, Research Information, October 23, 2013. Available from: https://www.researchinformation.info/news/elsevier-provides-textbooks-five-edx-moocs.

[233] C. Lambert, The 'Wild West' of Academic Publishing: The troubled present and promising future of scholarly communication, Harv. Mag. (2015). January–February 2015, http://harvardmagazine.com/2015/01/the-wild-west-of-academic-publishing.

References

[1] R. Litwin, Librarians' knowledge and attitudes about print-on-demand: an informal study, Library Juice: On the Intersection of Libraries, Politics and Culture (March 11, 2017). https://libraryjuicepress.com/blog/?p=5498. (see Appendix 1).

[2] M. Deegan, The Academic Book of the Future: A Report to the AHRC and British Library, Litwin Press, London, 2017. p. 30.

[3] J.B. Thompson, Books in the Digital Age, Polity Press, Cambridge, UK, 2005. p. 405.

[4] P.F. Drucker, Innovation and Entrepreneurship, reissued 1999, Butterworth-Heinemann, Oxford, UK, 1985. pp. 135–138.

[5] J.L. Bower, C.M. Christensen, Disruptive technologies: catching the waves, Harv. Bus. Rev. (January 1995). https://hbr.org/1995/01/disruptive-technologies-catching-the-wave.

[6] R. Adner, Match your innovation strategy to your innovation ecosystem, Harv. Bus. Rev. (April 2006). https://hbr.org/2006/04/match-your-innovation-strategy-to-your-innovation-ecosystem.

[7] Definition of prepress, n. Oxford English Dictionary Online. Oxford University Press, Oxford, UK, June 2017. Web. August 11, 2017.

[8] M. Kelper, The Handbook of Digital Publishing Volume II, Prentice Hall, Princeton, NJ, 2001. pp. 564.

[9] F.J. Romano, M.B. Cary, Pocket Guide to Digital Pre-Press, Delmar Cengage Learning, New York, 1995.

[10] TeX, Wikipedia online, August 2017. https://en.wikipedia.org/wiki/TeX.

[11] LaTeX, Wikipedia online August 2017. https://en.wikipedia.org/wiki/LaTeX. For more information about TeX and LaTeX see https://tex.stackexchange.com.

[12] J. Hammersley, J. Lees-Miller, H. Oswald, J. Allen, Exciting News—ShareLaTeX is joining Overleaf, 2017. Overleaf website. August 2017. https://www.overleaf.com/blog/518-exciting-news-sharelatex-is-joining-overleaf#.WZtBVq2ZOFg.

[13] Wikipedia, Adobe Systems website accessed August 2017: https://en.wikipedia.org/wiki/Adobe_Systems.

[14] Aries/Editorial Manager website accessed August 2017: http://www.ariessys.com/software/editorial-manager/.

[15] May 2016 Author Earnings Report: the definitive million-title study of US author earnings; http://authorearnings.com/report/may-2016-report/.

[16] L. Campbell, Self-Published Titles '22% of UK e-Book Market', 2016. March 23, 2016. http://www.thebookseller.com/news/self-published-titles-22-e-book-market-325152.

[17] United States Court of Appeals for the Federal Circuit. 05-1074, - 1075, - 1100 On Demand Machine Corporation, Plaintiff-Cross Appellant, v.Ingram Industries, Inc. and Lightning Source, Inc., Defendants-Appellants, and Amazon.com, Inc., Defendant-Appellant, p. 5. http://www.finnegan.com/files/Publication/67c79514-405d-4a6a-8aff-ff646d2f2ad9/Presentation/PublicationAttachment/f54c42f8-8c01-411e-a28f-0025992db7c3/05-1074%203-31-06.pdf.

[18] M. Kelper, The Handbook of Digital Publishing Volume II, Prentice Hall, Princeton, NJ, 2001.

[19] M. Kelper, On-Demand Publishing Technology, in: The Handbook of Digital Publishing Volume II, Prentice Hall, Princeton, NJ, 2001. (Chapter 24).

[20] J.B. Thompson, Books in the Digital Age, Polity Press, Cambridge, UK, 2005. pp. 422–425.

[21] J.B. Thompson, Books in the Digital Age, Polity Press, Cambridge, UK, 2005. pp. 426–27.

[22] (2017) Interview with publishing services provider based in Chennai, India.

[23] Process Standard Digital Handbook 2016, Step by Step Toward Printing the Expected, FOGRA Graphic Technology Research Association, Munich, Germany, 2012, updated 2016.

[24] C. Appleby, Donnelley's digital edge, J. Bus. Strateg. 15 (1994) 33.

[25] R.R. Donnelly Annual Report 1995.

[26] R.R. Donnelly Annual Report 2001.

[27] R.R. Donnelly Annual Report 2002.

[28] LSC Communications Results June 2017.

[29] S. Nias, CPI co-founder Bovard in surprise departure from company, Print Week (2008) (October 9, 2008).

[30] F.J. Romano (Ed.), Delmar's Dictionary of Digital Printing & Publishing, Delmar Publishers, Albany, NY, 1997.

[31] F.J. Romano, H. Fenton, On-Demand Printing: The Revolution in Digital and Customized Printing, Graphic Arts Technical Foundation, Sewickley, PA, 1998. p. 3.

[32] F.J. Romano, H. Fenton, On-Demand Printing: The Revolution in Digital and Customized Printing, Graphic Arts Technical Foundation, Sewickley, PA, 1998. p. 4.

[33] Romano, Frank J. editor (1997) Delmar's Dictionary of Digital Printing & Publishing Albany, NY: Delmar Publishers, p. 556; Romano, Frank J. and Fenton, Howard On-Demand Printing: The Revolution in Digital and Customized Printing (Graphic Arts Technical Foundation 1998), p. 6; Thompson, John B (2005) Books in the Digital Age. Cambridge, UK: Polity Press, pp. 427–426.

[34] J.B. Thompson, Books in the Digital Age, Polity Press, Cambridge, UK, 2005. pp. 429–431.

[35] K. Johansson, P. Lundberg, R. Ryberg, A Guide to Graphic Print Production, third ed., John Wiley & Sons, Hoboken, NJ, 2011. p. 289.

[36] K. Johansson, P. Lundberg, R. Ryberg, Case Study Lightning Source Inc. (Ingram) and John Wiley & Sons, 2009. http://www.stm-assoc.org/2009_12_03_Eproduction_Lightning_Source_Wiley_Case_Study.pdf.

[37] K. Johansson, P. Lundberg, R. Ryberg, John Wiley & Sons Annual Report 2015, 2009. http://www.wiley.com/legacy/about/corpnews/fy15_10kFINAL.pdf.

[38] K. Johansson, P. Lundberg, R. Ryberg, John Wiley & Sons Annual Report 2016, 2016. http://www.wiley.com/legacy/about/corpnews/FY16-10K.pdf.

[39] Interview with Simon Morley, Purchasing Manager, Gardner's Books, July 2017.

[40] C. Anderson, The long tail, Wired Magazine (2004). October 1, 2004. https://www.wired.com/2004/10/tail/.

[41] C. Anderson, The Long Tail, Hyperion, New York, 2006. pp. 47–49.

[42] J. Epstein, Book Business Publishing Past, Present and Future, WW Norton, New York, 2002 edition. p. xi.

[43] Dorotea Szkolar, Espresso Book Machines: Should Libraries Offer On Demand Publishing? Reference: April 4, 2012, Infospace—The official blog of Syracuse University iSchool.

[44] John Wiley & Sons' Media Release, April 21, 2009. http://eu.wiley.com/WileyCDA/PressRelease/pressReleaseId-49224.html.

[45] R. Anderson, The good, the bad, and the sexy: our espresso book machine experience, The Scholarly Kitchen (2011). August 2, 2011. https://scholarlykitchen.sspnet.org/2011/08/02/the-good-the-bad-and-the-sexy-our-espresso-book-machine-experience/.

[46] The Internet Bookshop (Oxford) Limited, (1998) Full accounts made up to December 31, 1997. Companies House, UK. November 23, 1998. (Retrieved July 2017).

[47] Wikipedia, Alibaba Group entry accessed July 2017.

[48] CreateSpace, a DBA of On-Demand Publishing, LLC. (An Amazon Company) website: accessed August 23, 2017. https://www.createspace.com/AboutUs.jsp.

[49] Springer Nature website. MyCopy printed ebooks service. http://www.springernature.com/gp/librarians/products/product-types/books/my-copy (Accessed August 22, 2017).

[50] R. Adner, The Wide Lens: What Successful Innovators See That Others Miss, 2013. (Portfolio, Revised edition June 25, 2013).

[51] R. Adner, The Wide Lens: What Successful Innovators See That Others Miss, 2013. (Portfolio, Revised edition June 25, 2013), p. 3.

[52] W.T. Dennis, Parcel and Small Package Delivery Industry, CreateSpace, North Charleston, SC, 2011. pp. 3 and 93.

[53] W.T. Dennis, Parcel and Small Package Delivery Industry, CreateSpace, North Charleston, SC, 2011. pp. 10–11.

[54] Deleted in review.

[55] Reference to a famous quote by Mae West: "If a little is great, and a lot is better, then way too much is just about right!".

[56] X. Tian, Book Publishing in Australia: The Potential impact of Digital Technologies on Business Models, A Thesis Submitted to RMIT University for the Degree of Doctor of Philosophy (Section 7 only), School of Business Information Technology Business Portfolio, RMIT University, Melbourne, 2008. June 2008. https://researchbank.rmit.edu.au/eserv/rmit:13382/Tian.pdf. And here is an associated article: X. Tian, B. Martin, Business models in digital book publishing: some insights from Australia, Publ. Res. Quart. 25 (2) (June 1, 2009) 73–88.

[57] P.F. Drucker, Innovation and Entrepreneurship, reissued 1999, Butterworth-Heinemann, Oxford, UK, 1985. p. 105.

[58] M. Jubb, Academic Books and Their Futures (June 2017): A Report to the AHRC and British Library, 2017. London (June 2017), p. 88. https://academicbookfuture.org/end-of-project-reports-2/.

[59] M. Deegan, The Academic Book of the Future: A Report to the AHRC and British Library, 2017. London (June 2017), p. 56 https://academicbookfuture.org/end-of-project-reports-2/.

[60] J. Howard, Ditch the monograph, Chron. High. Educ. (October 14, 2012). http://www.chronicle.com/article/Ditch-the-Monograph/135108.

[61] British Library Digital Scholarship Blog: September 27, 2016, http://blogs.bl.uk/digital-scholarship/2016/09/multimedia-phd-research-and-non-text-theses.html.

[62] JSTOR Labs, Reimagining the Digital Monograph: Design Thinking to Build New Tools for researchers, 2017. A JSTOR Labs Report http://labs.jstor.org/monograph/.

[63] C. Wolff, A.B. Rod, R.C. Schonfeld, Ithaka S + R, Jisc, RLUK UK Survey of Academics 2015, ITHAKA (2016) 101. (June 15, 2016). http://dx.doi.org/10.18665/sr.277685.

[64] M. Deegan, The Academic Book of the Future: A Report to the AHRC and British Library, 2017. London (June 2017) p. 7. https://academicbookfuture.org/end-of-project-reports-2/.

[65] M. Deegan, The Academic Book of the Future: A Report to the AHRC and British Library, 2017. London (June 2017) p. 38. https://academicbookfuture.org/end-of-project-reports-2/.

[66] M. Jubb, Academic Books and Their Futures (June 2017): A Report to the AHRC and British Library, 2017. London (June 2017) pp. 13–14 .https://academicbookfuture.org/end-of-project-reports-2/.

[67] F. Pinter, L. White, in: R. Campbell, E. Pentz, I. Borthwick (Eds.), Development of Book Publishing Business Models and Finances, Chandos Publishing, Elsevier, Academic and Professional Publishing, Oxford, 2012, pp. 17. http://www.pinter.org.uk/pdfs/Development%20of%20Book%20Publishing.pdf.

[68] N.L. Maron, C. Mulhern, D. Rossman, K. Schmelzinger, The Costs of Publishing Monographs, Toward a Transparent Methodology, 2016. February 5, 2016. http://www.sr.ithaka.org/publications/the-costs-of-publishing-monographs/.

[69] C. Lynch, The Battle to Define the future of the book in the digital world, First Monday 6 (6) (June 4, 2001).

[70] Wiley Media Release: "Wiley establishes print on demand solution for online only journals through The Sheridan Press", November 5, 2012. http://eu.wiley.com/WileyCDA/PressRelease/pressReleaseld-106031.html.

[71] Definition of "textbook", n. Oxford English Dictionary Online. Oxford University Press, Oxford, UK. Web. accessed August 11, 2017.

[72] J.B. Thompson, Books in the Digital Age, Polity Press, Cambridge, UK, 2005. p. 12.

[73] J. Esposito, How to reduce the cost of college textbooks, The Scholarly Kitchen (2017). March 27, 2017. https://scholarlykitchen.sspnet.org/2017/03/27/reduce-cost-college-textbooks/.

[74] J. Esposito, Elsevier provides textbooks for five edX MOOCs, Res. Inf. (2013). October 2013. https://www.researchinformation.info/news/elsevier-provides-textbooks-five-edx-moocs.

[75] Primis Online: Mechanical Engineering Design, 7/e, Joseph E. Shigley, University of Michigan, Charles R. Mischke, Iowa State University and Richard Budynas, Rochester Institute Technology, Copyright year: 2004 http://highered.mheducation.com/sites/0072520361/information_center_view0/primis_online.html.

[76] N. Venkatraman, J. Strock, Part 1: From Mass Production to Mass Customization: The Origins of Primis, Boston University Management School, Boston, MA, 2012. http://smg.bu.edu/exec/elc/documents/Primis%20PLI%20(2).pdf.

[77] M. Deegan, The Academic Book of the Future: A Report to the AHRC and British Library, 2017. London (June 2017), p. 37. https://academicbookfuture.org/end-of-project-reports-2/.

[78] Open Book Publishers website accesses August 21, 2017: https://www.openbookpublishers.com.

[79] Open Book Publishers website accesses August 21, 2017: http://www.openbookpublishers.com/section/4/1/our-vision.

[80] Wikibooks Collections from the Wikibooks website in August 2017. https://en.wikibooks.org/wiki/Wikibooks:Collections.

[80a] C. Wolff-Eisenberg, A.B. Rod, R.C. Schonfel. UK Survey of Academics 2015: Ithaka S+R | Jisc | RLUK. Ithaka S+R. Last modified 15 June 2016. https://doi.org/10.18665/sr.282736.

[81] M. Deegan, The Academic Book of the Future: A Report to the AHRC and British Library, 2017. London (June 2017) p. 43.

[82] M. Jubb, Academic Books and Their Futures (June 2017): A Report to the AHRC and British Library, 2017. London (June 2017), p. 189. https://academicbookfuture.org/end-of-project-reports-2/.

[83] S.M. Ward, R.S. Freeman, J.M. Nixon, E-Books in Academic Libraries: Stepping Up to the Challenge, Purdue University Press, West Lafayette, IN, 2015. Project MUSE https://muse.jhu.edu/results?section1=author&search1=%20Judith%20M%20Nixon.
[84] 4th Drupa Global Trends, March 2017, p. 6. http://www.drupa.com/cgi-bin/md_drupa/lib/pub/tt.cgi/Global_Trends_Overview.
[85] E. Harvey, Reporting on the digital book printing conference, Book Business Magazine (2017).
[86] 4th Drupa Global Trends, March 2017, p. 8. http://www.drupa.com/cgi-bin/md_drupa/lib/pub/tt.cgi/Global_Trends_Overview.
[87] 4th Drupa Global Trends, March 2017. p. 9. http://www.drupa.com/cgi-bin/md_drupa/lib/pub/tt.cgi/Global_Trends_Overview.
[88] SmithersPira, Growth in digital printing to remain strong until 2024, in: The Future of Digital Printing to 2024, SmithersPira, Surrey, UK, 2014. www.smitherspira.com/news/2014/april/digital-printing-to-remain-strong-until-2024.
[89] InfoTrends survey, workflow issues have increased threefold since 2013.
[90] 82% of print service providers have turned to cloud-based software in recent years.
[91] The Fogra (Research Institute for Media Technologies in Munich, Germany) has published Process Standard Digital (PSD).
[92] EDP Media release 2017 Award winners: http://edp-award.com/index.php?Pos=202.
[93] KBA Website accessed August 22, 2017. https://www.kba.com/en/kba-your-partner/.
[94] KBA Media Release April 20, 2010 “KBA Commander CT for market leader in mono book printing: CPI group in France opts for innovative KBA technology”. Website accessed August 22, 2017. http://www2.kba.com/gb/news/detail/article/cpi-group-in-france-opts-for-innovative-kba-technology/.
[95] Bookmaster invests in new Canon Oce Varioprint. http://www.24-7pressrelease.com/press-release/bookmasters-upgrades-digital-fleet-with-the-installation-of-canons-oce-varioprint-i300-color-sheetfed-inkjet-press-and-the-oce-colorstream-3900-continuous-feed-inkjet-press-437512.php.
[96] July 2017 issue of Research Information David Ross, Executive Director of Open Access at Sage Publishing.
[97] Alliant University’s Alliant Press supported by Author House.
[98] R. Pool, A monograph for tomorrow, Res. Inform. (2017). August/September 2017, Cambridge, UK. https://www.researchinformation.info/feature/monograph-tomorrow.
[99] American bible society website accessed August 22, 2017.
[100] Wycliffe Associates website accessed August 22, 2017, Donate: Three Letters that are Revolutionizing Bible Translation—POD. https://give.wycliffeassociates.org/p-1472-print-on-demand.aspx.
[101] Wycliffe Associates website accessed August 22, 2017: Resources Print-on-demand https://resources.wycliffeassociates.org/translation-tools/print-on-demand-pod/.
[102] D. Berze, Independent publishing: the next big thing? Res. Inform. (2016). December 13, 2016 and Independent publishing: breaking the mould? February/March 2017. https://www.researchinformation.info/news/analysis-opinion/independent-publishing-next-big-thing.

Index

Note: Page numbers followed by *f* indicate figures, *t* indicate tables and *b* indicate boxes.

Printed and bound by CPI Group (UK) Ltd, Croydon, CR0 4YY
08/06/2025
01896869-0001